D/

Something to

you laugh out

loud.!!

S xx

James Hardy Vaux's
1819
DICTIONARY
of
CRIMINAL
SLANG

and other **IMPOLITE TERMS** as used by the
Convicts of the British Colonies of Australia

***

with additional **TRUE STORIES,**
REMARKABLE FACTS & ILLUSTRATIONS *by*
SIMON BARNARD

TEXT PUBLISHING MELBOURNE AUSTRALIA

textpublishing.com.au
textpublishing.co.uk

The Text Publishing Company
Swann House, 22 William Street, Melbourne Victoria 3000, Australia

The Text Publishing Company (UK) Ltd
130 Wood Street, London EC2V 6DL, United Kingdom

Published by The Text Publishing Company, 2019
A New and Comprehensive Vocabulary of the Flash Language by James Hardy Vaux originally published by John Murray, London, 1819

Book design by Simon Barnard
Illustrations by Simon Barnard
Typeset by J&M Typesetting

Printed and bound in Australia by Griffin Press, part of Ovato, an accredited ISO/NZS 14001:2004 Environmental Management System printer

ISBN: 9781925773897 (hardback)
ISBN: 9781925774665 (ebook)

A catalogue record for this book is available from the National Library of Australia.

This book is printed on paper certified against the Forest Stewardship Council® Standards. Griffin Press holds FSC chain-of-custody certification SGS-COC-005088. FSC promotes environmentally responsible, socially beneficial and economically viable management of the world's forests.

JAMES HARDY VAUX was born in 1782 in Surrey, England. A habitual offender, he was transported to Australia on three occasions: in 1801, 1810 and 1831. In 1812, while imprisoned at the Newcastle Penal Station, he collated a dictionary of convict slang, which was published in 1819 as *A New and Comprehensive Vocabulary of the Flash Language*.

SIMON BARNARD is a writer, illustrator and collector of colonial artifacts. He was born and raised in Launceston but now lives in Melbourne. His first book, *A-Z of Convicts in Van Diemen's Land*, won the Eve Pownall Award for Information Books in the Children's Book Council of Australia's Book of the Year awards in 2015.

simonbarnard.com.au

The Secret Language of Australia

Australia's first dictionary, *A New and Comprehensive Vocabulary of the Flash Language* by James Hardy Vaux, printed in London in 1819, was a collection of words and terms used by convicts to describe and sometimes disguise their crimes. For the administrators of the convict system it provided a valuable insight into criminal life and the means to understand convicts charged with further offences.

Approximately 164,000 convicts were transported from British and Irish ports to the Australian colonies. Their slang, formally termed cant and informally known as flash, was an ever-evolving language steeped in the cultural melting pot of the British underworld. In the early days of colonisation a court-appointed interpreter was often required to translate the depositions of the witnesses and the accused.

The dictionary proved to be hot property. After it was released in Australia it appears to have sold out. In 1821, a Van Diemonian lawyer misplaced his copy and tendered a reward of five shillings—the cost of a new copy. Twenty years later the dictionary was in its fourth printing. Another Van Diemonian lawyer was wryly reported to be in dire need of a copy when he struggled to explain the terms 'on the *cross*' and 'on the *square*' to a jury.

The dictionary's author, James Hardy Vaux, was a convict himself, a habitual offender transported from Britain to New South Wales three times—in 1801, 1810 and 1831. By his own admission he was guilty of 'buzzing, dragging, sneaking, hoisting, pinching, smashing, jumping, spanking, and starring; together with the kid-rig, the letter-racket, the order-racket, and the snuff-racket'.

Vaux was born in Surrey in England in 1782. Well educated and of respectable parentage, he rejected an apprenticeship, gainful employment and naval service for a rakish life of villainy. In 1812, while imprisoned at the Newcastle Penal Station and employed as a clerk, he compiled the dictionary, which he cheekily dedicated to the station's commandant:

> I trust the Vocabulary will afford you some amusement from its novelty; and that from the correctness of its definitions, you may occasionally find it useful in your magisterial capacity.
>
> I cannot omit this opportunity of expressing my gratitude for the very humane and equitable treatment I have experienced, in common with every other person in this settlement, under your temperate and judicious government.

Vaux's dictionary was instructive but also entertaining. It was read more widely than just within the court system, and as people became familiar with the terms it described, the usage of those terms increased. 'The true language of English thieves is becoming the established language of the colony,' wrote British colonial administrator Edward Gibbon Wakefield in 1829.

Fearing that slang would normalise and perpetuate criminal behaviour, many authors, journalists, diarists and clerks ignored, omitted or edited it out of their writing. 'Indecent', 'profane' and 'abusive language', as specified in the rules and regulations governing the major sites of imprisonment in colonial Australia, was forbidden.

The effect that language had on children was of particular concern. When Vaux's dictionary was first released it was deemed 'dangerous to the young'. After visiting Australia in 1836, Charles Darwin concluded that female convicts taught their masters' children 'the vilest expressions, and it is fortunate if not equally vile ideas'. But attempting to silence convicts was futile. Informal language was a vital form of expression—approximately half of all convicts were illiterate. Sung, shouted, screamed and whispered, slang was also scrawled into bibles, stippled onto coins, scratched into cell walls and pricked into convicts' skin.

The language of the convicts endures. Words such as *seedy*, *serve*, *snitch*, *snooze*, *square* and *stash* are now commonplace. Slang contributed to the shaping of an Australian identity: *danna*, meaning human excrement, gave way to *dunny*. *Togs* became 'swimming costume'. *Ridge*—gold—became *ridgy didge*—'genuine, good'. *Larking* probably became 'larrikin'. *Swag* is the origin of 'swagman'. And *grog* still means grog.

───────────

This book contains Vaux's original dictionary, reproduced in its entirety, entry by entry, along with stories of convicts and their crimes, quoting the language used to report them in court documents, newspaper articles, diaries and letters of the time. Some entries also include etymological information, tracing the possible origins of Vaux's terms. Vaux's writing is reprinted verbatim in all entries except E, X and Z, which were omitted by Vaux. Here, they have been collated from contemporaneous sources.

The year of this book's publication, 2019, marks the 200th anniversary of Vaux's original work. In 2012, first edition copies of his two-volume set sold for US$13,750. In one volume the original owner noted:

I knew this Gentleman in Sydney—He lives near me & I saw him frequently. But notwithstanding his intentions of reform, he had been recently turned out of the Police Office, where he had an appointment as Clerk. At this period he was

gentleman at large. He dresses well, & looked genteelly—
but nobody knowing how he lived, he was still regarded as a
suspicious character.

Vaux, whose name was synonymous with crime, was infamous the world
over. Yet he remains an elusive figure. Following his release in 1841, the
then fifty-nine-year-old disappeared. But thanks to his handiwork the
whids and *games* of *lag'd coves, mollishers* and *kids* remains *out-and-out flash*.

ANDREW MILLER'S LUGGER: A king's ship or vessel.

A lugger is a small sailing ship fitted with a four-cornered lugsail, and Andrew Miller was an eighteenth-century naval lieutenant who was jokingly said to have conscripted such a multitude of sailors that he owned the Royal Navy. A total of 825 vessels transported convicts from British and Irish ports to the Australian colonies. The vast majority were not Andrew Miller's luggers, but rather privately owned vessels contracted by the British government.

AREA SNEAK, or AREA SLUM: The practice of slipping unperceived down the areas of private houses, and robbing the lower apartments of plate or other articles.

London blacksmith George Colben was 'well known to the police as an area sneak'. In 1839, aged twenty-two, he snuck down the side of a house, slipped into a kitchen and stole silver spoons and forks. He was caught and sentenced to ten years transportation to New South Wales. Silverware, known as 'plate', may have been especially tempting for Colben, as convict blacksmiths were known to melt down silverware to produce counterfeit coins.

ARM-PITS: To *work* under *the arm-pits*, is to practise only such kinds of depredation, as will amount, upon conviction, to what the law terms single, or petty larceny; the extent of punishment for which is transportation for seven years. By

following this system, a thief avoids the halter, which certainly is applied *above* the arm-pits.

The noose fitted around the neck of a person sentenced to death by hanging was known as a halter. Criminals repeatedly convicted of petty larceny—stealing goods worth less than a shilling—could be transported to Australia  for seven years. The more serious crime of grand larceny, including the theft of goods worth more than a shilling, could result in fourteen years' transportation, transportation for life, or death by hanging. Anthony Jackson, a coalminer from Birmingham, kept his crime under the arm-pits, but after his third offence he was charged with felony and transported to Van Diemen's Land. He died in 1825 after he was buried up to his neck in a freak mining accident.

AWAKE: An expression used on many occasions; as a thief will say to his accomplice, on perceiving the person they are about to rob is aware of their intention, and upon his guard, *stow it*, the *cove's awake*. To be awake to any scheme, deception, or design, means, generally, to see through or comprehend it.

James Allen was preparing to pick the pocket of a sleeping sailor who suddenly woke and said, 'It won't do. I am awake to that.' But he nodded straight back to sleep, and Allen stole his money. Allen was later caught and sentenced to life in Van Diemen's Land.

BACK-JUMP: A back-window. See: JUMP.

While languishing on death row in Kent County Gaol, John Ingram, a burglar, received a letter from one of his victims requesting the whereabouts of his property. Ingram wrote a reply: he entered the man's '*crib*' through a back 'jump' then crept through the '*slavy's*' '*back-slums*' and stole '*wedge*' that he '*planted*'. Ingram included precise instructions for unearthing the buried silverware, but police failed to find it. Ingram, it seems, was something of a comedian. The night before his execution Ingram carefully arranged his bedding, telling his gaolers that he needed a comfortable night's sleep because the following night he would be 'put to bed with a shovel'. On the day of his execution he told jokes that offended the gaol minister, who refused him Holy Sacrament, and when the hangman drew the execution cowl over his head, Ingram said: 'I wish you all goodnight.'

BACK-SLANG: To enter or come out of a house by the back-door; or, to go a circuitous or private way through the streets, in order to avoid any particular place in the direct road, is termed *back-slanging it.*

Criminals often travelled roundabout routes to avoid scrutiny, while convicts were ordered to take indirect routes to prevent them associating with the general public. At the Penitentiary Chapel in Hobart Town, convicts were back-slanged through two back doors and a screen was positioned to keep them out of the view of the rest of

the congregation. Badly behaved convicts were locked in cells situated beneath the chapel pews.

BACK-SLUM: A back room; also the back entrance to any house or premises; thus, *we'll give it 'em on the back slum*, means, we'll get in at the back-door.

John Jones, known to the police as 'a little red-haired vagrant' who frequented the 'back-slums' of Stonehouse, England, broke into a house through a back-slum window. He stole money, cutlery, a snuffbox and clothing. When he pawned the clothing for cash, police arrested him, and he was sentenced to seven years' transportation.

BAD HALFPENNY: When a man has been upon any errand, or attempting any object which has proved unsuccessful or impracticable, he will say on his return, It's a *bad halfpenny*; meaning he has returned as he went.

The term bad halfpenny may have originally indicated counterfeit money that was deemed bad and returned to the person who dealt it. Theresa Halfpenny, at her fifty-third court appearance, was wryly referred to as a 'bad halfpenny' for returning yet again for misdemeanours. She was sentenced to three months' gaol for drunkenness.

BANDED: Hungry.

Banded is derived from band, meaning belt, because a starving man tightened his belt around his diminishing waist. Dennis Collins was a one-legged ex-sailor who became homeless and banded after his invalid pension was revoked. He lobbed a rock at the king in protest and was charged with treason and sentenced to be hanged, beheaded and quartered. But the sentence was commuted to transportation to Van Diemen's Land for life. When Collins arrived, he declared that he would no longer 'perform the King's task, nor eat the King's food' and over the course of three wretched weeks he slowly starved to death.

BANDS: To *wear the bands*, is to be hungry, or short of food for any length of time; a phrase chiefly used on board the hulks, or in jails.

Convict Linus Miller wrote in his memoir that he was 'half-starved' and that he wore the bands for a week. He had discarded his 'government slops,' preferring to wear his own clothing, but after he learned that convicts caught out of uniform were subject to punishment, he traded nine dinners for a pair of old knee breeches. (Slops, derived from the Middle English *sloppe*, refers to cheap ready-made clothing. But *slop* is also slang for tea.)

BANG-UP: A person, whose dress or equipage is in the first style of perfection, is declared to be *bang up to the mark*.

A man who has behaved with extraordinary spirit and resolution in any enterprise he has been engaged in, is also said to have *come bang up to the mark*; any article which is remarkably good or elegant, or any fashion, act, or measure which is carried to the highest pitch, is likewise illustrated by the same emphatical phrase.

In 1832, the *Sydney Herald* reported that convict Mary Prince was more of a 'Princess' than a 'Prince', because of her '*toggery*', which was 'in bang up style'. Prince, who was caught roaming the streets of Sydney, was punished with one month's imprisonment in a Female Factory. As she was leaving court she 'tried to *gammon* a faint,' but her trickery did not fool her gaolers.

BARKING-IRONS: Pistols; an obsolete term.

Pistols were called barking irons because they made a sound similar to a barking dog. During a heated argument at Glebe in Sydney in 1848, Constable William Giles brained Watchman Joseph Ward with a wooden club known as a shillelagh. Ward charged Giles with assault, but because Ward had threatened to slash Giles with his cutlass and unleash his 'brace of barking irons,' the judge dismissed the case.

BARNACLES: Spectacles.

Barnacles is rhyming slang for spectacles. John Hart was a 'barker', a peddler, arrested for maltreating a passer-by who refused to buy his wares. Hart, according to his victim, threatened to remove his 'barnacles' and 'thrash him'. But Hart was also accused of speaking language that was too 'gross' to repeat in court. Peddlers who spruiked secondhand clothes were called 'barkers' because they yelled loudly and aggressively, similar to a barking dog.

BASH: To beat any person by way of correction, as the woman you live with, etc.

Bash may derive from *baske*, a Danish word that means 'to beat'. But it may have also come from *basa*, Swedish for 'smack'. In New South Wales in 1837, Harriet Purcell attempted to stop John Blackman 'bashing' his wife. But when Purcell intervened, Blackman bashed her as well. Purcell charged Blackman with assault and Blackman was fined ten shillings but not convicted of a crime. Women had few rights under colonial law, though a female convict assigned to her husband had greater rights than a free married woman. A convict wife could lodge complaints about her husband and be removed if found to be suffering abuse.

BASTILE: Generally called, for shortness, *the Steel*; a cant name for the House of Correction, Cold-Bath-Fields, London.

Many convicts were imprisoned in Coldbath Fields Prison—nicknamed the Bastille, after the infamous fourteenth-century Parisian fortress—before being transported to Australia. Owen Suffolk, while imprisoned there for vagrancy, 'resolved to become a thief' and went on to become one of Australia's most infamous bushrangers. Solomon Gorman was sent to the 'district Bastille' in New South Wales for drunkeness, while in 1838, William Lushington Goodwin, editor of the *Cornwall Chronicle*, called the 'Aboriginal settlement' on Wybalenna 'the Flinders Island Bastille', and described it as a place of 'ignominious and cowardly imprisonment' for 'poor kidnapped blacks'.

BEAK: A magistrate; the late Sir John Fielding, of police memory, was known among *family* people by the title of the blind *beak*.

Beak, slang for magistrate, may have originated in the seventeenth century when magistrates wore beak-shaped masks stuffed with herbs and spices to prevent them contracting the  bubonic plague from prisoners. It's also possible that beak is derived from *beag*, a Middle English word for a necklace or gold collar, as magistrates often wore gold necklaces as symbols of their authority.

Seaman John Fielding was blinded in an accident, so he left the Royal Navy to pursue a career in law and was appointed as a magistrate in the Bow Street district of London in 1754. Due to the loss of his eyesight, he was said to have developed a remarkable sense of hearing—he could identify three thousand criminals solely by their voices.

BEAN: A guinea.

Bean, meaning guinea, may derive from kidney bean, as guinea rhymes with kidney. In 1838, impoverished carpenter William Blick was carrying a piece of beef home for his children's Christmas dinner when he was tackled by two thieves who stuffed mud in his mouth and stole his beef as well as his cash. Blick accused Charles 'Guinea Bean' Bowles of the crime, but Bowles was acquitted for lack of evidence, and Blick's children had nothing but a small loaf of bread for Christmas dinner.

BEEF: Stop thief! To *beef* a person, is to raise a hue and cry after him, in order to get him stopped.

Beef, short for hot beef, is rhyming slang for 'stop thief'. In 1832, a London policeman heard a cry of 'stop thief' and leapt into action. But when he discovered that the group of children crying 'hot beef' had tricked him, he arrested them. At their trial, the children testified they'd been calling for 'hot taters', 'hot mutton' and 'hot pies' for a *'lark'* and the judge released them without charge.

Pickpocket Mary Ann Jones was transported to Van Diemen's Land after she was tackled by a Londoner who heard the cry 'stop thief'. Members of the public were required by law to assist in catching criminals, and calling for assistance was known as 'raising a hue and cry'. *Hue and Cry* was also the name of a police gazette that detailed information about criminals who were wanted by the law.

BELLOWSER: See: WIND.

BENDER: A sixpence. See: CROOK.

BENDER: An ironical word used in conversation by *flash* people; as where one party affirms or professes any thing, which the other believes to be false or insincere, the latter expresses his incredulity by exclaiming *bender*! Or, if one asks another to do any act which the latter considers unreasonable or impracticable, he replies, O yes, I'll do it—*bender*; meaning, by the addition of the last word, that, in fact, he will do no such thing.

Bender may stem from the phrase 'bend the truth', meaning to lie or exaggerate. In 1856, James Sherry was charged with stealing wood. He did not exclaim bender, but rather admitted to the crime, thanks to which he may have avoided gaol time—he was fined 'five *bob* and a bender' (sixpence). Sixpence coins were known as benders because they were poorly manufactured and prone to bending.

BEST: To *get your money at the best*, signifies to live by dishonest or fraudulent practices, without labour or industry, according to the general acceptation of the latter word; but, certainly, no persons have more occasion to be industrious, and in a state of perpetual action than *cross-coves*; and experience has proved, when too late, to many of them, that honesty is the best policy; and, consequently, that the above phrase is by no means *a-propos*.

Ben Hall, one of Australia's best-known bushrangers, worked tirelessly to live best; some sources credit him with more than six hundred robberies. In April 1865, the New South Wales government introduced the Felons Apprehension Act for the sole purpose of proclaiming Hall and his associates outlaws—being 'outside the law' meant that they could be killed by anyone at any time. Hall decided to quit bushranging, but in May he was ambushed by police and fatally shot. The act did not come into force until six days after Hall's death, so his killers, who shared in a reward of £1000, could be described as having got their money at the best.

BETTY: A picklock; to *unbetty*, or *betty* a lock, to open or relock it, by means of the *betty*, so as to avoid subsequent detection.

Betty may be a corruption of bess, another slang word for 'picklock', which is probably derived from *best*, meaning outwit. John Flynn was caught with skeleton keys and a betty. He was charged with felonious intent and sentenced to six months in Sydney Gaol, but after Inspector James Singleton discovered that Flynn's picklocks fitted the locks of a slew of recently burgled properties, he was resentenced to two years' gaol with hard labour. Singleton then decided to try the keys on the door lock of a notorious gambling den. With twenty-six police in tow, he crept up to the entrance, and, to his great delight, discovered a key that unlocked the door. His troops stormed the building and arrested seventeen men for illegal gambling.

BILLIARD SLUM. *The mace* is sometimes called *giving it to 'em on the billiard slum.* See: MACE, and: LETTER Q.

BISHOP. See: CHRISTEN.

BIT: Money in general.

Bit, meaning money, probably originated in a small sum of money, such as a portion, share or *bit*. According to his memoirs, notorious pickpocket David Haggart stole 'bit' when he bludgeoned his victim and '*fork't*' cash.

BIT-FAKER: A coiner. See: FAKE.
BIT-FAKING: Coining base money.

During the voyage of the *Charlotte* to New South Wales in 1788, convict and bit-faker Thomas Barrett was caught bit-faking coins from buckles, buttons and spoons. The ship's surgeon, John White, was impressed by Barrett's skill. It is thought that White commissioned Barrett to make the Charlotte Medal to commemorate the voyage. The memento is celebrated as the first work of Australian colonial art. Barrett was executed at Sydney Cove in 1788 for stealing food, earning him further fame as the first European executed in the colony.

BLACK DIAMONDS: Coals.

The term black diamonds reflects the desirability and value of coal. The New South Wales press dubbed the Newcastle Penal Station the 'black diamond settlement', and  convicts there were sentenced to mine coal as a form of punishment. It was hot, filthy and exhausting work, and many convict-colliers worked naked. When Reverend Henry Phibbs Fry ventured into the Van Diemonian coalmines, he remarked that the 'naked figures, faintly perceptible in the gloom' filled him with 'horror'.

BLEEDERS: Spurs.

Spurs are small spikes attached to the heels of horseriding boots, used to urge the horse to go faster. Cockspurs are small blades fitted to the legs of cockerels to inflict damage during cockfights. Convicts could be sentenced to wear 'cock spurs', a slang term for a set of leg irons joined with two links of chain on either side of a central ring, rather than the standard four-link chains. According to convict William Thompson, men clapped in bleeders 'shuffled along' because walking was 'impossible'.

BLOODY-JEMMY: A sheep's head.

James Lincomb, an English butcher who sold sheep heads and was constantly 'bedaubed with blood', may have inspired the term; Jemmy is a slang name for James. But blood-soaked men named James were also nicknamed bloody Jemmy. Ararat publican James

Smith became known as 'bloody Jemmy' in 1858, when he brutally murdered his wife, Mary. The doctor who performed the post-mortem examination noted that 'her left leg, both arms, and seven ribs were broken, her collar-bone smashed, her skull terribly fractured'. Smith insisted that the injuries were self-inflicted. He was convicted of manslaughter and sentenced to seven years' hard labour.

BLOW THE GAFF: A person having any secret in his possession, or a knowledge of any thing injurious to another, when at last induced from revenge, or other motive, to tell it openly to the world and expose him publicly, is then said to have *blown the gaff upon* him.

Gaff may be a corruption of gab, meaning to talk at length. In 1832, convict Philip Ryan was discovered drinking claret and eating anchovy

toast, fare too fine for a convict. The authorities demanded to know how he acquired the tasty morsels, but Ryan 'politely declined to blow the gaff' on his associates. He was ordered to 'try Mr Murray's fare for seven days'—a slang term for seven days' solitary confinement with only bread and water at Carters' Barracks, controlled by Superintendent Andrew Murray.

BLOWEN: A prostitute; a woman who cohabits with a man without marriage.

Blowen may derive from the German word *blühen*, meaning bloom or blossom, or from *beluni*, Romani for 'a sister in debauchery'. Prostitutes may have also been called blowens because their reputation had been 'blown'. According to nineteenth-century author James O'Connell, colonists wanting a wife could obtain a marriage certificate from the bishop of New South Wales, then go to the Parramatta Female Factory and select a bride. Factory women made fun of the 'farcical scene' and teased their prospective husbands about their age, appearance and unpopularity among the free women of the colony. One woman imprisoned at Parramatta reportedly taunted, 'Ha! Old boy, couldn't you find a moll to suit? Is there never a blowen in the lot good enough for an old stringy-bark settler like you?'

BLUE-PIGEON: Lead.
BLUE-PIGEON FLYING: The practice of stealing lead from houses, churches, or other buildings, very prevalent in London and its vicinity.

Lead roof tiles are blueish-grey in colour and so were referred to as pigeons, which are similarly coloured. In 1787, watermen patrolling the River Thames accused John Cox of 'flying the blue-pigeon' when they found a ladder, a chisel and two hundred pounds of lead inside his boat. Cox was charged with stealing and transported to New South Wales for seven years.

BLUNT: Money.

Blunt may stem from the blunted edge on timeworn coins, or from blond, meaning gold. The term has also been attributed to Sir John Blunt, an eighteenth-century baronet notorious for his role in the disastrous 1720 stock market crash. When convict Elizabeth Cox was charged with drunkenness, she paid a five-shilling fine to avoid a stint in the Sydney stocks, saying, 'Here, take the blunt'. But when James O'Neil was punished for drunken revelry he chose not to pay the fine and was instead ordered to sit in the stocks for six hours, the maximum period. 'I shall have the blunt, however, when I come out. That's one comfort,' he said.

BOB, or BOBSTICK: A shilling.

Bob may derive from *baubee*, a Scottish coin. Alternatively, shillings might have been nicknamed after a bob, a type of grub used as fish bait, as they were often used as a bribe. When Robert Paterson was arrested for riding his horse at breakneck speed along a footpath in Ballarat, he offered the policeman 'five bob' to let him go. But the policeman declined the bribe and Paterson was fined twenty bob for 'furiously riding', ten bob for 'obstructing the footpath', forty bob for 'offering the bribe', and ten bob for the 'cost of forage for his horse'.

BODY-SLANGS. See: SLANGS.

BODY-SNATCHER: A stealer of dead bodies from church which are sold to the surgeons and students in anatomy.

John Bishop was an infamous 'body-snatcher'. He confessed to selling between five hundred and one thousand bodies to London hospitals. To keep up with demand, he even took to murder. In 1831, he was executed for the murder of a boy.

BOLT: To run away from or leave any place suddenly, is called *bolting*, or *making a bolt*: a thief observing an alarm while attempting a robbery, will exclaim to his accomplice, *Bolt*, there's a *down*. A sudden escape of one or more prisoners from a place of confinement is termed *a bolt*.

Joseph Syme, a memoirist and prison officer, suspected that convicts sentenced to solitary confinement did not reflect on their bad behaviour but plotted their next 'bolt'. Luke Roberts was a notorious bolter, but in 1837 his escapades came to an abrupt end when he was struck dead by a bolt of lightning.

BOLT-IN-TUN: A term founded on the cant word *bolt*, and merely a fanciful variation, very common among *flash* persons, there being in London a famous inn so called; it is customary when a man has run away from his lodgings, broke out of a jail, or made any other sudden movement, to say, The *Bolt-in-tun* is concerned; or, He's gone to the *Bolt-in-tun*; instead of simply saying, He has *bolted*, etc. See: BOLT.

Images of a beer tun (a large cask) with a crossbow bolt penetrating its bung (a stopper) adorned the Bolt-in-Tun Inn in Fleet Street, London. When, in 1834, John West stole a greatcoat belonging to the coachman of the Bolt-in-Tun, he didn't effect a bolt-in-tun and so was caught and sentenced to seven years' transportation to Van Diemen's Land.

BONED: Taken in custody, apprehended; Tell us how you was *boned*, signifies, tell us the story of your apprehension; a common request among fellow-prisoners in a jail, etc., which is readily complied with in general; and the various circumstances therein related afford present amusement, and also useful hints for regulating their future operations, so as to avoid the like misfortune.

Bone, meaning take, refers to the way a dog runs off with a bone. In 1869, convict Thomas Dinton discovered a one-legged human skeleton in bushland near the Port Arthur Penal Station. A wooden leg was found nearby, and the remains were identified as one-legged William Lovett, an impoverished ex-convict. Having absconded from the station's invalid depot in

1862, Lovett was, after seven long years, boned.

BONNET: A concealment, pretext, or pretence; an ostensible manner of accounting for what you really mean to conceal; as a man who actually lives by depredation, will still outwardly follow some honest employment, as a clerk, porter, newsman, etc. By this system of policy, he is said to have a good *bonnet* if he happens to get *boned*, and, in a doubtful case, is commonly discharged on the score of having a good character. To *bonnet for* a person, is to corroborate any assertion he has made, or to relate facts in the most favourable light, in order to extricate him from a dilemma, or to further any object he has in view.

When Mary Fercley was arrested for stuffing eighteen yards of ribbon into her bonnet, she insisted the ribbon had become entangled with her hat after she sat it on the shop counter. For her clever bonnet, she avoided punishment. Mary Malone wasn't so lucky. The *Sydney Herald* reported that for stealing flowers and 'bonneting' a '*charley*', she was sentenced to 'botanize at Gordon's gardens'—two months' hard labour at the Parramatta Female Factory, supervised by Ann Gordon.

BOUNCE: To bully, threaten, talk loud, or affect great consequence; to *bounce* a person out of any thing, is to use threatening or high words, in order to intimidate him, and attain the object you are intent upon; or to obtain goods

of a tradesman, by assuming the appearance of great respectability and importance, so as to remove any suspicion he might at first entertain. A thief, detected in the commission of a robbery, has been known by this sort of finesse, aided by a genteel appearance and polite manners, to persuade his accusers of his innocence, and not only to get off with a good grace, but induce them to apologize for their supposed mistake, and the affront put upon him. This masterstroke of effrontery is called *giving it to 'em upon the bounce*.

BOUNCE: A person well or fashionably drest, is said to be a *rank bounce*.

James McDonald was charged with 'bouncing the constables that he was free'. McDonald was probably well dressed and not wearing a convict uniform. He was ordered to 'study Bell's Book of Fate'—imprisonment at Carters' Barracks, under the supervision of Assistant Superintendent Thomas Bell—for two months. The Book of Fate is an ancient manuscript believed to prophesise the future.

BOWLED OUT: A man who has followed the profession of thieving for some time, when he is ultimately taken, tried, and convicted, is said to be *bowled out* at last. To *bowl* a person *out*, in a general sense, means to detect him in the commission of any fraud, or peculation, which he has hitherto practised without discovery.

In 1832, convict Mary Jeffries was 'bowled out' when police caught her in Sydney Domain 'reading Ovid's *Art of Love*' with her 'rigging clasped over her masthead'. Rigging is slang for clothing, masthead refers to the head, and the *Art of Love* is a series of books about love and courtship written by ancient Roman poet Ovid. It seems that Jeffries was caught while engaged in prostitution.

BRACE UP: To dispose of stolen goods by pledging them for the utmost you can get at a pawnbroker's, is termed *bracing* them *up*.

Many convicts were convicted of stealing goods and pawning them for cash. In 1837, Joseph Lawrence was charged with bracing up and transported to Van Diemen's Land for a fourteen-year term. He was awarded a conditional pardon and opened up a pawnshop, but was soon caught forging cheques and sent to the Port Arthur Penal Station.

BRADS: Halfpence; also, money in general.

Brads may be back slang derived from darby, a slang term for ready money. Alternatively, since halfpenny coins were small and made of copper, they may have been named after the small copper nails called brads. Convict George Neale loaded a shotgun with copper nails and bailed up colonists for brads. In 1855, he was caught and sentenced to life in the Port Arthur Penal Station.

BREAKING UP OF THE SPELL: The nightly termination of performance at the Theatres Royal, which is regularly attended by pickpockets of the lower order, who exercise their vocation about the doors and avenues leading thereto, until the house is emptied and the crowd dispersed.

The term spell may derive from the German words *schauspiel* and *spielen*, meaning 'play' and 'perform', while the name Theatre Royal is a title universally applied to theatres in Britain and Australia, but which originally specified theatres for dramatic productions.

George Barrington, 'the prince of pickpockets', was infamous for picking pockets during the breaking up of the spell. He posed as a well-to-do gentleman and stole from 'the brightest luminaries in the globe of London'. But in 1790, he was caught and transported to New South Wales for a seven-year term.

BREECH'D: Flush of money.

Breech'd is a pun both on breach, meaning split, and on breeches, a style of short trousers that end at the knee. After police discovered  Thomas Lawrence and Charles Cornell 'well dressed and well breeched', in stark contrast to their usual 'rags and poverty', they were charged with theft and sent to gaol. Savvier criminals, however, dressed in tattered clothing to conceal their ill-gotten gains. In 1792, William Pound was charged with pretending to be a maimed and impoverished beggar. Wrapped in rags and stuffed in his breeches police found more than £630 in assorted bills and cash, a sum approximately thirty times the average annual wage earned by his fellow Englishmen.

BRIDGE: To *bridge* a person, or *throw* him *over the bridge*, is, in a general sense, to deceive him by betraying the confidence he has reposed in you, and instead of serving him faithfully, to involve him in ruin or disgrace; or, three men being concerned alike in any transaction, two of them will form a collusion to *bridge* the third, and engross to themselves all the advantage which may eventually accrue. Two persons having been engaged in a long and doubtful contest or rivalship, he, who by superior art or perseverance gains the point, is said to have *thrown* his opponent *over the bridge*. Among gamblers, it means deceiving the person who had back'd you, by wilfully losing the game; the money so lost by him being shared between yourself and your confederates who had laid against you. In playing three-handed games, two of the party will play into each other's hands, so that the third must inevitably be *thrown over the bridge*, commonly called, *two poll one*. See: PLAY ACROSS.

In 1832, the battered body of flagellator George Grover was discovered lying beneath the Richmond Bridge in Van Diemen's Land. With his dying breath, he accused four men of bridging him. But despite a lengthy investigation, no charges were laid. Convicts who volunteered to be flagellators were despised for bridging their fellow convicts.

BROADS: Cards; a person expert at which is said to be a good *broad-player.*

Playing cards were called broads because they have length and breadth without depth. William Chapman was a notorious 'broad *sharp*'. But in 1857 he was arrested after police discovered that he was carrying a 'roll of paper done up like a bundle of notes', which was a phony gambling stake, and a pack of broads that he'd trimmed to aid cheating—high-numbered cards had convex edges and low-numbered cards had concave edges. Chapman was sent to Pentridge Prison.

BROOMSTICKS. See: QUEER BAIL.

BROWNS and WHISTLERS: Bad halfpence and farthings; (a term used by coiners.)

Counterfeit halfpennies and farthings acquired their nickname because they were brown in colour and emitted a telltale ring when tapped against a hard surface, which drew attention in the manner of a whistle. In 1796, Newgate Prison officials were astonished to discover an inmate operating an elaborate coin-counterfeiting operation. James Pullen, dubbed the 'king of coiners', was living in 'great luxury'—discovered in his cell was £100 in counterfeit cash and an array of tools and machinery, including moulds to produce browns and whistlers.

BUB: A low expression signifying drink.

Addison William Blakey, an 'inveterate drunkard' with a wooden leg and a 'head like a prize cabbage', was repeatedly punished for drinking-related incidents. In 1853, he was prosecuted by his wife, Ann, for failing to provide her with adequate 'bub and *grub*'. Blakey was supposed to supply Ann with five shillings per week, but because he blew all their money on booze, he'd taken to stumbling home drunk and slip-

ping her only a few pence. The magistrate granted Blakey time to remunerate his 'ill-used wife' but soon after the ruling, he was charged with drunkenness and sentenced to six weeks in Sydney Gaol.

BUCKET: To *bucket* a person is synonymous with *putting* him in the *well*. Such treatment is said to be a *bucketting concern*. See: **WELL**.

BUFF: To *buff* a person or thing is to swear to the identity of them; swearing very positively to any circumstance, is called *buffing it home*.

Buff may be inspired by a witness who polishes—buffs—the truth. But the term may also come from the sense of a person revealing or uncovering the truth, since 'in the buff' means naked. In 1835, Alexander Saunders, the 'keeper of a house of notorious accommodation', was charged with renting a room to convict Houghton Hinton. Convicts were not permitted in pubs, and publicans caught breaking the rules were penalised. Saunders pleaded not guilty, but after Hinton 'buffed it home' to curry favour with the judge and lessen his punishment, Saunders was fined £10.

BUFFER: A dog.

Buffer may derive from bufe, a slang word for dog that originated from the sound of barking. In colonial Australia, dogs were invaluable. They provided colonists with game, protection, labour, entertainment  and companionship—thirteen-year-old John Eedwetch owned a 'dear old dog named buffer'. But some dogs were recruited to crime. In 1889, West Australian shopkeeper Leonard Hicks spotted a dog trotting out of his shop with a frying pan in its mouth. A few minutes later the dog returned and carried away a mat. Waiting on the other side of the road was the owner, William Rogers. For enticing his 'very clever dog' into thievery, Rogers was sentenced to six months in Fremantle Prison.

BUG or BUG OVER: To give, deliver, or hand over; as, He *bug'd* me a *quid*, he gave me a guinea; *bug over the rag*, hand over the money.

Bug may be a corruption of bung, meaning 'to pass something'. Charles Hogan was sentenced to life in Van Diemen's Land for forcing a person to bug over their property. At the Port Arthur Penal Station, he was recruited to bug over leeches to medics, who required hundreds of the critters every month. Leeches were applied to patients to clean their wounds and cleanse them of impure blood. When John Sallows arrived in Van Diemen's Land, he bore 'Marks on Pit of stomach of Leeches'. He had been treated for rheumatism and scurvy with leeches during the voyage out.

BULL: A crown, or five shillings. See: HALF A BULL

Slang names for coins often referred to the number of lashes that convicts were sentenced to receive. Bull was slang for seventy-five lashes; a sixpence, or *tester*, was twenty-five lashes; a shilling, a *bob*, was fifty lashes; and a sovereign, a *canary*, was one hundred lashes. Convict George Britton was punished with testers, bob, bulls and canaries—a total of 766 lashes.

BULL-DOG: A sugar-loaf.

Sugar loaves are large cone-shaped masses of moulded sugar, nicknamed bull-dogs perhaps because of their dog-like toughness and squat shape. After a fire broke out in the city of Port Adelaide, Catherine Whitesides was caught stealing a bull-dog from a burning shop. She was sentenced to one months' gaol with hard labour.

BULL-HANKERS: Men who delight in the sport of *bull-banking*; that is, bull-baiting, or bullock-hunting, *games* which afford much amusement, and at the same time frequent

opportunities of depredation, in the confusion and alarm excited by the enraged animal.

Bull-hanker stems from hank, meaning a coil of thread. In a brutal form of entertainment called bull-bating, bull-hankers pitted attack-dogs  against a tethered bull. According to William Day, a bull-hanker transported to Van Diemen's Land, bulls would catch dogs on their horns and toss them 'through windows or over low roofs'. In bull-hunting, more commonly known as bull-running, a wild bull was let loose in public streets. Any form of entertainment that drew crowds provided thieves with cover to perpetrate crime—thirteen-year-old John Copping was sentenced to ten years' transportation for picking pockets during a bull-hunt.

BUM-CHARTER: A name given to bread steeped in hot water, by the first unfortunate inhabitants of the *English Bastile*, where this miserable fare was their daily breakfast, each man receiving with his scanty portion of bread, a quart of boil'd water from the cook's coppers!

The English Bastille was a slang name for London's Coldbath Fields Prison. Prison-issue food was notoriously unappetising, but in Australia, convicts received a better quality of food than many free people living in Britain. Convicts were typically issued bread, vegetables and salt-cured meat each day. But that didn't stop convicts wanting to escape. In 1897, a prisoner nearly suffocated when he attempted to escape Parramatta Gaol by hiding in a refuse tank containing the leftover bum-charter slop.

BUM-TRAP: A sheriff's officer or his follower.

A sheriff's officer, more commonly termed a bailiff, was notorious for following closely at a sheriff's bum. For this reason, bailiffs were called bum-bailiffs and members of the 'catch club' (because they were said to 'catch' farts). But they were also known as bull-dogs, hawks, lurchers and, from the manner in which they escorted debtors, shoulder clappers. Bailiffs were  unpopular; colonists attacked them with knives, swords and pistols. In 1853, South Australian John Bevis was fined £1 for kicking a 'bum bailiff' and pelting him with stones.

BUNCE: Money.

Costermongers—street vendors—typically sold fruit and vegetables. Child costermongers hawked their masters' goods on commission, and the money they earned was known as 'bunts', a corruption of 'bonus'. Bunce has also been linked to 'bunts': apples unfit for retail that the costermonger boys scavenged to sell cheaply for themselves. According to social commentator Henry Mayhew, 'the costermongers' boys will, I am informed, cheat their employers, but they do not steal from them.' But Richard Jewson, a costermonger transported for picking pockets, was sentenced to two years on a road gang in Van Diemen's Land for embezzling money on a transaction he conducted on behalf of his master. To exclude outsiders, costermongers spoke their own cant and back slang—Jewson may have referred to the pound and four shillings he stole as one 'dunop' and 'rouf-gens'.

BURICK: A prostitute, or common woman.

Burick may derive from *bure*, a Scottish word that means 'loose woman', or it might stem from the Romani words *burk* or *burkdari*, meaning 'breast' or 'breasts'. According to an 1850 issue of the *Westminster Review*, 'grinding poverty approaching to actual want' was the driving force of prostitution in Britain and all other countries. To improve their wretched living conditions, some buricks stole from their clientele. But stealing with impunity was no easy thing. Susan Grey had her friends throw a blanket over her victim's head while they  'entirely stript' him of his clothes, to prevent him identifying her to the police. Lizzy MacCluskey, who, according to the New South Wales' press, had 'eyes like two burnt holes in a blanket' and a 'waist like a hogshead of porter', rendered her clients unconscious with opiate-laced booze. When they recovered they could not definitively prove she was the person who robbed them. But all Elizabeth 'Bouncing Betsey' Smith had to do was front up to court—her accuser, it was said, was too embarrassed to show his face.

BUSH'D: Poor; without money.

In his memoirs, James Laurence describes his fellow convicts 'taking to the Bush' to escape the brutality of the Moreton Bay Penal Station. To survive bush'd in the bush, convicts hunted game that provided them with meat and skins

to trade or sell, or wear. Absconder Henry Shippey survived five years on a tiny sub-Antarctic island south of New Zealand; when he surrendered to the authorities he was clothed in seal skins. At the time of bushranger Michael Howe's capture, he was wearing a 'dress made of kangaroo skins', while Robert James McKay, the 'wild man' of Ben Lomond, wore 'badger skins'—*badger* was colonial parlance for 'wombat'. John Perry, a member of the Jeffries Gang, was rumoured to have worn 'moccasins made of human skin'.

BUSHY-PARK: A man who is poor is said to be *at Bushy park*, or *in the park*.

Ex-convict Martin McDonald was at bushy-park. He lived in an actual hollow tree in the Hobart Town Domain. When, in 1862, he purloined a mantelpiece and window blinds from a vacant house to refurbish his tree, he was charged with theft and sentenced to two years' gaol with hard labour.

BUSTLE: A cant term for money.
BUSTLE: Any object effected very suddenly, or in a hurry, is said to be *done upon the bustle*. To *give it to* a man *upon the bustle*, is to obtain any point, as borrowing money, etc.; by some sudden story or pretense, and affecting great haste, so that he is taken by surprise, and becomes duped before he has time to consider of the matter.

Money may have been nicknamed bustle because people bustled to acquire it. Convicts who lacked the money to pay fines were subject to punishment at the whim of the court. Anne Smith was an 'incorrigible drunkard' who was fined five shillings for public intoxication; as she was without 'the bustle' to pay her fine, she was bustled off to the Sydney stocks.

BUZ: To buz a person is to pick his pocket. *The buz* is the *game* of picking pockets in general.

Buz may be a corruption of *bustle*. In 1851, Daniel Squibb was drinking in a London pub when a thief yelled 'Buz', hit him on the head with a pint pot and knocked him to the ground. Three men, including Michael 'Goosey' Bryant, ransacked Squibb's pockets and then fled. But Bryant returned to the pub a few hours later, where he was identified and arrested. In 1858, he was transported to Fremantle Prison in Western Australia. Bryant may have been nicknamed goosey because of his 'long' face, 'sallow' skin and 'stout' body.

BUZ-COVE, or BUZ-GLOAK: A pickpocket; a person who is clever at this practice, is said to be *a good buz*.

Gloak, slang for man, may derive from *glokh*, the Shelta word for man; Shelta is a cant spoken by Romani, Irish and Welsh travellers.

In 1827, Harry Prendergast and his '*pal*' were arrested on suspicion of stealing an elderly woman's purse. At their trial, a policeman testified that Prendergast, who was nicknamed 'Elephant', was a 'notorious *swell* buzzman'. The magistrate was unfamiliar with the term, and the police officer explained that 'by a swell buzzman was meant a genteel thief, who talked to, or buzzed his victim while robbing him'. But because there were no witnesses to the crime, the duo was acquitted. Prendergast probably acquired his nickname because of his corpulent physique.

CABIN: A house.

Ex-convict James Munro lived on Preservation Island in Bass Strait, alongside Indigenous women who lived in cabins that formed 'a little village'. Whether relations between the women and Munro were mutually beneficial is not known. But in 1830, Munro was accused of leading raiding parties to capture Indigenous women. Dubbed the 'King of the Eastern Straits', 'Governor of the Straits' and the 'Tasmanian Crusoe', Munro was known for speaking 'crack jaw dictionary words' and a regional language called 'island slang'. Some people speculated that he also was a pirate who lured ships into shore to scavenge the wrecks. When the *Britomart* disappeared in 1840, a visitor to the island noted that Munro's pigpen comprised part of the *Britomart's* 'cabin'.

CADGE: To beg. *The cadge* is the *game* or profession of begging.

Because many beggars also were peddlers, who carried wares in baskets, cadge may derive from *cage*, French for basket. But some beggars were also thieves. Fourteen-year-old James 'the cadger' Norton copped a four-year sentence after a woman discovered he'd hitched up her dress to rifle through her pocket. Norton's true name was Dennis Burke; he was a member of the Field Lane Gang, a group of London pickpockets who specialised in '*covering*'.

CADGE-GLOAK: A beggar.

In 1833, Kate Gibson was charged with drunkenness and vagrancy when she was discovered 'dead drunk' in Sydney. At her court appearance she wore a sling for her left arm and stated that she only drank 'a little rum to assuage her pain'. But court officials inspected her arm, concluded that it wasn't broken, and sentenced the cadge-gloak to a three-hour stint in the stocks. According to author William Shaw, many convicts feigned illness or injury to bilk money from colonists. Shaw, who declined a meal from a 'cadger's scran-bag', concluded that Sydney was a 'moral lavatory' inhabited by more 'knaves' than any other city. *Scran* is slang for left over food.

CANT OF DOBBIN: A roll of riband.

Cant means a 'portion' or 'share', while dobbin may derive from *dobby*, a mechanism that attached to a loom to weave small patterns. A gang of pickpockets known as The Forty Thieves distracted their victims by offering to sell them a dog tethered to a cant of dobbin. The Forty Thieves were children—gang member Joseph Saunderson was twelve years old when he arrived in Van Diemen's Land to complete a seven-year sentence for pickpocketing. Tattooed on his left hand were five dots, an insignia that marked his affiliation to the gang.

CAP: Synonymous with BONNET, which see.

CARDINAL: A lady's cloak.

Cardinals were named after the red cloaks worn by cardinals of the Catholic Church. When William Henry Nightengale was charged

with stealing silk, cloak-maker Martha Chadwell testified that Nightengale's friends, two 'women of the town', had supplied her with silk to tailor 'cardinals'. The judge was unfamiliar with the term, so Chadwell explained, 'Cardinals, sir, are dresses or cloaks made of silk, and are very fashionable at present.' Nightengale was released without charge, however, as red silk was so common that the prosecutor could not definitively prove where the silk supplied to Chadwell had originated.

CARRY THE KEG: A man who is easily vexed or put out of humour by any joke passed upon him, and cannot conceal his chagrin, is said to *carry the keg*, or is compared to a *walking distiller*.

Keg—a small barrel—is a pun on *cag*, slang for 'sulkiness' and 'ill humour'. In 1835, Convict-Constable James Leach prosecuted a Van Demonian for transporting a barrel of rum without a permit. But when the man failed to appear in court, the *Colonial Times* drolly reported that Leach 'cheerfully carried the keg'.

CASTOR: A hat.

Castor is Latin for beaver, and milliners prized beaver fur to make hats. Margret Donnally was punished with a six-month stint at the Parramatta Female Factory after she donned a 'beaver castor' and disguised herself as a man. Hats were also made from the skin of animals endemic to Australia. Bushranger Thomas Jeffries wore a kangaroo skin hat. When, in 1821, soldiers dressed in uniforms tailored from kangaroo skins mistook each other for bushrangers, Corporal John Dean was shot dead. Animal skins were well suited to the Australian climate, but also excellent camouflage. According to a colonist, men in a 'kangaroo skin cap, jacket, and trowsers' could 'easily be mistaken for one of the wild animals of the forest.' In 1822, convicts were officially forbidden to wear clothing made of skins.

CAT and KITTEN RIG: The petty *game* of stealing pewter quart and pint pots from public-houses.

Publicans served booze in pewter mugs known as pots. A quart pot, nicknamed a cat, contained a quarter of a gallon, while a pint pot—a kitten—held one eighth of a gallon. The pots may have got their nickname from the resemblance their bulbous shape and curved handles bore to a cat's body and tail. When, in 1828, nineteen-year-old William Dixon was charged with stealing pots, the term 'cat and kitten stealer' had to be explained to the magistrate. Pot thieves melted down pots to sell the pewter. When police searched pot-thief Elizabeth Jenkins' flat and discovered a frying pan filled with molten pewter, she was sentenced to seven years' transportation to New South Wales.

CAZ: Cheese; *As good as caz*, is a phrase signifying that any projected fraud or robbery may be easily and certainly accomplished; any person who is the object of such attempt and is known to be an easy dupe, is declared to be *as good as caz*, meaning that success is certain.

Caz may come from *caise*, Irish for 'cheese'. In 1850, Joseph William Hoosen was charged with insulting newsman George Cavenagh with language 'too gross a nature to repeat'. Hoosen blamed his behaviour on drunkenness and a war injury that affected his memory. As testament to his condition he emptied his pockets of four pounds of caz, and declared that he had no recollection of purchasing it. Hoosen's defence, as reported in the Melbourne press, proved 'as good as cheese' and he was let off with a small fine.

CHANDLER-KEN: A chandler's shop. See: KEN.

A chandler was a merchant who dealt in a specific type of goods. But some chandler-kens concealed unlawful gambling clubs and brothels. According to the *New Sprees of London*, Bob Dorkings' 'chanderkin' in Bainbridge Street, Saint Giles, concealed 'The Cadger's Palace', the 'daily and nightly resort' of '*cracksmen*', '*dragsmen*', and 'beggars of all description'.

CHANT: A person's name, address, or designation; thus, a thief who assumes a feigned name on his apprehension to avoid being known, or a swindler who gives a false address to a tradesman, is said to *tip them a queer chant*.

CHANT: A cipher, initials, or mark of any kind, on a piece of plate, linen, or other article; any thing so marked is said to be *chanted*.

CHANT: An advertisement in a newspaper or hand-bill; also a paragraph in the newspaper describing any robbery or other recent event; any lost or stolen property, for the recovery of which, or a thief, etc., for whose apprehension a reward is held out by advertisement, are said to be *chanted*.

In 1829 Philip Hicks was sentenced to seven years' transportation for stealing a pickled tongue; a newspaper chant detailing his crime informed the British public that he also went by the alias Philip King. But when he arrived in New South Wales, his name was chanted as Philip King, and Hicks was listed as his alias. Convicts typically tipped a queer chant to conceal their criminal histories. In 1832, for exchanging a stolen saw for a pig, King was sent to a chain gang for three months. The saw was identified as stolen because it bore a broad arrow—a chant emblematic of the British Government.

CHARLEY: A watchman.

Watchmen may have been nicknamed after Charles I who made improvements to the London night watch. Many 'charleys' were serving convicts; those with police or military experience were deemed the most suitable. Bryan McMahon, a deserter from the 39th regiment, was employed as a charley on a weekly wage of eight shillings. But in 1825, McMahon was discovered asleep on his master's kitchen floor with stolen goods spilling out from under his hat. He was dismissed and sentenced to a road gang.

CHARLEY-KEN: A watch-box. See: KEN.

A watch-box was a small hut that sheltered watchmen. In 1847, convict watchman Richard Pyle was discovered dead in a charley-ken in Hobart Town. The coroner ruled out foul play and declared Pyle had 'died of natural causes from the visitation of God'.

CHATS: Lice.
CHATTY: Lousy.

Because lice were 'the chief live stock or chattels of beggars, gypsies, and the rest of the canting crew', chats comes from chattel, meaning livestock. An infestation of chats generally resulted in sore, itchy skin, but chats could also cause death. They spread disease, such as typhus, commonly called gaol fever. Ridding oneself of chats was difficult. In 1843, George Baker was reprimanded for the chatty state of his head. When he was discovered infested with chats a second time, he was charged with misconduct and his sentence of hard labour was extended by two months.

CHAUNT: A song; to *chaunt* is to sing; to *throw off a rum chaunt*, is to sing a good song.

Chaunt derives from chant, meaning 'to sing'. Convict James Laurence, nicknamed 'Blind Larry' because he was blind in his left eye, was so admired for his 'chaunting' that he entertained officials such as Governor Thomas Brisbane. But Laurence also was proficient in cant language. According to his memoirs, he acquired money 'on the *sly*' to 'keep a girl by no means on the *square*' as per the custom of the 'Stage Struck *Coves*' of the London theatre.

CHEESE IT. The same as *Stow it*. See: STOW.
CHEESE THAT. See: STOW THAT.

CHINA STREET: A cant name for Bow Street, Covent Garden.

Bow Street, a thoroughfare in Covent Garden in London, was probably nicknamed after 'China oranges', a type of orange imported from China. In 1830, a China Street policeman arrested Elizabeth Turpin for stealing a basket of ninety oranges from a Covent Garden market. She was transported to New South Wales for a seven-year term.

CHIV: A knife; to *chiv* a person is to stab or cut him with a knife.

Chiv, a term applied to any improvised bladed weapon, may derive from *chivomengro*, Romani for knife. William Courtney accused George Bradley of stabbing him in his chest at the Impression Bay Probation Station in Van Diemen's Land. According to Courtney's testimony, Bradley's accomplice, Charles Fisher, instructed him to '*ding* the chiv'.

Bradley and Fisher were convicted of attempted murder, with the jury recommending that they be executed. But the two convicts appealed the sentence and successfully argued that Courtney stabbed himself. They were pardoned and Courtney was sentenced to nine months' hard labour in chains. Courtney had a history of self-harm—during his imprisonment, he was punished for rubbing caustic lime into his eyes, injuring his foot and cutting his own throat.

CHRISTEN: Obliterating the name and number on the movement on a stolen watch; or the crest, cipher, etc., on articles of plate, and getting others engraved, so as to prevent their being identified, is termed having them *bishop'd* or *christen'd*.

Christening, meaning 'to label', comes from christen—'to give a baby a Christian name at a baptism as a sign of admission into Christianity'. Ex-convict and Sydney jeweller Alexander Dick was notorious for

 're-christening' his wares. But Richard Waters, a watchmaker transported to Van Diemen's Land, was permitted to christen clocks—he was recruited to install clocks in the Penitentiary Chapel and St David's Church, both of which he inscribed with his name to provide a record of his handiwork.

CHUM: A fellow prisoner in a jail, hulk, etc.; so there are *new chums* and *old chums*, as they happen to have been a short or a long time in confinement.

Chum may derive from chamber-fellow, 'a person who shares a room with another person'. When Martin McNamara arrived in New South Wales, he was charged with drunkenness and disobedience, and punished with a twenty-eight-day stint on the treadmill. To alert  newly arrived convicts to the rigours of working the treadmill, an old chum scrawled a warning on a wall in the treadmill yard:

> Beware new chum,
> Avoid the stepper
> By God you'll find it
> Bloody pepper

Pepper, slang for 'assault' or 'hard blow' comes from the pepper-like shot discharged from a gun, and the fiery taste of pepper. Stepper is slang for treadmill.

CHURY: A knife.

Chury comes from *chury* and *cheiiri*, Romani words for knife. When John Lowe was walking to the triangles to undergo a flogging, flagellator Stephen Maypole called him a 'crawling bugger' and told him to quicken his pace. Lowe was furious and attempted to stab Maypole with a concealed chury forged from a barrel hoop. But by blocking the blow with his hand, Maypole avoided serious injury.

CLEANED OUT: Said of a gambler who has lost his last stake at play; also, of a *flat* who has been stript of all his money by a coalition of *sharps*.

By the mid-nineteenth century, newspaper reports detailing the exploits of '*sharpers*' who 'cleaned out' hapless '*flats*' were commonplace. Members

of the public appealed to the colonial government to clamp down on illegal gambling, but the authorities had a long history of turning a blind eye. When, in 1803, Governor Philip Gidley King issued a last-minute reprieve for one of three condemned convicts, but did not specify

which man, the hangman made them draw lots. Francis Simpson was not permitted to enter the lottery because of his 'unbecoming levity', so when Patrick Gannon drew the short straw, he was fatally cleaned out.

CLOUT: A handkerchief of any kind.

Clout is a corruption of cloth, meaning a piece of fabric. In 1838, a gang of teen-aged pickpockets led nine-year-old Joseph Williams into the streets of London to tutor him in the arts of pickpocketing. But when Williams was nearly caught '*drawing the*

clout' out of a man's pocket, a girl in the gang said 'give it to him, Jack, over the nob, for being such a Johnny Raw', so Jack, the gang's leader, slapped Williams across his face. (Nob is slang for head, and a Johnny Raw is slang for a 'naïve or inexperienced person'.) To improve his pick-pocketing skills, Williams was then instructed by Jack to take a tobacco pipe out of his coat pocket. Williams succeeded in extracting Jack's pipe 'without awakening any suspicion', but police watching from afar swooped on the young thieves and arrested them.

CLOUTING: The practice of picking pockets exclusively of handkerchiefs.

Notorious brute and pickpocket William Bristol mentored children in the art of clouting in an area of London nicknamed Thieves' Kitchen. Bristol, to ensure his students developed a light touch, instructed them to pick handkerchiefs from the pockets of a jacket suspended in midair—if the jacket moved, the child was beaten. When, in 1851, Bristol was sentenced to eighteen months' gaol for attempting to pick a man's pocket, the judge remarked that he 'regretted that the court had not the power of passing such a sentence as would rid the country of the prisoner'.

CLY: A pocket.

Because pickpockets clawed at their victims' pockets, cly may come from *cleye*, a Middle English word for 'claw'. When, in 1832, William Harrison was accused of stealing his master's house key, he refuted the allegation with 'saucy' language. Harrison's master then insisted on '*frisking*' Harrison's 'clye', and, during the scuffle, the key fell from his jacket. Harrison was charged with insolence and sentenced to seven days' solitary confinement in Sydney Gaol.

CLY-FAKER: A pickpocket.

When William Tanner was spotted 'cly-faking', he hid behind a woman's large, bell-shaped dress. But the notorious '*fogle* hunter' was discovered and sentenced to six months' hard labour in Sydney Gaol.

COACH-WHEEL: A dollar or crown-piece.

A crown-piece got its nickname from the large rear wheels of a coach, while a half crown— known as a fore coach wheel—was nicknamed

after the smaller wheels positioned at the front of a coach. Thomas Lucas, a convict serving a life sentence, was well acquainted with coach-wheels—he was a coachman and wheelwright transported to Van Diemen's Land for stealing a cache of money that included a coach-wheel.

COME. A thief observing any article in a shop, or other situation, which he conceives may be easily purloined, will say to his accomplice, I think there is so and so *to come.*
COME IT: To divulge a secret; to tell any thing of one party to another; they say of a thief who has turned evidence against his accomplices, that he is *coming* all he knows, or that he *comes it as strong as a horse.*

In 1835, ex-policeman Thomas Tipper spotted Thomas Swindle stealing a pocket-book. But instead of alerting the police, Tipper decided there would be a pocket-book to come and purloined it from Swindle. When Swindle relinquished the pocket-book he said, 'Tipper, you won't come it upon us?' to which Tipper replied, 'No, of course not,' and let Swindle go. But after police discovered Tipper with the pocket-book, he informed on Swindle to save himself.

COME TO THE HEATH: A phrase signifying to pay or give

money, and synonymous with *Tipping*, from which word it takes its rise, there being a place called Tiptree Heath, I believe, in the County of Essex.

Tip, meaning bribe, is a play on Tiptree Heath, a hamlet in the county of Essex where smugglers would come to store contraband in cellars concealed beneath the locals' cottages.

COME TO THE MARK: To abide strictly by any contract previously made; to perform your part manfully in any exploit or enterprise you engage in; or to offer me what I consider a fair price for any article in question.

Benjamin Hinks boasted that he 'would come to the mark' when selling stolen items to '*staunch*' people. Hinks, who lived 'on the *cross*' for three years, and his accomplice, James Francis, a '*cross cove*' of twenty years' standing, were convicted of stealing and selling a saddle. Hinks was sentenced to seven years' transportation, while Francis copped fourteen years.

CONCERNED: In using many cant words, the lovers of *flash*, by way of variation, adopt this term, for an illustration of which, see: BOLT-IN-TUN, ALDERMAN LUSHINGTON, MR. PALMER, etc.

CONK: The nose.

CONK: A thief who impeaches his accomplices; a spy; informer, or tell-tale. See: NOSE, and WEAR IT.

Conk may come from *concha*, the Latin word for shell, or from *kogcha*, Greek for 'anything hollow'. Some convicts, such as pugilist Tom Way,  were celebrated for punching their opponents on the 'conk'. But others, like Thomas Tweddle, were despised for biting off conks. Tweddle, after arguing with John Fennel about religion, bit off his conk, spat it on the ground and remarked, 'who is your God now?' Fennel accused Tweddle of assault and provided damning evidence: the conk pickled in a bottle of wine and the testimony of conks. But Tweddle escaped punishment, successfully arguing that Fennel's nose detached when he fell on broken glass.

COVE: The master of a house or shop, is called *the Cove*; on other occasions, when joined to particular words, as a *cross-cove*, a *flash-cove*, a *leary-cove*, etc., it simply implies a man of these several descriptions; sometimes, in speaking of any third person, whose name you are either ignorant of, or don't wish to mention, the word *cove* is adopted by way of emphasis, as may be seen under the word AWAKE.

Cove may derive from *cofe*, Scottish for pedlar, or from *cova* and *covo*, Romani for man. At a Yarrawonga pub, John Murphy and John Raleigh were arrested for attempting to rob Officer Patrick O'Sullivan, who'd disguised himself as an intoxicated '*flash cove*'. Murphy was sentenced to nine months' gaol, while Raleigh got six months'.

COVER: To stand in such a situation as to obscure your *Pall*, who is committing a robbery, from the view of by-standers or persons passing, is called *covering* him. Any body whose dress or stature renders him particularly eligible for this purpose, is said to be *a good cover.*

At the Bolt-in-Tun Inn, eighteen-year-old Henry Taylor stole a man's handkerchief while his accomplices were 'covering him to prevent anybody from seeing what he was doing'. But Constable William Owen, who was observing from afar, arrested the boys and they were transported to New South Wales for life.

COVESS: The mistress of a house or shop, and used on other occasions, in the same manner as *Cove,* when applied to a man.

In 1819, Elizabeth Martin, the covess of a London linen shop, sold a pair of stockings to fifteen-year-old Sarah Lyon and fourteen-year-old Esther Levy. But as the two girls were leaving the shop, a customer overheard Levy say: 'If the cove had turned her back we might have had half the shop.' Discovered with eleven stolen handkerchiefs, they were sentenced to seven years' transportation.

CRAB: To prevent the perfection or execution of any intended matter or business, by saying any thing offensive or unpleasant, is called *crabbing it,* or *throwing a crab*; to *crab* a person, is to use offensive language or behaviour as will highly displease, or put him in an ill humour.

CRAB'D: Affronted; out of humour; sometimes called, being in *Crab-street*.

The term crab is derived from the snapping pincers of an irate crab. At Launceston's St John's Hospital, Margaret White, nee Kennedy, was arrested for pinching a £1 note. Kennedy, who was 'feeble from age' and a 'helpless cripple', was carried seated on a chair into court. Once there, she insisted that she'd mistaken the £1 note for a scrap of paper to light her pipe, but after she was accused of stealing the note she was 'crabbed' and decided to keep it. She was sentenced to one year's gaol. Kennedy, a convict, may have been maimed when she was scalded with boiling water preparing laundry en route to Van Diemen's Land.

CRABSHELLS: Shoes.

Shoes may have been nicknamed crabshells because of their shape and toughness. When intoxicated sailor Harry McCann woke to discover a prostitute running away with his clothing and cash, he called for the police. The case went to trial the following morning, but because McCann was required for sea service he offered to drop the charges and let the woman keep the money providing she returned his 'crab shells' and 'rigging'. But Magistrate John Smith Fleming decided to prosecute the woman, so she was remanded in Newgate Prison and McCann's clothing and shoes were retained as evidence. Rigging is nautical slang for clothes.

CRACK: To break open; *the crack* is the *game* of house-breaking; *a crack* is a breaking any house or building for the purpose of plunder.

In 1851, Frederick Dowden was gaoled for burglary. A prisoner in a nearby cell reportedly asked him, 'What have they got you here for?' to which Dowden replied, 'For a Crack'. He lamented that if police discovered his '*swag*' he would surely be '*lagged*'. Dowden was correct in this assumption, and he was transported to Fremantle Prison in Western Australia for a fifteen-year term.

CRACKSMAN: A house-breaker.

Van Diemonian convict James Lowe, a housebreaker and machinist proficient at making picklocks, was caught red-handed with 'false keys and picklocks' and banished to the Port Arthur Penal Station for two years' hard labour. Soon after his release he was arrested again, this time under suspicion of breaking into a warehouse with a 'cracksman's knife'—a tool that Lowe insisted was a 'horse-pick' for removing stones from horses' hoofs. But a locksmith testified the tool was a picklock, so Lowe was sentenced to life at the Norfolk Island Penal Station.

CRACK A WHID: To speak or utter: as, he *crack'd* some *queer whids*, he dropt some bad or ugly expressions: *crack a whid* for me, intercede, or put in a word for me. See: WHID.

In 1835, John George caught James Whitelock and Thomas Johnson stealing a sack of flour from his master's bakery. Johnson warned George 'not to crack a weed' but George informed his master and the two thieves were arrested. Johnson copped six months' gaol, but nineteen-year-old Whitelock was transported to Van Diemen's Land for a seven-year term.

CRACKER: A small loaf, served to prisoners in jails, for their daily subsistence.

According to convict and memoirist Louis Garnerary, crackers served to convicts imprisoned on English hulks were no bigger than the size 'of a fist' and often inedible due to their 'coarse' texture. But for many convicts, transportation to the Australian colonies afforded them little respite from unsavory hulk rations. Van Diemonian convict and memoirist John Leonard noted that convicts at the Grasstree Hill Road Station were 'half-starved' because their cracker ration was so putrid it could stick to a wall.

CRAP: The gallows.
CRAP'D: Hanged.

Crap may derive from crop, meaning harvest, or from *krap*, Dutch for clasp. Solomon Blay, a convict crap-merchant—hangman—is alleged to have hanged his victims with little regard. When John 'Rocky' Whelan was crap'd, he dropped through the crap and struggled for twenty-one agonising

minutes. During his fifty-year reign as hangman, Blay hanged over two hundred Van Diemonians, becoming the longest serving hangman in British history.

CRIB: A house, sometimes applied to shops, as, a *thimble-crib*, a watch-maker's shop; a *stocking-crib*, a hosier's, etc.

Crib may come from *cribbe*, a Middle English word for manger. Rowland McGill copped a ten-day stint on the Sydney treadmill for '*cracking* his master's crib' in order to '*mill*' him.

CROAK: To die.

Croak is attributed to the 'gurgling sound a person makes when the breath of life is departing'. In 1882, an elderly man croaked in Croaker Creek, New South Wales. The man, whose face had been 'eaten away by birds and cats' was, by his clothes, identified as an itinerant worker named Jack. But the remains of other wayfarers discovered during the colonial era defied identification. Locals could only speculate as to who the person was and how they may have died. In 1889, a skeleton was  discovered at Darlot in Western Australia with boots laced to its feet and a water bag tucked beneath its skull. A scrap of weatherworn paper was found nearby but the only legible word was 'Locke.' The skeleton of another West Australian was discovered scattered beneath a tree. Initials carved into the tree trunk were assumed to be those of the deceased, but because the carving was so old the letters had all but grown over.

CROOK: A sixpence. See: BENDER

A sixpence bent to form a crook was a token of good luck. But coins were also inscribed with messages. Love tokens, as they were known, were popular with convicts. Before twenty-one-year-old George Needham was executed for burglary in 1818, he inscribed a crook with his name and gifted it to a loved one.

CROSS: Illegal or dishonest practices in general are called *the cross*, in opposition to *the square*. See: SQUARE. Any article which has been irregularly obtained, is said to have been *got upon the cross*, and is emphatically termed a *cross article*.

Cross, meaning dishonest, may come from criminals who are at cross-purposes with, or opposed to, societal norms. In 1886, George Donovan

 made the mistake of befriending a pair of undercover policemen patrolling the streets of Melbourne. Donovan offered to sell the policemen a silver bracelet that he 'got on the cross'. But when the group walked passed a watchhouse in Little Collins Street, the police arrested Donovan and escorted him to gaol.

CROSS-COVE, or CROSS-MOLLISHER: A man or woman who lives *upon the cross*.

English artist and social satirist George Cruikshank disguised himself as a criminal so he could study his subjects more intimately. According to Cruikshank, a thief might refer to himself as a 'cross cove', and an honest man as a '*square cove*'. But thieves also communicated with secret signs, such as 'putting their fingers across' when greeting each other.

CROSS-CRIB: A house inhabited, or kept by *family* people. See: SQUARE CRIB.

When convict George Price was discovered drinking booze in an 'accommodating crib', he was sentenced to six days on 'Mr. Gunn's circular motion'—the Hobart Town treadmill, supervised by Lieutenant William Gunn.

CROSS-FAM: To *cross-fam* a person, is to pick his pocket, by crossing your arms in a particular position.

David Haggart was a practitioner of the cross-fam—he passed his arm across his body to pick the pocket of a person standing beside him. Pickpockets developed strategies to perpetrate theft undetected. Edward Davies, while holding his hat, draped his arm over his victim's shoulder to conceal his other hand picking their pocket. Mary Blakeman wore a pair of false arms embedded in a muff to provide cover for her hands as she picked the pockets of unsuspecting theatregoers. Some pickpockets, however, had no arms. Joseph Hall, an armless man, was accused of knocking a man's hat over his eyes and then clasping him with his 'stumps' while his accomplices emptied the man's pockets of cash.

CUE. See: LETTER Q.

CUT THE LINE. See: LINE.
CUT THE STRING. See: STRING.
CUT THE TARN. See: YARN.

CUTTING-GLOAK: A man famous for drawing a knife, and cutting any person he quarrels with.

Spanish sailor Pedro Aldanoes threatened to stab a policeman when he was caught picking pockets. Aldanoes was sentenced to seven years' transportation to New South Wales, arriving in 1815. In 1818, he was sentenced to be hanged for stabbing a policeman to death. When the infamous cutting-gloak stood on the gallows, he drew a razor that was hidden in his hair and attempted to slash the hangman.

DAB: A bed.

Dab, meaning bed, may be back slang derived from dab, 'a soft mass'. Author Alexander Harris observed an ex-convict 'make the dab' with a blanket, sheepskins and clothes. But convict John Broxup slept on a pile of ferns and branches, and Nicholas Doyle on a piece of bark. Convicts typically slept in canvas hammocks or beds made from wooden boards, though they often went without beds and slept on the ground. Bedding was usually two blankets, a rug and a canvas mattress, called a palliasse, which was filled with wool, straw, sawdust or hair.

DAB IT UP: To *dab it up* with a woman, is to agree to cohabit with her.

According to Scottish sailor and memoirist John Nicol, 'every man on board took a wife from among the convicts' of the *Lady Julian* as she sailed to New South Wales in 1789. Nicol agreed to dab it up with Sarah Whitlam, a nineteen-year-old burglar on a seven-year sentence. During the 309-day voyage, Whitlam gave birth to their son, John Jnr, but soon after their arrival the family separated; Nicol shipped out, so Whitlam took a new partner.

DANCERS: Stairs.

Stairs were called dancers because people 'danced' up and down them. For neglect of duty, James Coyle was sentenced to 'dance on the tread-mill' —a long rotating cylindrical wheel fitted with steps. Attached to the wheel was a system of gears that turned millstones to grind grain. Convicts climbed the treadmill as though they were walking up dancers. Slang names for a treadmill included stepper, shin-scraper, cock-chafer, wheel-of-life, roundabout, Jack the slipper, the stairs without a landing, the never-ending staircase, and the Cubit, so named after its inventor, William Cubit.

DANNA: Human, or other excrement.

Danna may be a corruption of dung. In 1843, Thomas Baker, the publican of Sydney's Crown and Anchor Pub, was rumoured to be re-locating to a site unfit for a 'dunniken' to take advantage of its proximity to a newly erected theatre. Dunniken, derived from *danna* and *ken*, is slang for 'toilet'.

DANNA-DRAG: Commonly pronounced *dunnick-drag*. See: KNAP A JACOB, etc.

DARBIES: Fetters.

Darbies may derive from *Father Darby's bands*, a rigid seventeenth-century bond that bound the borrower to the moneylender. When convict Ellen King attacked a witness at the Hobart Town Police Court, she was clapped in handcuffs. But the handcuffs were too big, so King 'slipped the darbies' and attacked the witness a second time.

DARKY: Night.
DARKY: A dark lanthorn.

Richard Gould, suspected of perpetrating burglary and murder under the cover of darky, was arrested at England's Gravesend docks attempting to flee to New South Wales. When the case went to trial, witnesses testified that Gould was planning to '*serve*' an 'old man' after acquiring '*screws*' and a 'darkey'. He was sentenced to life in New South Wales. A lanthorn is a handheld lantern.

DEATH-HUNTER: An undertaker.

Twenty-seven-year-old William Player was transported to Van Diemen's Land for stealing a blanket from a death-hunter. Player died in 1867, at the age of seventy-six. Because he was a pauper, he was probably placed in a plain wooden coffin, and, with minimal ceremony, interred in an unmarked grave.

DICKY, or DICK IN THE GREEN: Very bad or paltry; any thing of an inferior quality, is said to be *a dicky concern.*

Richard 'Dicky' Hart, released from back-to-back stints on Cockatoo Island and in Darlinghurst Gaol, was said to be in a 'dickey state'. So Johanna Dacey, a benevolent Sydneysider, allowed him to lodge in her house. But when she discovered she was missing £21, she accused Hart of stealing and evicted him. Hart was then caught picking pockets, charged with being a 'rogue and a vagabond', and returned to Darlinghurst Gaol.

DIMMOCK: Money.

Dimmock may stem from *dime*, French for tithe, one-tenth of a sum of money. In 1835, a letter written by convicts James Phillips and James Moony was found lying on a country road in New South Wales. The letter revealed, that, when flush with 'dimmick', the two convicts had purchased contraband tobacco from the cook assigned to their chain gang.

DING: To throw, or throw away; particularly any article you have stolen, either because it is worthless, or that there is danger of immediate apprehension. To *ding* a person, is to drop his acquaintance totally; also to quit his company, or leave him for the time present; to *ding* to your *pall*, is to convey to him, privately, the property you have just stolen; and he who receives it is said to *take ding*, or to *knap the ding*. DINGABLE: Any thing considered worthless, or which you can well spare, having no further occasion for it, is declared to be *dingable*. This phrase is often applied by *sharps* to a *flat* whom they have *cleaned out*; and by abandoned women to a keeper, who having spent his all upon them, must be discarded, or *ding'd* as soon as possible.

Ding may derive from dung, meaning worthless. When John Williams stole a basket of raisins, his accomplice instructed him to 'ding it' after he spotted Constable Daniel Cartwright hot on their tail. But Cartwright collared Williams and arrested him. At Williams' trial, the judge asked him: 'What does ding it mean?' He replied: 'To throw the property away'. Williams was sentenced to seven years' transportation.

DISPATCHES: False dice used by gamblers, so contrived as always to throw a nick.

Gamblers used false dice to 'dispatch' their opponents, while a nick is a winning roll in the dice game known as hazard. James White, a resident at George Alderson's hotel in Melbourne, played hazard with his landlord most evenings. White usually lost the games, and eventually discovered that he'd been cheated with 'despatch die'. White prosecuted Alderson to recover his losses, but the judge deemed the two gamblers as bad as each other and so dismissed the case.

DO: A term used by *smashers*; *to do a queer half-quid*, or *a queer screen*, is to utter a **counterfeit half-guinea**, or a forged bank-note.

When convict James Gavaghan was gaoled for viciously biting a policeman, he was overheard plotting to 'do' the officer with a '*chiv*'. Gavaghan was sentenced to two years' at the Port Arthur Penal Station.

DO IT AWAY: To *fence* or dispose of a stolen article beyond the reach of probable detection.

In 1870, John Entwistle Holden and John Martin, counterfeiters who had absconded from Fremantle Prison, were apprehended walking along the North Fremantle Bridge. Holden threw a bundle of incriminating counterfeit coins into the river, but the arresting officer retrieved them. The two men begged the officer to 'do away with the coins' but he refused. Holden copped a seven-year sentence and Martin copped three years. But ex-convict John Ollis was then also arrested for doing away with the two convicts—he was charged with 'having knowingly harbored two convicts illegally at large' and sentenced to nine months in Fremantle Prison.

DO IT UP: To accomplish any object you have in view; to obtain any thing you were in quest of, is called *doing it up for* such a thing; a person who contrives by *nob-work*, or ingenuity, to live an easy life and appears to improve daily in circumstances, is said to *do it up in good twig*.

 Convict John Gough was arrested 'doing it up' when a *'charley'* recognised the 'cut of his *mug*'. Gough, who'd changed out of his parti-colour uniform, was discovered smoking a cigar while escorting a woman to the theatre. He was sentenced to twelve months' hard labour in chains.

DO THE TRICK: To accomplish any robbery, or other business successfully; a thief who has been fortunate enough to acquire an independence, and prudent enough to *tie it up* in time, is said by his former associates to have *done the trick*;

on the other hand, a man who has imprudently involved himself in some great misfortune, from which there is little hope of his extrication is declared by his friends, with an air of commiseration, to have *done the trick* for himself; that is, his ruin or downfall is nearly certain.

John Leader and John Cane escaped from a chain gang to 'do the trick' on Chief Justice Francis Forbes of New South Wales. After sneaking into his house, they stole thirty-six shirts, twenty-four pairs of trousers, eighteen waistcoats and twelve pairs of stockings. But the Forbes family woke and interrupted the two thieves, who were arrested fleeing the scene. They were sentenced to seven-years terms.

DOBBIN: Riband. See: CANT.

DOLLOP: A *dollop* is a large quantity of any thing; *the whole dollop* means the total quantity.

The standard reward for the apprehension of runaway convicts was £2. But according to the *Launceston Advertiser*, some bounty hunters colluded with convicts to obtain the money—after the absconder was caught and sentenced to a judicial 'dollop' he was paid a share of the 'gilt'. (Gilt, slang for money, derives from gold.) For allowing a prisoner to escape custody and share a reward, Convict-Constable Howell Howell was sentenced to three years' hard labour at the Port Arthur Penal Station.

DONE: Convicted; as, he was *done* for *a crack*, he was convicted of house-breaking.

In 1835, 'a very wretched looking old man' was caught clambering through the ceiling of a bakery in Hounslow, England. The man, who was dressed as a sailor, identified himself as Charles Noble; a twenty-year veteran of the Royal Navy. Noble confessed that he had committed the crime because he was 'starving', and then resigned himself to the fact that he was 'done'. He was charged with breaking and entering and condemned to death. But the jury recommended mercy, so Noble was instead sentenced to a hulk for five-years' imprisonment. To alleviate congested prisons, decommissioned warships were transformed into floating prisons called hulks. Hulk life was dank and gloomy, and the conditions were foul. Prisoners worked onboard doing odd jobs such as making and mending shoes, or were ferried ashore for dock work.

DORSE: A lodging; to *dorse* with a woman, signifies to sleep with her.

Dorse may come from *dorsus*, a Latin word referring to the 'back' on which the sleeper lies. According to an exposé of the English underworld published in an 1852 edition of the *Kendal Mercury*, 'coves' and 'molls' could 'dorse' for a '*darkey*' in a 'padding *ken*'—a lodging house that catered to criminals and vagabonds. Convicts transported

to the Australian colonies, however, were required to marry and obtain a respectable dorse if they wished to dorse together. In 1853, convicts Thomas Johnson and Ellen Lynch were married in Hobart Town. But two years later, Charles Waters, also a convict, was discovered hiding beneath the Johnsons' bed. Waters and Lynch were sentenced to six months' hard labour in a government dorse.

––––––––––

DOUBLE: To *double* a person, or *tip* him *the Dublin packet*, signifies either to run away from him openly, and elude his attempts to overtake you, or to give him the slip in the streets, or elsewhere, unperceived, commonly done to escape from an officer who has you in custody, or to *turn up a flat* of any kind, whom you have a wish to get rid of.

Dublin is a pun on double, meaning 'to turn sharply and run away'. A Dublin Packet was a boat that ferried mail to and from Ireland. But packets were also contracted to freight stolen or illegal goods, including dead bodies. The illegal exportation of Irish cadavers for use in anatomical study was said to have been carried out to a 'shameful extant'. In 1826, a shipment of casks was discovered to contain eleven cadavers packed in salt. And in 1829, seven cadavers were discovered in a cask labelled 'hams'. In 1830, James Henry, a fourteen-year-old delivery  boy, narrowly avoided a murder charge after he was discovered at the Dublin docks with a trunk containing the body of a woman—the trunk's owner had abruptly done a double.

––––––––––

DOUBLE-SLANGS: Double-irons. See: SLANGS.

Two sets of leg irons prevented a convict from running or swimming to freedom. When John Scott leapt from his transport ship, the weight of his double-slangs dragged him to the bottom of the Derwent River. A month later his body washed up in such a 'putrefied state' that it had to be buried on the spot. Convicts could also be sentenced to wear three sets of leg irons. During the voyage of the *Royal Charlotte* in 1825, ten convicts who plotted to seize the ship were clapped in triple irons.

———————————

DOWN: Sometimes synonymous with *awake*, as, when the party you are about to rob, sees or suspects your intention, it is then said that *the cove is down. A down* is a suspicion, alarm, or discovery, which taking place, obliges yourself and *palls* to give up or desist from the business or depredation you were engaged in; to *put a down upon* a man, is to give information of any robbery or fraud he is about to perpetrate, so as to cause his failure or detection; to *drop down to* a person is to discover or be aware of his character or designs; to *put* a person *down to* any thing, is to apprize him of, elucidate, or explain it to him; to *put a swell down*, signifies to alarm or put a gentleman on his guard, when in the attempt to pick his pocket, you fail to effect it at once, and by having touched him a little too roughly, you cause him to suspect your design, and to use precautions accordingly; or perhaps, in the act of *sounding* him, by being too precipitate or incautious, his suspicions may have been excited, and it is then said that you have *put* him *down, put* him *fly,* or *spoiled* him. See: SPOIL IT. To *drop down upon yourself,* is to become melancholy, or feel symptoms of remorse or compunction, on being committed to jail, cast for death, etc. To sink under misfortunes of any kind. A man who gives way to this weakness, is said to be *down upon himself.*

James Hallen, it was said, was 'too downey a *cove* to be caught'. But in 1837, he was convicted of embezzling four hundred yards of fabric and sentenced to fourteen years' transportation to Van Diemen's Land.

DOWN AS A HAMMER; DOWN AS A TRIPPET. These are merely emphatical phrases, used *out of flash*, to signify being *down, leary, fly*, or *awake* to any matter, meaning, or design.

Convict Edward Brammer was notorious for knocking off his leg irons and escaping, but overseers who were down as a hammer thwarted his escapes. Because of his misconduct, Brammer wound up hewing coal in the dreaded Van Diemonian coalmines. In 1841 he was struck a fatal blow after a convict dropped his pickaxe down the mineshaft.

DRAG: A cart. *The drag*, is the *game* of robbing carts, waggons, or carriages, either in town or country, of trunks, bale-goods, or any other property. *Done for a drag*, signifies convicted for a robbery of the before-mentioned nature.

A cart was called a drag because it was dragged by horses, but stealing from a cart may have been termed 'the drag' because thieves dragged off the goods. When a warehouseman spotted John Roberts 'drag a truss of tea from a cart', he was done for a drag and

sentenced to seven years' transportation. To deter such thieves, the rear platforms on carts and carriages were studded with iron spikes. Drags armed with spikes were extremely dangerous—in 1818, a boy who jumped on the back of a carriage had his leg impaled and was nearly dragged to his death. Spiked carriages were outlawed in 1832.

DRAG-COVE: The driver of a cart.

Australia's first passenger railway was established in 1836, at Port Arthur. Convicts propelled small wooden carts that ran along narrow wooden rails. Passengers paid one shilling for a one-way trip. Luke Marshall was a drag-cove who, in 1877, fractured his spine when he leapt from a cart during a downhill run. Marshall died six years later, laid up in an invalid depot. The cause of his death was attributed to 'an old injury to the spine'.

DRAGS MAN: A thief who follows the *game* of *dragging*.

An 1833 edition of the *Colonial Times* printed a letter warning the mailman to be more careful securing his mailbags to the mail cart. To call attention to the game of dragging, the letter was signed 'A. DRAGSMAN'. Twelve months later, however, the mailbags were stolen in the largest mail robbery in the history of Van Diemen's Land.

DRAKED: Ducked; a discipline sometimes inflicted on pick-pockets at fairs, races, etc.

Draked probably comes from drake, the name for a male duck. In 1837, when two members of the *Swell* Mob were caught picking pockets at a fair in Greenwich, England, they were bound hand and foot, draked in a river and then rolled along a dusty road. Draking, it was said, saved 'the trouble and expense of prosecuting' and, by rendering pick-  pockets a sodden mess, prevented the perpetrators from inconspicuously blending in with the public. But draking could be fatal. Thomas Wakin, a boy, was drowned when he was 'ducked' in a pond.

DRAW: To *draw* a person, is to pick his pocket, and the act of so stealing a pocket-book, or handkerchief, is called *drawing* a *reader*, or *clout*. To obtain money or goods of a person by a false or plausible story, is called *drawing* him *of* so and so. To *draw a kid*, is to obtain his *swag* from him. See KID-RIG.

When William Nicholls passed out in an English pub, George Saunders picked his pocket. Saunders boasted that he'd 'drawn the *cove*' and bought a round of drinks for his friends. When Nicholls sobered up he contacted the police, but because he was so drunk at the time of the crime, his testimony was unreliable and Saunders escaped prosecution.

DRIZ: Lace, as sold on cards by the haberdashers, etc.

Driz may derive from *doriez*, a Romani word for lace. Scrawled above a fireplace in a Dartford lodging house were the words: 'Scotch Mary with driz, bound to Dover and back, please God.' Instances of travellers scrawling their names and vocations in lodging houses were commonplace, but because this lodging house was formerly a gaol, it's possible that the author was a Scottish woman named Mary, who, after being gaoled for stealing lace, prayed for a safe return to Dover.

DROP: The *game* of ring-dropping is called *the drop.*
DROP: To give or present a person with money, as, he *dropp'd* me a *quid,* he gave me a guinea. A *kid* who delivers his bundle to a sharper without hesitation, or a shopkeeper who is easily duped of his goods by means of a forged order or false pretence, is said to *drop the swag in good twig,* meaning, to part with it freely.

On London Bridge in 1836, Sarah Bush saw a man pick up a small parcel from the footpath. Inside the parcel appeared to be a gold ring, earrings  and a brooch. The man, George Adams, offered to sell the items to Bush for a cheap price, so she agreed to drop him six shillings and six pence. But later that day, Bush discovered she'd been duped into buying worthless jewellery smeared in gold paint. When, a few days later, Adams attempted the drop on Bush again, she alerted the police and the notorious 'ring dropper' was arrested and sentenced to seven years' transportation.

DROP A WHID: To let fall a word, either inadvertently or designedly.

When Thomas Faxton and Thomas Smith were arrested on suspicion of committing highway robbery, Faxton fell to his knees to drop a whid and confess to their crime. Smith replied: 'Ye whiddling Dog, now you have

hang'd your self, and me too, but if I had a Knife, I'd cut your Throat.'
Both men were executed at Tyburn, England, in 1732.

DROP-COVE: A *sharp* who practises the *game* of ring-dropping.

The day before Valentines Day in 1858, Elizabeth Brookes accepted a ring from a passer-by named William Taylor, who claimed to have found it in the street. But Taylor was a drop-cove—when Brookes kissed him goodbye, he slipped his hand into her pocket, stole all her money and took back the ring.

DROP-DOWN. See: DOWN.

DRUMMOND: Any scheme or project considered to be infallible, or any event which is deemed inevitably certain, is declared to be a *Drummond*; meaning, it is as sure as the credit of that respectable banking-house, Drummond and Co.

Goldsmith Andrew Drummond founded the English banking firm Drummond and Company in 1717. The Bank of Australia, founded in 1826, was nicknamed the 'pure Merino' after its non-convict clientele who were deemed as fine as purebred merino sheep. But in 1828, convicts crawled through a sewer that ran beneath the bank, tunnelled into the vault and stole approximately £14,000. They were caught and banished to Norfolk Island. The mastermind, however, was convict stonemason Thomas Turner, who'd assisted in the construction of the vault and sewer but didn't participate in the robbery—for his clever drummond, he received a lesser punishment and stayed put in Sydney.

DUB: A key.

Dub may be a corruption of dup, meaning open, derived from *do ope*, slang for 'to open'. Many convicts were experts at picking locks with specially

crafted keys called 'queer dubs'. In 1893, gaolers at Melbourne's Pentridge Prison were shocked to discover that Charles Ballard, an inmate, had unlocked a 'secret lock made expressly and solely for the Penal department by a firm of English locksmiths'. Ballard, it transpired, had dedicated his ten-year term to perfecting the perfect dub—discovered in the drain connected to his cell was a pile of reject keys that hadn't flushed.

DUB AT A KNAPPING-JIGGER: A collector of tolls at a turnpike-gate.

A turnpike-gate, commonly called a tollgate, was a barrier positioned across a road that prevented travellers from proceeding unless they paid a toll. Rueben Joseph, a convict so notorious for dealing in stolen goods that he was nicknamed 'the *fence*', was, rather aptly, the dub at a knapping-jigger in Van Diemen's Land. He collected tollgate tokens imprinted with a picture of his tollhouse, tollgate and fence.

DUB-COVE, or DUBSMAN: A turnkey.

A gaoler was known as a 'turnkey' because they turned keys. At Nenagh Gaol, Ireland, highwayman James Ryan gave 'the dubsman a holiday', a slang term for 'escaped from gaol'. After prying up a flagstone in his cell, Ryan crawled through the sewer and into the gaol yard. There, he purloined a ladder, scaled the twenty-four-foot wall and, using his bedding, lowered himself over the other side. But when he landed he broke his right leg, and, after crawling two and a half miles, he was discovered hiding in a bog. Ryan was transported to Van Diemen's Land for a fifteen-year term.

DUBLIN-PACKET. See: DOUBLE.

DUB UP: To lock up or secure any thing or place; also to button one's pocket, coat, etc.

Dub up was also slang for paying money. In 1842, notorious inebriate Eugene Rogers was fined £3 for assaulting a policeman. But because Rogers did not have 'cash to dub up', he was sentenced to dub up for a month in Sydney Gaol.

DUCE. Twopence is called a duce.

Duce comes from *duos*, Latin for two. In an 1852 edition of the *Kendal Mercury*, the English public was alerted to 'professional *cadgers*' who perpetrated 'dodges'—cons. In the 'maimed dodge', beggars scoured their skin with blue stone and smeared the abrasions with gobs of fat to fabricate hideous wounds and bilk money from sympathetic Brits. But the most lucrative con was the 'escaped slave dodge': black sailors on shore leave pretended to have escaped from slave colonies, and, by professing a religious conversion, profited especially well from religious groups such as the Wesleyan Society. After a busy day scamming, such conmen lodged in a '*cadgers* hotel' after '*tipping* the deuce' to the hotelier.

DUDS: Women's apparel in general.

Duds comes from the Middle English word *dudde*, meaning 'clothes'. Mary Carroll, a noted 'duds' thief, was sentenced to three months'  gaol with hard labour. But Elizabeth Farrell was sentenced to seven years' transportation for stealing clothes. During the voyage to New South Wales, she was punished with a 'wooden jacket'—a barrel with two holes cut for her arms. When Farrell donned the unusual duds she amused her shipmates with turtle impersonations, but because the barrel prevented her sitting or lying comfortably, the joke soon wore off, and, after promising to behave, she was released.

DUES. This term is sometimes used to express money, where any certain sum or payment is spoken of; a man asking for money due to him for any service done, or a *blowen* requiring her previous compliment from a *family-man*, would say, Come, *tip us the dues*. So a thief, requiring his share of booty from his *palls*, will desire them to *bring the dues to light*.

DUES. This word is often introduced by the lovers of *flash* on many occasions, but merely *out of fancy*, and can only be understood from the context of their discourse; like many other cant terms, it is not easily explained on paper: for example, speaking of a man likely to go to jail, one will say, there will be *quodding dues concerned*, of a man likely to be executed; there will be *topping dues*, if any thing is alluded to that will require a fee or bribe, there must be *tipping dues*, or *palming dues concerned*, etc.

In 1829, thieves looted Henry Wilson's drapery shop in Bishopsgate, London. After leasing an adjacent property, the gang tunnelled through the adjoining wall and stole goods valued at more than £300. Following a tipoff from Mrs Dobson, a local weaver, Wilson discovered some of his missing silk in the house of Richard Chick. When police arrested Chick, he swore to his innocence and stated that 'piping dues are on', meaning that Dobson supplied him with the silk then informed on him to score a reward (piping is slang for speaking). But Chick was not believed and he was sentenced to *topping* dues—execution by hanging. His wife, Mary, then suffered *quodding* dues—she was gaoled for smashing twenty panes of glass in Dobson's ground floor windows.

DUMMY: A pocket-book; a silly half-witted person.

A pocket-book containing banknotes is dumb, meaning mute, unlike a purse containing coins that loudly chink together. When, in 1872, John Duffy refuted a charge of highway robbery at the Melbourne Magistrates' Court, the prosecutor produced the plaintiff's dummy and pointed out that Duffy had written his name in it, but neglected to erase the plaintiff's name. Duffy the dummy was sentenced to eight years' hard labour with two years in leg irons.

DUMMY-HUNTERS: Thieves who confine themselves to the practice of stealing gentlemen's pocket-books, and think, or profess to think, it paltry to touch a *clout*, or other insignificant article; this class of depredators traverse the principal streets of London, during the busy hours, and sometimes meet with valuable prizes.

In 1835, ex-policeman Thomas Tipper was indicted for receiving a stolen pocket-book from Thomas Swindle, a dummy-hunter. Tipper, who swore to his innocence, insisted that he'd confiscated the pocket-book to reunite it with its rightful owner. But Swindle, who was adamant that Tipper was double-dealing, declared: 'God perish me blind if he did not take the dummy from me when we *drawed* it'. Tipper escaped prosecution but Swindle was transported to Van Diemen's Land for a seven-year term. Soon after Swindle arrived he was appointed to the police force, but after a spate of scandalous incidents he was dismissed.

EARWIG: To overhear.

In 1849, Mary Kinsdale slipped her arm behind Robert Harvey, an off-duty policeman, and cut the ribbon securing his watch around his neck. But Harvey heard 'the click of scissors' and accosted her. The would-be watch thief then discreetly coughed to summon her accomplice, Albert Prior, to rescue her. But Harvey punched them both in the head, arrested them, and locked them in adjacent cells to listen in on their conversation. Kinsdale told Prior that he would get 'ten *stretch*', but when Prior realised that police were listening he cried, 'earwig, earwig'. Kinsdale was sentenced to twelve months' hard labour, but Prior, as predicted by Kinsdale, copped ten years' transportation.

FADGE: A farthing.

A farthing is a low-value coin. Eighteen-year-old Laura Whittaker, an impoverished prostitute from London's Quadrant, charged her clients two shillings and one penny—100 fadge. In 1831, for stealing a man's clothing, she was transported to Van Diemen's Land for a seven-year term. In the *Flare-Up Songster,* a book of verse published in 1834, the farthing's paltry status is used to mock the plight of Quadrant prostitutes such as Whittaker:

> I am a fine *Blowen tog'd* out so gay,
> And down the Quadrant I take my way,
> I never goes one fadge under my price
> They must pay for my mutton if they want a slice.

FAKE: A word so variously used, that I can only illustrate it by a few examples.

To *fake* any person or place, may signify to rob them; to fake a person, may also imply to shoot, wound, or cut; to *fake* a man *out and out*, is to kill him; a man who inflicts wounds upon, or otherwise disfigures, himself, for any sinister purpose, is said to have *faked himself*; if a man's shoe happens to pinch, or gall his foot, from its being overtight, he will complain that his shoe *fakes* his foot sadly; it also describes the doing of any act, or the fabricating any thing, as, to *fake* your *slangs*, is to cut your irons in order to escape from custody; to *fake* your *pin*, is to create a sore leg, or to cut it, as if accidentally, with an axe, etc., in hopes to obtain a discharge from the army or navy, to get into the doctor's list, etc.; to *fake a screeve*, is to write a letter, or other paper; to *fake a screw*, is to shape out a skeleton or false key, for the purpose of *screwing* a particular place; to *fake a cly*, is to pick a pocket; etc., etc., etc.

James Mason was sentenced to seven years' transportation for faking a house in Bristol, England. But because he continued to fake in Van Diemen's Land, he was banished to the Sarah Island Penal Station. There, he faked himself. Mason was charged with 'disabling himself by cutting off two of his fingers in order to deprive [the] government of his labour'. He was punished with fifty lashes.

FAKE AWAY, THERE'S NO DOWN: An intimation from a thief to his *pall*, during the commission of a robbery, or other act, meaning, go on with your operations, there is no sign of any alarm or detection.

In 1854, Van Diemonian convicts George Meadows and Charles Smith were arrested for speaking 'obscene and detestable language'. But when 'they managed to slip the *darbies* and fake away', they were also charged with absconding. Meadows was sentenced to six months' gaol, and Smith to four.

FAKEMAN-CHARLEY; FAKEMENT. As *to fake* signifies to do any act, or make any thing, so *the fakement* means the act or thing alluded to, and on which your discourse turns; consequently, any stranger unacquainted with your subject will not comprehend what is meant by *the fakement*; for instance, having recently been concerned with another in some robbery, and immediately separated, the latter taking the booty with him, on your next meeting you will inquire, what he has done with the *fakement*? Meaning the article stolen, whether it was a pocket-book, piece or linen, or what not. Speaking of any stolen property which has a private mark, one will say, there is a *fakeman-charley* on it; a forgery which is well executed, is said to be a *prime fakement*; in a word, any thing is liable to be termed a *fakement*, or a *fakeman-charley*, provided the person you address knows to what you allude.

When, in 1845, Constable Matthew Carroll caught Anne Brown 'out on the fakement', he arrested her. Stashed in her apron was an array of stolen items including boots, a decanter, a jug, and a book that the New South Wales press wryly suggested was *Popular Errors*—a sixteenth-century tome addressing medical malpractice. Brown was sentenced to six months' hard labour at the Parramatta Female Factory.

FAM: The hand.
FAM: To feel or handle.

Fam, short for famble, is a slang word for hand that may come from fumble, meaning to handle something clumsily. But the term has also been attributed to *fem*, a Danish word for 'five', meaning 'five fingers'. Bushranger Charles Routley was missing his left fam. To fam and fire his rifle, he wore a specialised 'fam-stick', slang for glove. With an iron hook protruding from a block of wood fastened to his arm, Routley 'took a sure and unerring aim, never missing his shot.'

FAMILY: Thieves, sharpers and all others who get their living *upon the cross*, are comprehended under the title of *"The Family."*

Many criminals cared for each other as though they belonged to the same family. 'The Royal Family' and 'The Family Men' were infamous gangs in mid-eighteenth-century England. Some people, such as fifteen-year-old John Ames, may have joined gangs to survive. When, in 1839, he was charged with stealing six brass castors, he declared: 'my father and mother have been dead eleven years.' But other children, such as Ames' associate, eleven-year-old John Hogan, may have been born into crime. Hogan was convicted of stealing the castors and transported to Australia, where two of his brothers had also been transported. Entire families could also be banished to Australia. When Sophia Gunyon stole £100 and gave it to her husband, she was convicted of stealing and him receiving. They were transported to Van Diemen's Land with their five children. The colonial authorities encouraged convict families to live peacefully and prosper away from the influences of The Family.

FAMILY-MAN, or WOMAN: Any person known or recognised as belonging to *the family*; all such are termed *family people.*

Most convicts transported to Australia did not return to their friends and families in Britain. Infirm ex-convicts ejected from government institutions had to beg, borrow or steal to survive. John Rossiter, a 'very old family man', was infamous in Van Diemen's Land for 'imposing on licensed victuallers'. Three weeks after he was released from his seven-year sentence of transportation, he was sent back to prison for purloining 'food, drink, clothes and money' from the publican of the aptly named Help Me Thro' the World Inn.

FANCY: Any article universally admired for its beauty, or which the owner sets particular store by, is termed a *fancy article*; as, a *fancy clout*, is a favourite handkerchief, etc.; so a woman who is the particular favourite of any man, is termed his *fancy woman*, and *vice versa*.

When Helen Gates stabbed her philandering husband with a shoemaker's knife, she said: 'Take that for drinking with your fancy woman.' The wound was deemed to be 'trifling', so Gates was not capitally convicted and instead sentenced to six months in the Parramatta Female Factory. But when Mary Ann Brownlow caught her husband drinking with a 'fancy woman', she stabbed him to death with a butcher's knife. She was charged with murder and executed.

FAWNEY: A finger-ring.

Fawney may derive from *foshono*, Romani for 'imitation' and 'ring'. In 1878, Sergeant William Thick was patrolling the Shoreditch region of London when he overheard two pickpockets arguing: James Fitzgerald was angry with his partner, William Collins, because he did not steal their victim's 'fawny'. But Collins argued that Fitzgerald had 'done nothing' to assist in the mugging so he was going to keep their victim's '*slang*'. Because Thick was well versed in slang, he ran to the nearest police station, confirmed that a man had recently been mugged for his watch chain, then raced back to the two thieves and arrested them. Fitzgerald was sentenced to eighteen months' gaol while Collins copped a seven-year term.

FAWNIED, or FAWNEY-FAM'D: Having one or more rings on the finger.

In 1880, Andrew George Scott, more famously known as 'Captain Moonlite', was executed for bushranging. At the time of his death he was fawnied with a ring woven from the hair of his partner in crime, James Nesbitt. The two bushrangers, according to Scott's death row correspondence, were 'united by every tie which could bind human friendship'. Scott's 'dying wish' was to be buried next to his 'beloved' in Gundagai Cemetery. The authorities did not approve his request so he was buried in Rockwood Cemetery. But in 1995, a group of Scotts' admirers successfully petitioned to reinter his remains near Nesbitt's unmarked grave.

FEEDER: A spoon.

When John Powers declared he'd '*nailed a feeder*', his friend did not know what he meant until he spotted a spoon poking out of Powers' sleeve. Items that could

be easily concealed were popular targets for thieves. For this reason, convicts were searched on a regular basis. In 1827, in New South Wales, notorious absconder Thomas Quinn was caught tunneling through his cell wall with a feeder. To prevent convicts using cutlery as tools and weaponry, cooking and eating equipment was returned to the convicts' superiors at the end of each meal.

FENCE: A receiver of stolen goods; to *fence* any property, is to sell it to a receiver or other person.

Fence is derived from defence—thieves fenced their booty to defend themselves against the possibility of the police connecting them to their crimes. Isaac Solomon, dubbed the 'Prince of Fences' is the most infamous fence in the history of convict transportation. In 1827, he was arrested for receiving stolen goods but escaped from London to Denmark, then America. From there he travelled to Rio de Janeiro and then to Van Diemen's Land, where his wife, Ann, had been transported with four of their children. But he was recognised, arrested and returned to England. There, Solomon was sentenced to fourteen years' transportation and shipped back to Van Diemen's Land. Notorious the world over, 'Ikey', as he was known, inspired the character of Fagin in Charles Dickens' novel *Oliver Twist*.

FIB: A stick. To *fib* is to beat with a stick; also to box.

Fib may derive from *fob*, meaning 'to put someone off by trickery'. Convict John Stone, who boasted that 'he would be carried dead off

the ground before he would give in,' died
after competing in a fibbing match in
New South Wales. Stone was drunk at
the time of the fight, and his opponent,
convict William Jacques, narrowly avoided

a charge of manslaughter—according to witness testimony, if spectators
had tried to stop the fight they would have been fibbed with a fib.

FIBBING-GLOAK: A pugilist.

A pugilist is a professional boxer. Boxing was a popular sport in seventeenth-century London, with some people of the opinion that it was
a noble sport that encouraged 'the spirit of fair play and honour',
while others denounced it as barbaric entertainment perpetuated by
'murderers, robbers, burglars, thieves, bullies, pickpockets, keepers of
flash and gambling houses of the lowest description, *body-snatchers*, and
vagabonds of every other description.' At least twenty fibbing-gloaks
were transported to Australia, including John 'the Sprig of Shamrock'
Husband, William 'Jack the Painter' Allen, and Dick 'The Pet of the
Fancy' Curtis. Some, such as John 'Perry the Black' Perry, fought profes-
sionally in Australia. Less well known, however, were convicts such as
Charles Barney, who did a ten-day stint on the Sydney treadmill for
'fibbing' his master's 'nob' most 'unmercifully'. (Nob is slang for head.)

FIBBING-MATCH: A boxing match.

Convicts have a long history of prizefighting. The first recorded fibbing-
match in Australia occurred in 1814, in New South Wales, between
Charles Sefton and John Berringer, convicts transported for burglary.

Convict Tom Way was famous for 'fibbing' in Van Diemen's Land, New South Wales and Victoria, though according to his conduct record he was also famous for 'frightening a Young Woman with a Frog'.

FILE: A person who has had a long course of experience in the arts of fraud, so as to have become an adept, is termed *an old file upon the town*; so it is usual to say of a man who is extremely cunning, and not to be over-reached, that he is a *deep file*. *File*, in the old version of cant, signified a pickpocket, but the term is now obsolete.

File, meaning thief, may originate from pickpockets who skimmed property from their victims, similar to the way a file removes the surface layer of an object. In 1858, the New South Wales press declared that fifty-three-year-old James Filewood was a 'queer-looking old file'. Filewood, and his older brother, George, were transported for trafficking shoes and boots. Bootmaker George pilfered footwear from his employer then palmed it off to James, who sold it. Over the course of eighteen months the Filewood boys embezzled forty-six pairs of boots and 150 pairs of shoes.

FINGER-SMITH: A midwife.

Midwives were nicknamed finger-smiths because they worked with their fingers, and because smith means 'maker' and 'worker'. Convicts were the first finger-smiths to arrive in Australia from Britain. Babies were delivered on board transport ships and in prisons. When Jane Skinner went into labour at Richmond Gaol in Van Diemen's Land, Mary Ann

Watson was released from solitary confinement to act as her finger-smith. But Skinner's baby died soon after it was born. Because of unwholesome living conditions and insufficient or inadequate medical training and equipment, the infant mortality rate among convicts was notoriously high. Watson, whose trade was listed as 'washerwoman', may not have been experienced in midwifery. She did, however, have finger-smith expertise—finger-smith is also slang for 'pickpocket'.

FI'PENNY: A clasp-knife.

The term fi'penny was probably derived from a knife with a value of five pence—Edward Ward was robbed of a 'six-penny pocket-knife' but John Ready attempted to cut his own throat with a 'two-penny knife'.

FLASH: The cant language used by the *family*. To speak *good flash* is to be well versed in cant terms.

Flash probably comes from the ostentatious appearance and swaggering attitude of English criminals. But the term also has been attributed to *Flash*, an area in the Staffordshire Moorlands where *flash-men* spoke *flash*. Criminals communicated in flash to exclude people outside their group. Ann Dunne, a convict who lived with a gang of burglars in Sydney, was required to testify against the gang in court. But because they spoke in 'flash terms', Dunne understood 'little of what they said'. She did, however, provide damning testimony: the gang committed burglaries with their *'tools'* but were caught after their *'plant'* was *'sprung'*.

FLASH: A person who affects any peculiar habit, as swearing, dressing in a particular manner, taking snuff, etc., merely to be taken notice of, is said to do it *out of flash*.

When convict John Jones was charged with burglary in 1841, Judge Algernon Sidney Montague sentenced him to life at the Port Arthur Penal Station, with a recommendation that he be 'worked in chains for five or six years'. Montague denounced Jones as an 'abandoned, profligate, bad, flash character; a very wicked man', and because Jones was 'flashibly attired' he was stripped of his 'ornaments'. But according to convict and memoirist William Thompson, 'flash' convicts sentenced to chain gangs formed a 'superior society' that was so 'particular about their appearance' that their leg irons were as 'clean and bright' as 'polished silver'.

FLASH: To be *flash* to any matter or meaning, is to understand or comprehend it, and is synonymous with being *fly*, *down*, or *awake*; to *put* a person *flash to* any thing, is to put him on his guard, to explain or inform him of what he was before unacquainted with.

In 1840, Elizabeth Evans accused Mary Morton of assault. But because the women spoke 'nothing but slang and vulgarity', the Hobart Town magistrate, who was not flash to their testimonies, dismissed the case. Other convicts, however, were gaoled because they spoke flash. In 1845, New South Wales police were about to release two men suspected of a mugging when a passer-by overheard them speaking 'flash language'. The police took a closer look, realised that the men were '*bolters*' and so sent them back to Hyde Park Barracks.

FLASH: To shew or expose any thing: as I *flash'd* him a *bean*, I shewed him a guinea. Don't *flash* your *sticks*, don't expose your pistols, etc.

Frances Smith, a so-called 'bold hussy', was charged with 'indecently exposing her person' in the streets of Hobart Town. For her flash she was sentenced to four months in the Cascades Female Factory. But Convict-Constable Williams was dismissed from the police force and sentenced to four months in a road gang for 'participating in the exposure'.

FLASH-COVE, or COVESS: The landlord or landlady of a *flash-ken*.

Richard Crampton, a noted '*flash cove*', licensed several pubs in Sydney, including the aptly named Red Bull. Crampton was infamous for assaulting people with broomsticks, curtain rods and horsewhips.

FLASH-CRIB, FLASH-KEN, or FLASH-PANNY: A public-house resorted to chiefly by *family people*, the master of which is commonly an old *prig*, and not unfrequently an *old-lag*.

Constable Samuel Furzeman, whose 'skill and prowess' in sending criminals to Australia was 'unequalled', was a watchhouse-keeper in the parish of St Giles, one of the most notorious hotspots in London. At the time of his death, in 1831, newsmen remarked that Furzeman knew all the *'coves'* in all the 'flash cribs' because he was once a *'flash cracksman'*.

––––––––––

FLASH-MAN: A favourite or *fancy-man*; but this term is generally applied to those dissolute characters upon the town, who subsist upon the liberality of unfortunate women; and who, in return, are generally at hand during their nocturnal perambulations, to protect them should any brawl occur, or should they be detected in robbing those whom they have *picked up*.

In 1857, prostitute Catherine Kelly was sentenced to two months' gaol for 'vagrancy'. Prostitution was not illegal, but police could charge a prostitute with vagrancy to remove her from the street. At Kelly's trial, a policeman informed the court that her 'flash man' was in Melbourne Gaol. But the judge deemed the term offensive so he admonished the officer: 'Don't say her flash man, officer, it is not an expression to use in a public court. Say her friend, or her male companion, or something of that kind'.

––––––––––

FLASH-MOLLISHER: A *family*-woman.

A faction of flash-mollishers known as 'The *Flash* Mob' defied prison regulations and rebelled against authority—they wore jewellery and styled their hair contrary to orders, and, according to their superiors, they spoke 'disgusting language' and sang 'very disgusting' songs that 'ridiculed authority'.

FLASH-SONG: A song interlarded with *flash* words, generally relating to the exploits of the *prigging* fraternity in their various branches of depredation.

Francis MacNamara, known as 'Frank the Poet', was famous for composing flash-songs that undermined authority and empowered his fellow convicts. When he was sentenced to seven years' transportation to New South Wales, he replied to the magistrate:

> I dread not the dangers by land or by sea,
> That I'll meet on my voyage to Bottany Bay;
> My labours are over, my vocation is past,
> And 'tis there I'll rest easy and happy at last.

FLESH-BAG: A shirt.

In 1844, the governor of Oakham Gaol overheard inmate and burglar William Bates divulge that, despite wearing his 'flesh-bag' over his clothes to alter his appearance, his victim recognised him at his preliminary hearing before the '*beaks*'. Bates was charged with burglary and transported to Van Diemen's Land for life.

FLAT. In a general sense, any honest man, or *square cove*, in opposition to a *sharp* or *cross-cove*; when used particularly, it means the person whom you have a design to rob or defraud, who is termed the *flat*, or the *flatty-gory*. A man who does any foolish or imprudent act, is called a *flat*; any person who is found an easy dupe to the designs of *the family*, is said to be a *prime flat*. It's a *good flat that's never down*, is a proverb among *flash* people; meaning, that though a man may be repeatedly duped or taken in, he must in the end have his eyes opened to his folly.

In 1818, Customs Officer Michael Kelly suspected that Thomas Saunders stole cash from a drunken sailor, so instructed him to return the money. But Saunders refused and called Kelly a 'flat' and a 'bloody *Jacob*'. Kelly informed the police and Saunders was arrested. He was transported to Van Diemen's Land for a seven-year term.

FLAT-MOVE. Any attempt or project that miscarries, or any act of folly or mismanagement in human affairs is said to be a *flat move*.

When convict Catherine McGeary was awarded her freedom in 1856, she married colonist John Hargraves. But in a fatal flat-move, Hargraves backed his wagon into Catherine and flattened her to death against a fence.

FLATS: A cant name for playing-cards.

Convicts were not permitted to gamble and playing cards were prohibited. In 1844, John Glanville was caught with flats cut from the pages of a bible. He was sentenced to thirty-six lashes.

FLIP: To shoot.

Flip may derive from fillip, meaning stimulus. But the term may also come from the flintlock mechanism of early firearms; when the trigger was squeezed, a spring-loaded hammer containing flint flipped forward to ignite the gunpowder. English highwaymen were infamous for commanding their victims to 'stand and deliver' under threat of being flipped. In Australia, highwaymen were called bushrangers and they said: 'bail up'. George Davis ordered Edward Hoile to 'bail up', but Hoile refused, so Davis flipped him once in each thigh. He was caught and sentenced to twelve years' hard labour in Adelaide Gaol.

FLOOR: To knock down anyone, either for the purpose of robbery, or to effect your escape, is termed *flooring him*.

When convicts George Barlow and Elijah Smith were discovered in a Sydney 'rookery', they pretended they were free colonists to '*bounce*' their way out of trouble. But their scheme failed, so Barlow 'floored' the officer and they  '*bolted*'. Smith copped fifty lashes and Barlow was sentenced to twelve months' hard labour in chains. A rookery—slang for brothel and gambling house—is a gathering-place for crows, also called rooks.

FLOOR'D: A person who is so drunk, as to be incapable of standing, is said to be *floor'd*.

When, in 1832, Eliza Charlton was charged with '*bolting*', she swore to her innocence, claiming she'd been 'floored' by alcohol and was powerless to return to her place of employment. Charlton was sentenced to one month in a Sydney Female Factory, third class.

FLUE-FAKER: A chimney-sweeper.

An 1841 edition of the *Worchester Chronicle* drolly reported that a 'flue-faker' toiled in a 'black and dismal line' of work. The work of child chimneysweeps, who clambered up flues to remove ash and soot, was especially awful. Children suffered accidents and developed deformities and disease, such as 'soot wart', the first recorded form of occupational cancer. In 1817, eleven-year-old John Fraser became wedged in the chimney of a Scottish chapel. The occupant sent for a stonemason to excavate Fraser but his master, Chimneysweep Joseph Rae, dismissed the mason and ordered another sweep up the chimney to hitch rope around Fraser's legs. Rae then lashed the rope to a crowbar and attempted to lever Fraser loose. But as Fraser was yanked violently downwards he was smothered in his jacket, and, after screaming for mercy, he suffocated. Rae was charged with murder and sentenced to fourteen years in Van Diemen's Land.

FLY: Vigilant; suspicious; cunning; not easily robbed or duped; a shopkeeper or person of this description, is called a *fly cove*, or a *leary cove*; on other occasions *fly* is synonymous with *flash* or *leary*, as, I'm *fly* to you, I was *put flash* to him, etc.

Fly may be a corruption of fla, short for *flash*, meaning comprehend. William Shaw, a social commentator of the 1850s, toured Sydney's notorious Rocks under the protection of 'Paddy the Bruiser', an ex-convict who arranged the tour after reassuring his associates that Shaw was not 'fly' to their '*flash* phrases'. Shaw concluded that 'Sydney Street society undoubtedly furnishes the blackest specimens of fallen humanity'. Paddy, short for Patrick, is a derogatory name for an Irishman.

FLY THE MAGS: To gamble, by tossing up halfpence. See: MAG.

In 1832, Thomas Cheesman, John Webster and Michael Reardon were sentenced to seven days' gaol for 'spinning the mags' in Bathurst Street, Sydney. As the magistrate was unfamiliar with the term, Convict-Constable Francis Sutland explained that it was slang for a game involving tossing a halfpenny. According to Sutland, 'a string of halfpence' were arranged on a 'flat piece of wood' to enable 'the twirler to give an equal gravitation to each'. Pitch and toss, also termed 'mag-flying', is the origin of the gambling game two-up.

FOGLE: A silk handkerchief.

Fogle may come from *foglio*, Italian for sheet. When John Holland's pickpocketing crew were caught stealing a silk handkerchief, Holland begged Constable Thomas Thompson to 'take the fogle, and let us go.' But Thompson refused and Holland and his accomplices were sentenced to life in New South Wales.

FORKS: The two forefingers of the hand; to *put your forks down*, is to pick a pocket.

In 1852, Henry Ansell was walking in Shadwell, London, when he was tripped up by pickpocket John Thomas who shouted for his accomplice to: 'fork it; fork it!' But a passing policeman heard the commotion and Thomas was arrested and sentenced to twelve months' gaol.

FOSS, or PHOS: A phosphorus bottle used by *cracksmen* to obtain a light.

Burglars who required light to see what they were doing uncorked a bottle of oxidized phosphorus, dipped in a sulphur-tipped matchstick, ignited the match by striking it against the cork, then lit their lantern. Burglar Edward Davis carried '*rooks*', '*iron crows*' and 'phos'. In 1800, he was executed for burglary.

FRISK: To search; to *frisk a cly*, is to empty a pocket of its contents; to stand *frisk*, is to stand search.

FRISK: Fun or mirth of any kind.

Convict John Maine was sentenced to a three-hour stint in the Sydney stocks for a drunken frisk. When he was locked in the stocks, Joseph Furney, also a convict, decided to stand frisk and frisk Maine's pocket. Furney was sent to a road gang.

GAFF: To gamble with cards, dice, etc., or to toss up.

GAFF: A country fair; also a meeting of gamblers for the purpose of play; any public place of amusement is liable to be called *the gaff*, when spoken of in *flash* company who know to what it alludes.

Gaff may derive from gaff, meaning capture. At the Ashfield gaff in New South Wales, in 1857, police spotted Elijah Molineux swindling punters with his 'wheel of fortune'. Molineux snatched up his winnings and fled, but he was caught, charged with 'gaffing' and sentenced to one months' gaol. Molineux was an ex-convict with a long history of illegal gambling—twenty years earlier, for gambling at a Van Diemonian gaff, he was sentenced to three months' gaol with hard labour.

GALANEY: A fowl.

Galaney may derive from *gallina*, a Spanish word for fowl. Some convicts, such as Benjamin Taylor, who was transported for stealing galaney, were 'cockatoo gentry'—convicts incarcerated on Cockatoo Island in Sydney Harbour. If Taylor wore a yellow uniform, he would also have been a 'canary bird'. But if he wore a uniform featuring alternating patterns of black and yellow, termed parti-colour, he was a 'magpie'. Convicts were issued humiliating and distinctive uniforms that prevented them from blending in with the general public.

GALLOOT: A soldier.

Galloot may be a corruption of *galeoto*, an Italian word for sailor. But galloot also means 'a clumsy, stupid person'. When the convict transport *Waterloo* sailed to New South Wales in 1833, Daniel Connolly, a galloot in the 21st Regiment, accidentally shot himself dead.

GAME: Every particular branch of depredation practised by the *family*, is called a *game*; as, what *game* do you go upon? One species of robbery or fraud is said to be a good *game*, another a *queer game*, etc.

In 1826, eighteen-year-old Lewis Merry Webley was arrested after police discovered him carrying thirty eggs beneath his hat and toting a sack stuffed with forty pounds of cheese. Webley stated that William Pelham, a shop boy, had given him the fare. Police questioned Pelham who confessed to purloining the goods from his master's store but insisted that Webley was the instigator. Webley, however, was adamant that Pelham had 'carried the game on long before'. Webley was not believed and was transported to Van Diemen's Land for a seven-year term.

GAMMON: Flattery; deceit; pretence; plausible language; any assertion which is not strictly true, or professions believed to be insincere, as, I believe you're *gammoning*, or, that's all *gammon*, meaning, you are no doubt jesting with me, or, that's all a farce. To *gammon* a person, is to amuse him with false assurances, to praise, or flatter him, in order to obtain some particular end; to *gammon* a man *to* any act, is to persuade him to it by artful language, or pretence; to *gammon* a shop-keeper, etc., is to engage his attention to your discourse, while your accomplice is executing some preconcerted plan of depredation upon his property; a thief detected in a house which he has entered, *upon the sneak,* for the purpose of robbing it, will endeavour by some *gammoning* story to account for his intru-

sion, and to get off with a good grace; a man who is, ready at invention, and has always a flow of plausible language on these occasions, is said to be a *prime gammoner*; to *gammon lushy* or *queer,* is to pretend drunkenness, or sickness, for some private end.

Gammon probably comes from *gamenian,* an Old English word for game. Phillip King was caught 'gammoning lame' and punished with a seven-day stint on the Sydney treadmill. Instances of convicts pretending to be sick or injured were commonplace. But when gaolers declared 'old *cove*' Simeon Richardson was 'gammoning'—and ignored his pleas for help—a doctor eventually discovered that his leg was 'shockingly fractured'.

GAMMON THE TWELVE: A man who has been tried by a criminal court, and by a plausible defence, has induced the jury to acquit him, or to banish the capital part of the charge, and so save his life, is said, by his associates to have *gammoned the twelve in prime twig,* alluding to the number of jurymen.

George Mason was notorious for his '*out-and-out ramps*', and because he wore fashionable attire, inducing a '*fawney*', he was alleged to be a 'captain of the *Swell* Mob'.

More infamous, however, was his ability to 'gammon the Jury'. At Mason's sixth court appearance, he faced a charge of stealing a watch—his hand had been seized withdrawing the watch from his victim's pocket—but because Mason slipped the watch to his accomplice, there was no witness to the crime and he avoided yet another conviction.

GAMS: The legs, to have *queer gams,* is to be bandy-legged, or otherwise deformed.

Gams probably comes from *jambe*, French for leg. British Army recruits—men in good health with no prior military history—were paid in cash and supplied with '*bub* and *grub*' and accommodation. But some recruits, to escape wretched living conditions, lied about their health and personal histories. John Dawley, who was 'a little *queer* about the gams', was notorious for enlisting in British regiments and concealing his disability. When, in 1836, he was charged with  enlisting three times within one week, the magistrate declared that he'd 'never heard of a more impudent case of fraud' and sentenced Dawley to six weeks' gaol.

GARNISH: A small sum of money extracted from a *new chum* on his entering a jail, by his fellow-prisoners, which affords them a treat of beer, gin, etc.

Gaoler James Cox was accused of drunkenness, embezzling convict rations to feed his chooks and 'extracting garnish' from convicts at the Newcastle Penal Station. Cox, a convict, refuted the allegations and no charges were laid. But according to a report in the *Australian*, convicts admitted into Sydney Gaol were '*frisked*' of all their possessions including their '*slop* clothes'.

GARDEN: To *put* a person *in the garden, in the hole, in the bucket,* or *in the well,* are synonymous phrases, signifying to defraud him of his due share of the booty by embezzling a part of the property, or the money, it is *fenced for*; this phrase also applies generally to defrauding anyone with whom you are confidentially connected of what is justly his due.

In 1837, the upper half of a man was discovered rotting on the banks of Launceston's Tamar River. Tattoos on the body corresponded with  the tattoos of missing convict George Mogg. Suspicion quickly fell on Mogg's housemate, John Gardiner, also a convict. Gardiner was charged with Mogg's murder and sentenced to death. But he denied the charge until shortly before his execution, when he confessed to putting Mogg in the garden 'for the sake of his money'—after axing Mogg to death, Gardiner buried him in his garden, then, nine days later, dug him up, chopped him up, and dumped him in the river.

GARRET: The fob-pocket.

A garret is an attic or top-floor room in a building, while a fob is a small chain that attaches a pocket watch to a person's clothing. Colonists carried their watches in a vest pocket or at the top of their trousers, somewhat like a turret clock positioned in the top of a tower. But John Arthur Whittingham stored a stolen watch in his boot, John Keenan concealed a watch in his stockings and John Williams was accused of burying a watch in manure.

GEORGY: A quartern-loaf.

Georgy may derive from Brown George, nautical slang for 'brown bread', which is attributed to the brown wig worn by King George III. A quartern is a loaf of bread that weighed four pounds. The weight of bread was strictly regulated—George Medland, a grocer in Queensland, was fined for selling an underweight georgy.

GILL: A word used by way of variation, similar to *cove*, *gloak*, or *gory*; but generally coupled to some other descriptive term, as a *flash-gill*, a *toby-gill*, etc.

Gill, meaning man, may be a corruption of *chal*, Romani for fellow. But gill can also mean woman, derived from Gillian, and a gill is a unit of liquid measure, which gave rise to the term gill-shop, slang for pub. William Dear operated a gill-shop in Sydney. In 1835, he instructed his convict servant, Mary Kennedy, to deliver a gill of rum to a customer. But Kennedy gulped it down instead so Dear charged her with stealing. Because Kennedy was such a gill-gill, each time the word 'gill' was mentioned in court her 'mouth and throat appeared to be performing the act of swallowing'. She was punished with a six-month stint in third class at a female factory.

GIVE IT TO: To rob or defraud any place or person, as, I *gave it* to him *for* his *reader*, I robb'd him of his pocket-book. What *suit* did you *give it* them *upon*? In what manner, or by what means, did you effect your purpose? Also, to impose upon a person's credulity by telling him a string of falsehoods; or to take any unfair advantage of another's inadvertence or unsuspecting temper, on any occasion; in either case, the party at last *dropping down*, that is, detecting your imposition, will say, I believe you have been *giving it to* me nicely all this while.

After a bout of heavy drinking, Thomas Vine, a gunner in the Royal Artillery, declared he was the 'Ben Hall of Victoria' and took potshots at pedestrians. When a man ducked for cover, Vine said: 'Now see me give it to him in the small of the back.' But Vine missed, and, after his gun jammed, he was overpowered and carried to gaol. Vine was punished with twelve months' gaol with hard labour. Ben Hall was a bushranger known for his audacious escapades.

GLAZE: A glass-window.

Glaze probably derives from *glas*, a Middle English word for glass. In 1831, William Power, in order to be imprisoned and receive free food and board, confessed to '*milling* the glaze of three lamps'. The judge obliged and Power was sent to Sydney Gaol.

Several convicts named William Power were transported to New South Wales. The Power who was gaoled in 1831 may have arrived in 1797. Accounts of elderly or infirm convicts committing crimes to find relief from their wretched living conditions were not uncommon.

GLIM: A candle, or other light.

Glim comes from glimmer, a 'faint or wavering light'. When Benjamin Corbley was refused entry to a Sydney pub, he hammered the pub door with a stick and threatened to 'smash the glim'. A patrolling policeman ordered Corbley to behave, but after he bellowed 'sundry oaths and execrations' and picked a stone off the ground to throw at the lamp, he was arrested and fined five shillings.

GLIM-STICK: A candlestick.

At a 'tripe and trotter shop' situated in The Rocks, convict James Kidd was dining with several female convicts when a policeman burst into the room. Kidd cried 'douse the glim', and, under the cover of darkness, he smothered the officer with tripe. The women fled through a back door but Kidd was caught and punished with a seven-day stint on the tread-mill. The Rocks, an area along the rocky western foreshore of Sydney Cove, was a notorious haunt for convicts.

GNARL: To *gnarl upon* a person, is the same as *splitting* or *nosing upon* him; a man guilty of this treachery is called a *gnarling* scoundrel, etc.

Gnarl, meaning 'inform', is a pun on bark—a gnarl is a knotty protuberance on a tree, and a gnarler is 'a little dog that, by his barking, alarms the family when any person is breaking into the house'. When Thomas Thrush was convicted of highway robbery, he confronted his accuser and said: 'you Bugger what did you narle for'. Thrush was transported to New South Wales for life. Convicts who gnarled were 'dogs'—Patrick Minnighan bludgeoned James Travis for informing and said: 'There lies one bloody dog, stiff enough.' Travis died and Minnighan was executed.

GO-ALONGER: A simple easy person, who suffers himself to be made a tool of, and is readily persuaded to any act or undertaking by his associates, who inwardly laugh at his folly, and ridicule him behind his back.

William 'King John' Edwards was first convicted at just seven years of age. At twelve he was prosecuted for picking pockets and transported to Van Diemen's Land for a seven-year term. When Edwards arrived, the

principal superintendent of convicts asked him how old he was, he replied that he was 'so young when he was born that he could not tell'. Edwards, who stood four feet and three and a half inches tall, was reputed to be a go-alonger—the 'unfortunate instrument' of 'old thieves' who concealed children in luggage and conveyed them into houses so they could unlock a door under the cover of night. Edwards was probably nicknamed after King John, who was much shorter than his brother, King Richard I.

GO OUT: To follow the profession of thieving; two or more persons who usually rob in company, are said to *go out* together.

Jonathon and Fanny Stead didn't leave their house to go out, they robbed their lodgers. But in 1834, the couple were convicted of stealing and sentenced to seven years in Van Diemen's Land.

GOOD: A place or person, which promises to be easily robbed, is said to be *good*, as, that house is *good upon the crack*; this shop is *good upon the star*; *the swell* is *good for* his *montra*; etc. A man who declares himself *good for* any favour or thing, means, that he has sufficient influence, or possesses the certain means to obtain it; *good as bread*, or *good as cheese*, are merely emphatical phrases to the same effect. See: CAZ.

Thieves and vagabonds alerted each other to good tidings by communicating with secret symbols. A diamond scrawled on a building signified 'good', and that the occupant would, at least, have food to spare. But 'x' meant 'no good', signifying the occupant was uncharitable. Maps and notes were left in homeless shelters and lodging houses to relay more detailed information. Some proprietors of these 'padding *kens*', as they were called, kept a 'beggar's directory' or 'pad book'—a ledger detailing the most benevolent people and trustworthy criminals in the neighbourhood. But such books also detailed the names, addresses and physical descriptions of law enforcement. When, in 1837, John Robertson was charged with stealing his master's clothes, a nefarious letter was discovered stashed in a pocket. Addressed to a convict named Thomas Mence, the letter contained the names of several well-known residents of New South Wales. But because the letter incorporated cant terminology, the authorities speculated on its meaning. 'Lobster', they concluded, referred to Mence's master, Lieutenant Henry Lugard. Robertson denied writing the letter but he was prosecuted for stealing the clothes and sentenced to wear leg irons for nine months. Soldiers were nicknamed 'lobsters' because they wore red jackets.

GORY: A term synonymous with *cove*, *gill*, or *gloak*, and like them, commonly used in the descriptive. See: **FLAT**, and: **SWELL**.

GRAB: To seize; apprehend; take in custody; to make a *grab* at any thing, is to snatch suddenly, as at a gentleman's watch-chain, etc.
GRAB'D: Taken, apprehended.

James Slattery, an 'ill-looking wretch', was '*bowled out*' for absconding and grabbing. When, in 1832 he was 'grabbed' for '*prigging*' cushions, he was sentenced to twelve months' hard labour in chains.

GRAY: A half-penny, or other coin, having two heads or two tails, and fabricated for the use of gamblers, who, by such a deception frequently win large sums.

Because *pony* is cant for money, gray may derive from *gry*, Romani for horse. Blacksmith Richard McAlister produced a 'gray' by 'the welding together of the half of two coins'—he was caught cheating punters playing pitch-and-toss at Bathurst.

GROCERY: Half-pence, or copper coin, in a collective sense.

Halfpence may have acquired its nickname because it was common grocery fare. When convict Ann Murphy *'prigged'* an earthenware jug valued at three pence, she offered the policeman two pence to let her go. But he refused the grocery and she was punished with six months in the *'stone jug'* at Sydney.

GRUB: Victuals of any kind; to *grub* a person, is to diet him, or find him in victuals; to *grub* well, is to eat with an appetite.

Grub may derive from the way a bird *grubs* a *grub*. Male convicts, as a general rule, were issued one pound of beef and one to one and a half pounds of bread on a daily basis. But in 1832, in New South Wales, 'new *chum*' Thomas Flanagan charged his master with issuing him 'shocking bad grub'. Flanagan complained that he and his two convict co-workers were issued a combined ration of eight pounds of beef over a five-day period. The court ruled in Flanagan's favour and forwarded the matter to

Governor Richard Bourke. Convicts were permitted to lodge complaints regarding their treatment but the penalties that masters received for proven charges were generally limited to small fines. Convicts who complained risked further abuse, or punishment. When Francis Wade refused to eat his beef, he was ordered to 'try Bell's catering'—a fourteen-day stint on the Carters' Barracks treadmill, under the supervision of Assistant Superintendent Thomas Bell.

GUN: A view; look; observation; or taking notice; as, there is a strong *gun* at us, means, we are strictly observed. To *gun* any thing, is to look at or examine it.

Gun, meaning 'observe', probably derives from the act of aiming a gun. In 1880, Arthur Blackmore was spotted fleeing a Van Diemonian stone-breaking gang, so a guard let fire with his rifle. But the shot missed Blackmore, blasted into a railway station, though a framed advertisement, across the passenger platform, through a plate-glass window and onto the floor of a first-class passenger carriage. No one was injured, but the guard, for failing to take a better gun with his rifle, came under fire in the press.

HADDOCK: A purse; a *haddock stuff'd with beans*, is a jocular term for a purse full of guineas!

Haddock is a term inspired by Saint Peter, who, according to the Gospel of Matthew, extracted money from the mouth of a fish. In 1793, a cry of help drew a night watchman to a lane in Holborn, London, where Mary Carty was wrestling with fishmonger John Ruff. Scattered beneath their feet were coins and a purse. Ruff accused Carty of picking his pocket, but Carty accused Ruff of drunkenness and mistaking her for a thief. Ruff was adamant that the money was his and that Carty had dumped it when she spotted the watchman, but Carty protested, stating that it was her money and that it fell from her dress after she was accosted by Ruff. When asked to account for the purse, Rush stated: 'I have had it seven years at least, it is greasy by my selling pickled salmon and putting the money backward and forward in it.' Ruff won out and was reunited with his filthy haddock, and Carty was transported to New South Wales for a seven-year term.

HALF A BEAN, HALF A QUID: Half-a-guinea.

Bean, meaning guinea, may derive from kidney bean, because guinea rhymes with kidney. In 1803, Bow Street Police infiltrated a gang of coin-counterfeiters who conducted business in the Blue Anchor Pub. To safeguard against getting caught, the gang concealed their wares in mugs of beer and communicated in cant—pocketbooks were referred to as '*readers*', and coins as '*spangles*' and 'half-beans'. Gadaliah Philips, the ringleader, was charged with '*smashing*' and sentenced to one years' gaol.

HALF A BULL: Half-a-crown.

A half crown was a silver coin nicknamed after the resemblance it bore to a bull's eye. But the term also has been attributed to the unflattering bull-like portrait of King George III that features on the coin. Seventeen-year-old Robert Howard and his two teenaged accomplices paid Howard's younger brother, fourteen-year-old Charles, 'half a bull' to steal bobbins of silk from his employer. But they were caught and, when Charles testified against the trio, they were transported to Van Diemen's Land for seven-year terms.

HALF-FLASH AND HALF-FOOLISH: This character is applied sarcastically to a person, who has a smattering of the cant language, and having associated a little with *family* people, pretends to a knowledge of *life* which he really does not possess, and by this conduct becomes an object of ridicule among his acquaintance.

Commandant John Price spoke '*flash*' to convicts incarcerated on Norfolk Island. But according to Reverend Thomas Rogers, when Price spoke 'the vulgar slang' convicts reacted with 'derision and contempt'. Some convicts thought Price was half-*flash* and half-foolish, but other convicts believed that Price was an ex-convict. Rogers, however, was adamant that Price learned cant in Hobart Town, where he disguised himself as a policeman and frequented 'public houses in search of disorderly characters'. Price, the inspiration for the despotic commandant in Marcus

Clarke's novel *For the Term of his Natural Life*, was despised—in 1857, at Melbourne's Williamston docks, convicts beat him to death.

HAMMERISH: *Down as a hammer.* See: DOWN AS A HAMMER.

HANG IT ON: Purposely to delay or protract the performance of any task or service you have undertaken, by dallying, and making as slow a progress as possible, either from natural indolence, or to answer some private end of your own, *To hang it on with* a woman, is to form a temporary connexion with her; to cohabit or keep company with her without marriage.

In 1834, a Sydney resident wrote his local paper complaining that convicts working in road gangs would 'hang it on'. But according to George Arthur, Lieutenant Governor of Van Diemen's Land, working in irons on the roads was a punishment 'as severe a one as could be inflicted on man'.

HANK: A bull-bait, or bullock-hunt.
HANK: To have a person *at a good hank*, is to have made any contract with him very advantageous to yourself; or to be able from some prior cause to command or use him just as

you please; to have the benefit of his purse or other services, in fact, upon your own terms.

HANK: A spell of cessation from any work or duty, on the score of indisposition, or some other pretence.

When a group of East-Enders was preoccupied with a hank, eighteen-year-old James Pinkett smashed a shop window and stole a watch. But he was caught and sentenced to life in Van Diemen's Land. There, in 1832, he was assigned to Hugh Munro, a landowner. Pinkett was a cart-driver by trade so Munro had him at a good hank. But because Munro did not supply Pinkett with the 'necessary provisions', he was granted a hank and returned to government service. Colonists who billeted convicts as assigned servants were required to supply them with food, clothes, bedding, lodging and medicine. Convicts provided cheap labour for the construction of infrastructure. But in 1838, the Assignment System was abolished. An inquiry concluded that the system was impossible to manage fairly and was akin to slavery.

HIGH-TOBY: The *game* of highway robbery, that is, exclusively on horseback.

Some bushrangers perpetrated 'high toby' in dashing style. Edward 'Teddy the Jewboy' Davis and his 'Jewboy Gang', wore satin scarves, brooches, rings and 'broad-rimmed Manila hats turned up in front with an abundance of broad pink ribbons'. But they also accessorised their horses with 'a profusion of pink ribbons'.

HIGH-TOBY-GLOAK: A highwayman.

A highwayman was a man who robbed a person on a road, street or highway. But some high-toby-gloaks were women and children. Eleven-year-old Mary Wade was charged with highway robbery when she stripped an eight-year-old girl of her clothing. 'Child-stripping', also termed 'lully-prigging',  was a serious offence—Wade was sentenced to death. But she was reprieved, and, in 1789, was transported to New South Wales with the Second Fleet. Wade, one of the youngest convicts transported to Australia, is considered a founding mother. At the time of her death, in 1859, more than three hundred of her descendants were living in Australia.

HIS-NABS: Him or himself; a term used by way of emphasis, when speaking of a third person.

Nabs, meaning 'man', is a corruption of nob, a term derived from nobleman—a man distinguished by his class, rank or title. In 1855, William Armstrong charged Henry Thompson, 'a respectable looking young man', with assault and intent to commit robbery. But Thompson declared that Armstrong, whom he referred to as 'my nabs there in the witness box', attacked him. Thompson was not believed and was ordered to pay a £5 fine or spend two months in Sydney Gaol.

HOBBLED: Taken up, or in custody; to *hobble* a *plant*, is to *spring* it. See: PLANT.

Hobble is inspired by a restraint fitted to the legs of livestock to impede their movement, known as a hobble. James Duck, for stealing cattle, was hobbled on the leg, slang for sentenced to transportation. But Duck, who wore a wooden leg, was also a hobbler—'a person with an awkward way of walking'. In 1864, when arguing that British convicts were as honour-

able as freeborn Australians, Duck was punched in the face by William Henry Rawling, a Van Diemonian publican. When Duck bent to retrieve his tooth from the pub floor, Rawling yanked off his wooden leg and beat him over the head with it. The police intervened and Rawling was hobbled and fined £5. Duck, however, wound up at Port Arthur Penal Station—he was charged with sheep stealing when police matched the 'print of a wooden leg' to his stump.

HOG: A shilling; five, ten, or more shillings, are called five, ten, or more *hog*.

A hog was named after the image of a pig that featured on a shilling coin. When Patrick Malone passed out in an Irish pub after eating '*grub*', his three '*pals*' picked his pockets and stole 'hogs' and 'clippers'. Malone prosecuted

the trio to recover his possessions but because he was an infamous pick-pocket, the magistrate asked him how he'd acquired the cash. Malone confessed that he'd '*faked* some *clyes*' after slicing '*fobs*' with the 'clip-pers'—clippers was slang for scissors. Malone was sent to the '*stone jug*'.

HOIST: The *game* of shop-lifting is called the hoist, a person expert at this practice is said to be a *good hoist*.

Mary Ann Trueman and Mary Ann Robinson, thieves who resided in The Rocks, Sydney, were nicknamed 'rock (h)oisters'. In 1847, they were arrested for picking Samuel Jackson's pockets. But because he failed to appear in court, they were acquitted.

HOLE. See GARDEN.

HOPPER-DOCKERS: Shoes.

Shoes may have been nicknamed hopper-dockers because barefoot people hop to 'dock' their feet. But shoes also were nicknamed hock-dockers, after hock, 'the joint in a quadruped's hind leg', and clod-hoppers, because people hop over earthen clods. In 1827, at Parramatta, convicts '*shook*' the 'clod-hoppers' and '*kicksers*' belonging to convict Nicholas Doyle, a so-called '*flat*'. The thieves also stole Doyle's certificate of freedom. Convict Robert Goodwin offered to '*spring the plant*' if Doyle paid him '*blunt*', but because Doyle was penniless he prosecuted Goodwin to recover his possessions. Doyle, however, failed to prove that Goodwin was the thief, so the judge dismissed the case for lack of evidence.

HORNEY: A constable.

Horney may come from *horny*, slang for devil. Because policemen wore blue uniforms and condemned people to punishment, they were nicknamed 'blue devils' and 'devils in blue'. In 1832, a New South Wales horney arrested John Jackson, who, in a 'representation of the London blue devil corp', was blowing his bugle in the early hours of the morning.

Jackson was fined five shillings, but because he was without the money to pay the fine, he offered his bugle as surety. The judge refused and Jackson was punished with a two-hour stint in the stocks.

HOXTER: An inside coat-pocket.

Hoxter derives from *oxter*, 'a person's armpit'. When police arrested pickpocket Robert Thomas they were astonished to discover a stolen purse stashed in a secret hoxter that led from Thomas's inside breast pocket to the centre of the back of his jacket. He was sentenced to three months' gaol.

IN IT: To let another partake of any benefit or acquisition you have acquired by robbery or otherwise, is called *putting* him *in it*: a *family-man* who is accidentally witness to a robbery, etc., effected by one or more others, will say to the latter, Mind, I'm *in it*: which is generally acceded to, being the established custom; but there seems more of courtesy than right in this practice.

In December 1890, the strange sounds of screeching geese drew guards to an alley behind Melbourne Gaol. There, two geese and two men were spotted fleeing the scene. One of the men was identified as Francis Ryan, a recently released prisoner, who, it transpired, was attempting to put his ex-cellmates in it by smuggling in geese and sixty tobacco sticks for a Christmas feast. But Ryan found himself in it—he was returned to gaol for a six-month term.

IN TOWN: Flush of money; *breeched.*

Mary Ann Brown was transported to Van Diemen's Land for a seven-year term for stealing money. According to her entry in the Black Books, she spent '12 months on the town'—colonial parlance for twelve months' working as a prostitute. Prostitution was not illegal but running a brothel was—in 1837, Brown was charged with 'keeping a disorderly house' and banished from Hobart Town. But in 1838, the 'well-known lady of easy virtue' copped a second seven-year sentence when she stole 'a large sum of money' from a Hobart Town publican who was in town.

JACOB: A ladder; a simple half-witted person.

Ladders were nicknamed after Jacob, who, according to the Book of Genesis, dreamt of a ladder that connected earth and heaven. In 1867, John Williams realised his dream of ascending the walls of Fremantle Prison. Disguised in a guard's uniform, he led eight prisoners through the gates, out the main yard, up several jacobs and over the wall. The *Herald* reported that the brazen gaol break surpassed 'the most improbable escape ever invented by a novelist'. The assistant-superintendent of the prison was dismissed, and the guards were reprimanded for being jacobs.

JACK: A post-chaise.

A post-chaise is a four-wheeled enclosed carriage. Jacks that accommodated convicts were fitted with a urinal so the convicts could be locked in overnight, and they were also fitted with chains—convicts towed jacks from place to place. Jacks were notoriously cramped—convict John Frederick Mortlock likened them to the 'cages of wild animals'.

JACK-BOY: A postillion.

A postillion is a rider positioned on the lead horse of a horse-drawn coach or post-chaise. Robert Callaghan, a jack-boy transported to New South Wales for stealing lace, was caught stealing iron and transported to Van Diemen's Land. Callaghan, by now a proficient sailor,

who may have learned the trade while imprisoned aboard the hulk *Phoenix* in Sydney Harbour, absconded from the colony in a whaleboat. After a stopover at Gabo Island, Callaghan and his crew rowed off into the distance, never to be seen again.

JACKET: To *jacket* a person, or *clap a jacket* on him, is nearly synonymous with *bridging* him. See: BRIDGE. But this term is more properly applied to removing a man by underhand and vile means from any birth or situation he enjoys, commonly with a view to supplant him; therefore, when a person, is supposed to have fallen a victim to such infamous machinations, it is said to have been a *jacketing concern*.

In 1842, police were called to the Cascades Female Factory to quell a riot. When they attempted to single out the ringleaders, however, the women formed a circle, danced, and  chanted, 'We are all alike, we are all alike'. But when threatened with a stint in solitary confinement, Ann Maloney, a self-confessed 'jacketer', gave up seventeen of her mates.

JASEY: A wig.

Jasey may derive from jersey, a type of flax used to manufacture wigs. When, in 1844, a magistrate at Woolloomooloo lost the key to the room that stored his jasey and gown, Governor Henry Keck released an 'expert *cracksman*' from Sydney Gaol to pick the lock.

JEMMY, or JAMES: An iron-crow.

In 1847, Convict-Constable Charles Chappell charged convict Henry Clarke and ex-convict Reuben Underhayes with burglary. Underhayes attempted to bludgeon Chappell with a jemmy, but Chappell seized it, brained Clarke, and escorted the duo to gaol. At their trial, Chappell informed the court that '*flash* men' referred to a crowbar as a 'jemmy'. Underhayes was sentenced to a fifteen-year term, and Clarke, a fourteen-year term.

JERRY: A fog or mist.

When a heavy jerry descended on Sydney, bushranger Frances 'Frank' Gardiner escaped from the Cockatoo Island Penal Station. He was apprehended swimming in Sydney Harbour but, because his captors refused to allow him into their boat, he clung to a rope and was towed back to the station.

JERVIS: A coachman.

Jarvis was a common surname that may have been especially prevalent among coachmen. Nicknames for coachmen include Jarvis, Jervis and Jervy. Joseph Chuck was a '*flash* jarvey' in Sydney. Notorious for drunkenness and for assaulting both the police and his patrons, Chuck was nicknamed 'Jehus' after King Jehu of Israel, famous for his furious attacks by chariot.

JERVIS'S UPPER BENJAMIN: A box, or coachman's great coat.

A greatcoat may have acquired its nickname because Benjamin was a name common to English tailors. George Rogers cut a hole in the left pocket of his 'upper benjamin' so he could slip his hand through the opening and pick people's pockets undetected. But in 1856, he was caught '*cly-faking*' at the Homebush Racecourse and sentenced to two years' hard labour in Sydney Gaol.

JIGGER: A door.

Jigger may derive from *stigga*, Romani for gate. Scottish thief David Haggart escaped from Dumfries Gaol after he bludgeoned the gaoler and stole a '*dub*' that unlocked the 'jiger'. Haggart fled to Leith, where he broke open a padlocked 'jigger' to retrieve his cache of stolen '*wedge*'.

JOB: Any concerted robbery, which is to be executed at a certain time, is spoken of by the parties as *the job*, or having *a job* to do at such a place; and in this case as regular

preparations are made, and as great debates held, as about any legal business undertaken by the industrious part of the community.

When notorious '*body snatcher*' John Sheering was incarcerated in Coldbath Fields Prison, he met John Nash, also a '*body snatcher*'. Nash said he knew of 'a *good* job' that would earn them 'plenty of *blunt*'—he proposed they steal the payroll from St Bartholomew's Hospital. When the duo was  released they teamed up with John Hurley, a thief, and Nash laid out his plan, stating: 'The time to do the job is between nine and ten o'clock in the morning.' Sheering, however, alerted the police and Hurley and Nash were arrested and sentenced to death. But their sentences were commuted to seven years' transportation to Van Diemen's Land.

JOGUE: A shilling; five jogue is five shillings, and so on, to any other number.

In 1837, 'turnkeys' at the Cascades Female Factory were accused of conducting transactions with the inmates. According to an exposé in the *True Colonist*, women wishing to change money to purchase contraband such as tobacco, tea, beer and 'choice foods of various kinds', were charged five jogue for the privilege.

JOSKIN: A country-bumbkin.

George 'Davy the Jew' Davis and William '*Lampy* Bill' Hodgin were notorious for preying on 'country joskins' newly arrived in Sydney.

When Thomas Rogers strode into town early one morning in 1859, the two 'old pilferers' plied him with booze and introduced him to a 'nymph' named Sarah Annie Maria Ashworth—nymph being slang for prostitute. Later that day, Rogers woke in Ashworth's shed to discover he was penniless. The trio was arrested on suspicion of drugging and robbing Rogers, but were acquitted for lack of evidence. Davis was nicknamed because of his Jewish heritage, while Hodgin may have acquired his nickname because of his poor eyesight.

JUDGE: A *family-man*, whose talents and experience have rendered him a complete adept in his profession, and who acts with a systematic prudence on all occasions, is allowed to be, and called by his friends, a fine *judge*.

Simeon Lord, a judge caught stealing, was transported to New South Wales in 1790. There, Lord prospered as one of the colony's wealthiest merchants. Because of his social status, in 1810 he was appointed as a magistrate—a civil court officer who oversees minor offences and preliminary hearings for more serious offences. A few months after he was appointed, convict James Ratty was, as Lord had been, charged with stealing cloth, but unlike Lord, he was executed.

JUDGEMENT: Prudence; economy in acting; abilities, (the result of long experience,) for executing the most intricate and hazardous projects; any thing accomplished in a masterly manner, is, therefore, said to have been done with *judgement*; on concerting or planning any operations, one party will say, I think it would be *judgement* to do so and so, meaning expedient to do it.

Samuel Marsden, a Church of England Chaplain appointed as a magistrate in New South Wales, is alleged to have severely punished a group of Irish convicts accused of plotting a rebellion. Patrick Galvin was sentenced to three hundred strokes of the cat-o'-nine-tails. Because the first one hundred lashes cut him 'to the bone' between his shoulder blades, the next batch was dealt across his lower back, which rendered the flesh 'to such jelly' that the final hundred were dealt across his legs. But Galvin received his punishment with judgment, maintaining his innocence. Marsden, who despised Irish Roman Catholics, was infamous for meting out severe floggings—he was nicknamed 'the flogging parson'. In 1822, Marsden and several other magistrates were dismissed for exceeding their judicial duties.

JUDY: A *blowen*, but sometimes used when speaking familiarly of any woman.

Judy, meaning 'woman', may be inspired by the female protagonist in the Punch and Judy puppet show. When, in 1833, convict Tim Carney was spotted drinking booze with a judy named Judy Hughes, he was sent to the treadmill for a seven-day stint, while Hughes copped one month in the Parramatta Female Factory. At the time of their arrest, Carney, who was probably Irish, was allegedly singing a song about Irish whisky:

> Och Judy dear, a fig for beer,
> The pleasure sure is greater,
> When you are dry, to bung your eye,
> With quartens of the cratur!

The verse can be translated as: My dear woman, I don't care for beer, I drink whisky because it's more potent. Fig is a dismissive term; cratur is a corruption of *creature*, slang for whisky; and a quarten is a measure of liquid equal to one quarter of a gallon.

JUGELOW: A dog.

Jugelow comes from *guggal*, *juckel* and *jucko*, Romani words for dog. In 1830, a resident of Westminster Abbey overheard her friend's missing spaniel barking from inside an unfamiliar house. The police were summoned and, after searching the house, they discovered eight more jugelows. The occupants, Mary Holland and Esther Wright, were 'dog-finders'. With a dish brimming with 'puddening'— liver paste—the duo lured jugelows away from their owners and then held them captive until a hefty reward was '*chanted*'. If rewards were not forthcoming, the  jugelows were sold or butchered for '*blunt*'. Dog-finders traded in skins and fat, which one dog-finder passed off as 'bear's grease', a so-called baldness curative. Holland and Wright, whose stinking, blood-spattered abode was described as a 'slaughterhouse,' constructed a 'gallows and apparatus for hanging the jugelows and skinning them afterwards'— stashed under their stairs were the carcasses of fifteen flayed jugelows.

Jugelow-stealing, however, was not a felony. Holland and Wright faced a fine of up to £20, plus the value of the jugelow, or a stint in prison not exceeding three months. Jugelow-stealing was also a thriving business in Australia—James Edmunds stole a jugelow and was sentenced to twelve months in a road gang.

JUMP: A window on the ground-floor.
JUMP: A *game*, or species of robbery effected by getting into a house through any of the lower windows. To Jump a place, is to rob it upon *the jump*. A man convicted for this offence, is said to be *done for a jump*.

A window may have been nicknamed a jump because thieves *jumped* it open and then *jumped* through it. Police Magistrate John Fielding warned the public that thieves who perpetrated 'The Jump' targeted houses with no lights visible in the windows. Joseph Bolitho Johns, suspected of a jump, was charged with burglary and transported to Western Australia for a ten-year term. Because Johns was an incessant absconder, he was chained by his neck to a jump at Fremantle Prison. 'Moondyne Joe', as he is known, is one of Western Australia's most infamous outlaws. He was nicknamed after Moondyne Springs, an isolated gorge on the Avon River where he is alleged to have corralled stolen horses.

KELP: A hat; to *kelp* a person, is to move your hat to him.

Kelp is a pun on cap. According to an eighteenth-century treatise on thieving, '*pinchers*' bumped into their victims and picked their '*cly*' when they raised their hands to secure their 'kelp'. Eighteen-year-old Martha Turner was transported to New South Wales for life for knocking off a man's kelp and running away with his money. But Van Demonian convict William Day wore a hat made of kelp. According to his memoirs, he concealed his head with seaweed then braved swimming across Eaglehawk Neck—a narrow isthmus guarded by dogs and soldiers. But a wave carried away his disguise and he was caught.

KEMESA: A shirt.

Kemesa may come from *camisa*, Italian for shirt. Ann Murphy, for stealing clothing including a 'camesa', was punished with a one-month stint in Sydney Gaol.

KEN: A house; often joined to other descriptive terms, as, a *flash ken*, a *bawdy-ken*, etc.

Ken may derive from kennel, a doghouse. William Roberts, on the day after he was released from prison, was caught 'shepherding' a drunken man into one of the numerous Melbourne '*flash* kens'. Roberts, who was charged with attempted robbery, 'begged hard for another chance' so the judge released him with a 'severe' warning. But a few months later Roberts was caught robbing a drunk and sentenced to two years' gaol. A flash ken was a brothel, gambling den or lodging house that catered to prostitutes, gamblers and criminals.

KENT: A coloured pocket-handkerchief of cotton or linen.

Kent comes from kenting, a type of cloth produced in Kent, England. In 1835, convict John Heffernan cut eyeholes in a kent, tied it around his head and bailed up a traveller outside Bathurst, New South Wales. But when Heffernan's disguise blew back in a gust of wind, he was identified and charged with highway robbery. Heffernan's sentence was listed as 'death recorded'—a formal sentence of death without the intention that it would be carried out. Aside from people charged with murder, a judge could grant clemency to offenders convicted of a crime punishable by death. Convicts who were listed as 'death recorded' were typically sentenced to a lengthy prison term.

KICK: A sixpence, when speaking of compound sums only, as, *three and a kick*, is three and sixpence, etc.

Kick is a play on six. Convict Charles Caesar stored his savings—eleven and a kick—in a handkerchief concealed beneath his hat. But at a Sydney watchhouse, Adam Riley asked Caesar for kick to buy bread and then stole the money. Riley, who was charged with a multitude of offences, was sentenced to a seven-year term. Caesar, who was black and spoke French, was born in Mauritius. He may have been an ex-slave—classical names were popular among slavers with aristocratic pretensions.

KICKSEYS: Breeches; speaking of a purse, etc., taken from the breeches pocket, they say, it was *got from the kickseys*, there being no cant term for the breeches pocket. To *turn out* a man's *kickseys*, means to pick the pockets of them, in which operation it is necessary to turn those pockets inside out, in order to get at the contents.

Kickseys, also termed 'kecks', may come from kecks, the hollow stalks of plants. In 1856, Richard Collier was working in his black-smith shop when he spotted Justice of the Peace James Ascough Esquire 'unbutton his kickseys, and indecently expose his person, to the utter disgust of some females.' Collier was horrified, so he charged Ascough with indecent exposure. Two eyewitnesses corroborated his testimony but the Attorney-General of New South Wales declared that a man of Ascough's social standing 'would not, and could not, do such a thing' and so dismissed the case. A Justice of the Peace is a person appointed to hear minor court cases, but according to some colonists, they were a 'just-ass of the peace'.

KID: A child of either sex, but particularly applied to a boy who commences to thieve at an early age; and when by his dexterity he has become famous, he is called by his acquaintances *the kid* so and so, mentioning his sirname.

KIDDY: A thief of the lower order, who, when he is *breeched*, by a course of successful depredation, dresses in the extreme of vulgar gentility, and affects a knowingness in his air and conversation, which renders him in reality an object of ridicule; such a one is pronounced by his associates of the same class, a *flash-kiddy* or a *rolling-kiddy*. *My kiddy* is a familiar term used by these gentry in addressing each other.

Kid probably comes from kid, a young goat. In 1833, a burglar snuck into John Mason's house, slid a key from beneath his sleeping wife's pillow, unlocked a strongbox that was stashed in their bedroom and slipped away with £400. Constable William Peel investigated the crime

 and matched 'remarkably small' shoe prints to '*Flash* kiddy Elliot', a convict. Elliot swore to his innocence but when incriminating silver coins were discovered in his pocket, he was charged with the burglary and sentenced to life at Port Arthur Penal Station.

KID-RIG: Meeting a child in the streets who is going on some errand, and by a false, but well fabricated story, obtaining any parcel or goods it may be carrying; this game is practised by two persons, who have each their respective parts to play, and even porters and other grown persons are sometimes defrauded of their load by this artifice. To *kid* a person *out of* any thing, is to obtain it from him by means of a false pretence, as that you were sent by a third person, etc.; such impositions are all generally termed *the kid-rig*.

In 1827, fourteen-year-old errand boy Samuel Eycott was walking through Smithfield, England, when fifteen-year-old Joseph Bishop asked him for directions. But Bishop was a practitioner of the kid-rig—he duped Eycott into setting down his delivery bags so his accomplices could steal them. A few weeks after Eycott was robbed, he was walking with his mother when he overheard a boy remark: 'That is the *cove* we *served* last week'. Eycott  spotted Bishop, and, with the help of his mother, detained him until police arrived. Bishop was charged with robbery and sentenced to life in New South Wales.

KINCHEN: A young lad.

Kinchen derives from *Kindchen*, a German word for 'a little child'. Billy Keefe, dubbed a 'kinchen' by the New South Wales press, was prosecuted for child maintenance. But Keefe, a sixteen-year-old waiter whose weekly wage amounted to just eight shillings, declared he could barely afford to pay for his own '*bub, grub* and *togs*'. He was ordered to pay Margaret Mandell six shillings per week.

KIRK: A church or chapel.

Kirk is Scottish for church. In 1838, John Simms prosecuted his wife, Ellen Johnson, for bigamy—the crime of marrying a person while still married to another. Simms testified that he married Johnson in a 'kirk' in New South Wales in 1831, but that she'd taken a new husband in 1835. But because Simms and Johnson were convicts married without government approval, the validity of their marriage was in question, so the judge dismissed the case. Convicts wishing to marry had to seek approval from the governor. Applicants could be refused if they were already married, had not displayed recent good conduct or had not served an ample portion of their term of transportation.

KNAP: To steal; take; receive; accept; according to the sense it is used in; as, to *knap a clout*, is to steal a pocket-handkerchief; to *knap the swag* from your *pall*, is to take from him the property he has just stolen, for the purpose of carrying it; to *knap seven or fourteen pen'worth*, is to receive sentence of transportation for seven or fourteen years; to *knap the glim*, is to catch the venereal disease; in making a bargain, to *knap* the sum offered you, is to accept it; speaking of a woman supposed to be pregnant, it is common to say, I believe *Mr. Knap* is *concerned*, meaning that she has *knap'd*.

Knap is a variation of *nab* and *nip*, meaning take. At Hyde Park Fair in 1838, nineteen-year-old James Smith was arrested for knapping George Waterton's silk handkerchief. Smith alleged that Waterton had '*done the trick*' on him, and that the '*cove*' who stole the handkerchief dropped it at his feet to avoid getting 'knapped'. Smith was not believed and was transported to New South Wales for a ten-year term.

KNAPPING A JACOB FROM A DANNA-DRAG: This is a curious species of robbery, or rather borrowing without leave, for the purpose of robbery; it signifies taking away the short ladder from a nightman's cart, while the men are gone into a house, the privy of which they are employed emptying, in order to effect an ascent to a one-pair-of-stairs window, to scale a garden-wall, etc., after which the ladder, of course, is left to rejoin its master as it can.

Nightmen traveled in carts equipped with ladders and buckets to lower themselves into cesspits and haul out 'night soil', a polite name for human faeces. The work was notoriously unpleasant and, because  of the revolting smell, nightmen worked at night when fewer people were around. When, in 1833, a ladder belonging to nightman William Dennis was stolen, his assistant remarked: 'Hallo, master, somebody has nippered the *jacob*.' The thief, William Griffith, was caught and charged with stealing, but because he was a 'respectable person' who purloined the ladder for a '*lark*', he escaped conviction.

KNIFE IT. See: CHEESE IT.

KNUCK, KNUCKLER, or KNUCKLING-COVE: A pickpocket, or person professed in the *knuckling* art.
KNUCKLE: To pick pockets, but chiefly applied to the more

refined branch of that art, namely, extracting notes, loose cash, etc., from the waistcoat or breeches pockets, whereas *buzzing* is used in a more general sense. See: BUZ.

Pickpockets acquired their nickname because they used their fingers and knuckles to steal from their victims. According to Police Magistrate John Fielding, 'some of the best Knuckles are women'. When, in 1832, Ann Craig was arrested for robbing her mistress, she knuckled a snuffbox from the policeman's waistcoat pocket. She was sentenced to twelve months in the Parramatta Female Factory.

 **LAG:** To transport for seven years or upwards.

LAG: A convict under sentence of transportation.

LAG: To make water. To *lag* spirits, wine, etc., is to adulterate them with water.

Lag may stem from leg, meaning journey, or from the notion that convicted felons lagged behind the movement and development of free people. Quaker John Tawell was an infamous 'lag' who was 'lagged' to New South Wales for passing forged banknotes. There, he prospered in the pharmaceutical business and championed the Quaker faith—in 1836, to protest against colonists' excessive alcohol consumption, he lagged six hundred gallons of liquor in the waters of Sydney Harbour. Tawell returned to London in 1838, where he recommenced lagging—to prevent his wife discovering that he was having an affair; he lagged his mistress' beer with hydrogen cyanide and murdered her. Tawell was executed in 1845.

LAGGER: A sailor.

Lagger may come from lugger, a small sailing ship. But according to Captain George Laval Chesterton, *Jack the Lagger* was slang for 'a transported person'. Richard Rose, a lagger nicknamed 'Jack the lagger', was transported to New South Wales for smuggling French prisoners of war out of London on his boat, the aptly named *Freeholder*.

LAGGING-DUES: Speaking of a person likely to be transported, they say *lagging dues* will be *concerned.*

When, in 1826, seventeen-year-old pickpocket Cornelius McCoy was charged with stealing a handkerchief, he refused to name his accomplices, declaring that 'he would rather be lagged for seven years, than he would *split*.' Lagging-dues were concerned, and McCoy was sentenced to seven years' transportation.

LAGGING MATTER: Any species of crime for which a person is liable on conviction to be transported.

Hundreds of crimes were punishable by transportation to Australia, including fishing in an enclosed pond, and making and selling fireworks. But most people convicted of a lagging matter were charged with petty theft. When, in 1851, at Clerkenwell Prison, a cache of stolen money was discovered wedged between the breasts of notorious pickpocket Mary Cummings, the gaoler said: 'It is not long since I had you at Clerkenwell?' Cummings replied: 'No, it is not; but I suppose I shall be lagged this time.' She was transported to Van Diemen's Land for a seven-year term.

LAG SHIP: A transport chartered by Government for the conveyance of convicts to New South Wales; also, a hulk, or floating prison, in which, to the disgrace of humanity, many hundreds of these unhappy persons are confined, and suffer every complication of human misery.

A lag ship, on average, took four months to sail from Britain to Australia.

Convicts were confined to the middle deck, notoriously cramped, dark and poorly ventilated. The mortality rate of the Second Fleet that left Britain in 1790 was the highest in the history of transportation to Australia. Convicts arrived 'wretched, naked, filthy, dirty, lousy, and many of them utterly unable to stand, to creep, or even to stir hand or foot'. New regulations were introduced, including bonuses paid to masters for landing convicts in good health,

and the appointment of a naval-trained surgeon to superintend each voyage. In later years, the mortality rate of lag ships was lower than that of emigrant ships.

LAMPS: The eyes; to have *queer lamps*, is to have sore or weak eyes.

George Jones, while imprisoned in hospital recovering from a buckshot blast to his face, is alleged to have said to his comrade Martin Cash, 'Me lamps is queer. Will they *scrag* a blind cove?' Jones was sentenced

to death for bushranging. At the time of his execution a newsman reported: 'he was perfectly blind, he yet raised his head, as if looking up to Heaven for protection and forgiveness'. But according to Cash's memoirs, Jones' sight had been 'partially restored', a

secret that he kept from his gaolers. Jones may have been hoping for a respited sentence, but the authorities did not grant convicts clemency on the grounds of ill health. When Joseph Greenwood was sentenced to one hundred lashes and death, he petitioned Lieutenant-Governor George Arthur for mercy, claiming it was torture to flog a condemned man. But his pleas were in vain—at the time of his death his back was still bleeding and, according to convict John Broxup, teeming with maggots.

LARK: Fun or sport of any kind, to create which is termed knocking up a lark.

Lark may derive from *lake*, Old English for play. Lark is also probably the origin of larrikin, 'a boisterous, often badly behaved young man'. When police discovered John Sullivan wearing a woman's dress, bonnet and boots, and carrying a bundle of stolen clothes, he was arrested. Sullivan claimed that he was delivering the bundle for a friend, and that he was wearing womens' clothing for a 'lark'. But he was not believed, so the judge sentenced him to ten years' transportation to Van Diemen's Land.

LAWN: A white cambric handkerchief.

Lawn is a fine linen or cotton fabric. Fifteen-year-old Elizabeth Cane, for stealing a 'lawn' and pawning her mistress' property, was sentenced to seven years' transportation.

LEARY: Synonymous with fly. See: FLY.

LEARY-COVE. See: FLY.

LEATHER-LANE: Any thing paltry, or of a bad quality, is called a *Leather-lane concern.*

Leather Lane, a market in Holborn, London, may allude to *Le Vrunelane*, a merchant, or *lither*, Old English for mud. Leather Lane was renowned as a place of poverty where Italian immigrants lived in leather lane conditions. Children, at the behest of 'cruel masters', begged for money with performing animals such as monkeys, poodles and mice. But in 1829, Giuli Giuseppe was gaoled for one month after his monkey, Jacko, savaged a child.

LETTER Q: The *mace,* or *billiard-slum,* is sometimes called *going upon the Q,* or *the letter Q,* alluding to an instrument used in playing billiards. See: MACE.

Letter Q is a pun on cue—a long wooden rod for striking billiard balls. Thieves who perpetrated the letter q paid a small fee to play billiards then purloined the valuable ivory balls. By 1830, billiard balls, it was said, were stolen to an 'amazing extent'. In 1831, John Smith, a sixteen-year-old 'wholesale stealer of billiard balls' was indicted twice on the same day. But due to his 'good character' he escaped a sentence of transportation. Billiard-ball thief Harry Bell wasn't as fortunate. In defence of his character, he stated: 'I have moved in as high a circle as any man in England—I have served my King and country many years.' But the judge was unmoved and Bell was sentenced to a fourteen-year term in New South Wales.

LETTER-RACKET: Going about to respectable houses with a letter or statement, detailing some case of extreme distress, as shipwreck, sufferings by fire, etc.; by which many benevolent, but credulous, persons, are induced to relieve the fictitious wants of the imposters, who are generally men, or women, of genteel address, and unfold a plausible tale of affliction.

William Hodgson, who was caught with fifty 'begging-letters', earned a substantial income—an estimated £25 per week. Alfred Talent, another professional 'begging-letter writer', was charged with the letter-racket and transported to Van Diemen's Land for a seven-year term. But in 1854, he was caught defrauding Van Diemonians. Talent posed as a fundraiser collecting money to support an impoverished widow. At the time of his arrest, he was 'well prepared with documentary evidence' to support his 'nefarious plans'. He was sentenced to a seven-year term.

LEVANTING, or RUNNING A LEVANT: An expedient practised by broken gamesters to retrieve themselves, and signifies to bet money at a race, cockmatch, etc., without a shilling in their pocket to answer the event. The punishment for this conduct in a public cockpit is rather curious; the offender is placed in a large basket, kept on purpose, which is then hoisted up to the ceiling or roof of the building, and the party is there kept suspended, and exposed to derision during the pleasure of the company.

William Brodie, a respected cabinetmaker, deacon and city councillor, was also a compulsive gambler and cockfight fanatic. Instead of levanting on his creditors, he turned to crime to supplement his income. But in 1788, he was arrested and sentenced to death. Before a crowd of forty thousand Scots, Brodie was hanged from a gallows, that, according to legend, he helped design. Burglar by night and respectable citizen by day, Brodie inspired Robert Louis Stevenson's novel *Strange Case of Dr Jekyll and Mr Hyde*.

LIFE: By this term is meant the various cheats and deceptions practiced by the designing part of mankind; a person well versed in this kind of knowledge, is said to be one that knows *life*; in other words, that knows the world. This is what Goldsmith defines to be a knowledge of human nature on the wrong side.

Eighteenth-century novelist Oliver Goldsmith penned *The Vicar of Wakefield*, the tale of an English vicar who suffers a series of misfortunes that lead him to question his understanding of theodicy—why God allows bad things to happen to good people. A character with 'a thorough knowledge of the world as it is called; or, more properly speaking, of human nature on the wrong side,' is instrumental in the vicar's downfall, but also his redemption. The novel can be viewed as a parable of the Book of Job.

LIGHT: To inform of any robbery, etc., which has been some time executed and concealed, is termed *bringing the affair to light*. To produce any thing to view, or to give up any stolen property for the sake of a reward, to quash a prosecution,  is also called *bringing* it *to light*. A thief, urging his associates to a division of any booty they have lately made, will desire them to *bring the swag to light*.

Henry Smart's master requested that he 'bring to light' a quantity of candles and tea. But Smart could not produce the items so was sentenced to twelve months' hard labour.

LILL: A pocket-book.

Lill is derived from *lil*, Romani for book. While imprisoned on death row, Scottish pickpocket David Haggart, with the assistance of a biographer, wrote his life story. According to his memoirs, a 'snib' picking the 'suck' of a 'gloach', must flick open the 'tuig' by nonchalantly raising his '*fam*' to his chin and then slip in his '*forks*' to 'bring the lil down between the flap of the coat and the body'. Snib was slang for pickpocket; suck meant breast pocket; gloach meant man; and tuig, coat.

LINE: To *get* a person *in a line*, or *in a string*, is to engage them in a conversation, while your confederate is robbing their person or premises; to banter or jest with a man by amusing him with false assurances or professions, is also termed *stringing* him, or *getting* him *in tow*; to keep any body in suspense on any subject without coming to a decision, is called *keeping* him *in tow, in a string*, or *in a tow-line*. To *cut the line*, or *the string*, is to put an end to the suspense in which you have kept anyone, by telling him the plain truth, coming to a final decision, etc. A person, who has been telling another a long story, until he is tired, or conceives his auditor has been all the while secretly laughing at him, will say at last, I've just *dropped down*, you've had me in a fine *string*, I think it's time to *cut* it. On the other hand, the auditor, having the same opinion on his part, would say, Come, I believe you want to *string* me all night, I wish you'd *cut it*; meaning, conclude the story at once.

William Ennis was caught 'in a string' at a brothel in Melbourne. His assailants, George Hopper, Thomas Martin, Letham Edwards and Sarah Southernwood, were sentenced to gaol with hard labour. Ennis, however, may have caught the police in a line—he claimed he was not engaged in prostitution but in the brothel 'to search for a friend'.

LOB: A till, or money-drawer. To have *made a good lob*, is synonymous with *making a good speak*.

Lob may have come to mean till because it is echoic of a solid, heavy object. In 1840, Elizabeth Dunn overheard her landlord, John Day, use the term when discussing a bank robbery: he robbed a '*crib*' for 'a *good lob*' then stashed the burglary tools in a '*plant*'. Dunn alerted the police and was awarded £50. But Day, for stealing £50, was sentenced to fifteen years in Van Diemen's Land.

LOCK-UP-CHOVEY: A covered cart, in which travelling hawkers convey their goods about the country; and which is secured by a door, lock, and key.

Lock-up-chovey may be a corruption of covey, meaning 'a small group of things'. When a lock-up-chovey transporting confectionary was upended in a traffic accident in Brisbane, a horde of greedy children stole all the lollies.

LODGING-SLUM: The practice of hiring ready furnished lodgings, and stripping them of the plate, linen, and other valuables.

John and Sarah Rose, notorious 'lodging robbers', perpetrated a six-month-long lodging-slum spree in London. They stole beds, bellows, blankets, candlesticks, cups, decorative shells, irons, kettles, paintings, pillows, quilts, saucers, sheets and teapots. John, it seems, was an unconscionable thief—his irate mother-in-law attempted to prosecute him for 'decoying away' her seventeen-year-old daughter. He was sentenced to fourteen years' transportation.

LOOK AT A PLACE: When a plan is laid for robbing a house, etc., *upon the crack*, or *the screw*, the parties will go a short time before the execution, to examine the premises, and make any necessary observations; this is called *looking at the place.*

Bushrangers, to ensure a successful raid, would methodically look at a place. To aid their surveillance, Michael Howe and his men stole telescopes. But in 1818, soldier William Pugh ambushed Howe, beat his brains out and then hacked off his head. Pugh lugged Howe's festering head into Hobart Town (a distance of more than one hundred kilometres) where it was hung from the gaol gates and ogled by the gratified public. Because they decapitated their victims, bounty hunters were called headhunters—Pugh was awarded £50 for Howe's head.

LOUR: Money.

Lour may derive from the Romani words, *luva* and *loaver*, meaning money, or from *loiuer*, French for reward. George Lyons and Thomas Hopkins, infamous forgers and burglars, were executed for stealing 'lour'. But forger William Henshall was rewarded for minting the first official currency in Australia. Governor Lachlan Macquarie imported 40,000 Spanish reales and instructed Henshall to strike the centre out of each coin to double the number. The outer ring was known as a 'holey dollar' and the central plug as a 'dump'. Hanshall stamped each coin with their new value and 'NEW SOUTH WALES 1813,' but he also signed the coins with his initials.

LUMBER: A room.

LUMBER: To *lumber* any property, is to deposit it at a pawn-broker's, or elsewhere for present security; to retire to any house or private place, for a short time, is called *lumbering yourself.* A man apprehended, and sent to gaol, is said to be *lumbered,* to be *in lumber,* or to be *in Lombard-street.*

Lumber comes from a system of banking developed in Lombardy, Italy. A lumber, was, originally, a Lombard Room—a storeroom for pawnbrokers and bankers. Lombard became synonymous with commerce—the Bank of England and the Royal Exchange are situated near Lombard Street in London. John Rose was lumbered in Lombard Street for lumbering property that he stole from a lumber.

LUSH: Beer or liquor of any kind. Speaking of a person who is drunk, they say, *Alderman Lushington is concerned,* or, he has been *voting for the Alderman.*

Lush derives from *lush* and *losher,* Romani words for 'drink'. Alderman Lushington may stem from the City of Lushington, an eighteenth-century drinking society comprising a 'Lord Mayor' and four 'aldermen', who presided over 'wards' called Juniper, Poverty, Lunacy and Suicide. But it's also possible that the term refers to Stephen Lushington, or his son, Stephen Lushington junior, both of whom were members of parliament. By the 1830s Australia was rife with alcoholism. Jane Agnes, charged with 'drinking too much lush', was sentenced to four weeks in third class at the Parramatta Female Factory, while 'lushington' Winefred Doyle copped six weeks at the factory. At this time, a colonist of New South Wales consumed, on average, 13.6 litres of spirits annually. Van Diemonians drank approximately 19 litres. Many colonists appealed for prohibitory legislation but because the taxes placed on spirits were a major source of revenue, support from the colonial government was not forthcoming. Alcohol was, in fact, a form of currency—military, police and convicts were, at times, paid booze in lieu of cash wages.

LUSH-CRIB, or LUSH-KEN: A public-house, or gin-shop.

Public houses, more commonly called pubs, were off limits to convicts—Edward Roberts was punished with a dozen lashes for frequenting 'lush *cribs*' in Hobart Town. To get around the rules, convicts wore disguises. John Watson dressed as a sailor, and William Bray, a soldier. For pretending to be a policeman, George Carbull was sentenced to labour in a road gang for three months.

LUSH, or LUSHY: Drunk, intoxicated.

When, in 1835, a New South Wales policeman threatened to 'shop' Mary McCooney because she was 'lushy', she threw mud in his face. McCooney was fined one crown then '*mizzled*' out of court. Shop is slang for arrest.

LUSHY-COVE: A drunken man.

The term was also applied to women. Esther Holmes, a 'lushy cove', was charged with drunkenness on twenty-seven separate occasions. Alcohol-related offences were among the most common committed by convicts.

MACE: To *mace* a shop-keeper, or *give it to* him *upon the mace*, is to obtain goods on credit, which you never mean to pay for; to run up a score with the same intention, or to spunge upon your acquaintance, by continually begging or borrowing from them, is termed *maceing*, or *striking the mace*. See: LETTER Q.

Mace may come from mace, a heavy club. When, in 1776, police discovered stolen clothing for sale in a London pawnshop, the pawnbroker confessed to purchasing the clothes from George Lewis, a thief who acquired them on 'the mace'. Lewis was arrested and sentenced to six months' gaol. But he also was glim'd in the fam—branded on the hand. Lewis was probably branded on his thumb with 'T' for theft. Branding was a painful and humiliating punishment designed to last a lifetime, preventing criminals from going undetected. Branding criminals was abolished in 1829, but branding persisted in the British army until 1871.

MACE-GLOAK: A man who lives *upon the mace*.

In 1832, George Holmes, infamous for 'macing about Hobart Town', was accused of stealing and selling his master's bullocks, but also stealing back the bullocks to return them to his master's property. But because his master denied that he'd been 'maced', Holmes escaped punishment Two years later, however, the mace-gloak was caught stealing bullocks and sentenced to life imprisonment.

MAG: A halfpenny.

Mag is a corruption of make, slang for a half-penny. In 1831, Duncan Gollan was walking through London when a gang of pickpockets seized his arms and emptied his pockets. Daniel Field, who stole Gollan's pocket-book, waved it in the air and remarked, 'My friends there aren't a bloody mag in it.' Field

was charged with highway robbery and transported to Van Diemen's Land for life.

MANCHESTER: The tongue.

Manchester is probably a pun on Tongue, an area of Bolton in Greater Manchester, England. When a policeman arrested Janet McDonald for speaking indecent language, he repeated her language in court and was reprimanded for his 'vulgar' manchester. McDonald's ticket-of-leave was revoked and she was sentenced to seven days' hard labour.

MANG: To speak or talk.

Mang is derived from *mong*, Romani for beg or pray. By speaking cant, criminals such as pickpocket David Haggart felt safe to 'mang' about their crimes in public. But when William Henry Jones was overheard boasting that he'd '*done*' a 'fiver' (£5), he was arrested. Jones, who expected to be '*turned up*', was sentenced to seven years' transportation.

MAULEY: The hand.

Mauley comes from maul, meaning handle roughly. At London's Kings Head Pub, three members of the *Swell* Mob conspired to steal a purse from Colonel Brook Brydges Parlby Esquire.  Thomas Gascoyne attempted to take the purse, but because Parlby's hand was in the way, he whispered to John Jones, 'I can't get his mauly off his pocket.' Jones was also obstructed by Parlby's hand, so he whispered to John Hutchins, 'Can't you get his damned mauly off?' Hutchins led the revellers in a round of applause and when the colonel threw his mauleys in the air, Hutchins coolly stole the purse. But Constable Thomas Madden, who'd been observing from afar, arrested the three pickpockets and they were sentenced to fourteen years' transportation.

MAX: Gin or hollands.

Max is short for maximum, meaning 'great strength'. Hollands, also known as Hollands Gin, is a juniper-flavoured liquor named after Holland, its place of origin. In 1858, Constable James Levick charged Alfred Bradford, the publican of Sydney's Blind Beggar pub, with unlawfully selling liquor on the Sabbath. According to Levick, a punter carrying an empty bottle walked into the pub and then exited with the bottle full of 'max'. Bradford denied the allegation, claiming that Levick was '*down* upon him' because he'd '*jacketted*' him to his superior officer on a previous occasion. The magistrate dismissed the case but cautioned Bradford to 'keep such remarks to himself'.

MILESTONE: A country booby.

Milestones inform travellers of the number of miles to a particular place, while a country booby is a naive person who lives in a rural area. Milestone may have been a sarcastic term, implying that country people were uninformed and ignorant, or it may have stemmed from the travellers who dotted country roads in the manner of milestones.

In 1803, several milestones absconded from Sydney and perished in the bush while attempting to walk to China. That Australia and China were connected was a common misconception in the early days of colonisation, despite the authorities' assertions to the contrary. One of the survivors, John Place, a convict who hailed from a country town in England, attempted the journey a second time. He copped five hundred lashes.

MILL: To fight. To *mill* a person is to beat him.

The term mill was inspired by the revolving vanes of a windmill that powered gears to mill grain. Kate Pitt, charged with drunkenness and 'milling' her fellow servants, was punished with six weeks in the Parramatta Female Factory, third class. But Walter Scott, a convict transported to New South Wales, was nearly killed when he was milled in the head by a windmill vane.

MILL A GLAZE: To break a window.

In 1843, eight-year-old John Licet was arrested when he 'milled the *glaze*'. Dubbed a 'brat', 'little reprobate' and 'the most anointedest young scamp' in Melbourne, he was ordered to behave or spend a month in gaol and receive 'a whipping every day'. Licet's parents, to stop him causing trouble, chained him to a wall.

MILL-DOLL: An obsolete name for Bridewell house of correction, in Bridge-street, Blackfriars, London.

The name comes from milling doll, slang for beating hemp. Mill-Doll inmates beat clumps of hemp—punnies—with mallets to remove the bark and separate the fibres. Hemp was used in rope and textile manufacture. Female inmates were expected to process eight punnies a day, and men twelve. According to inmate Jacob Llive, prisoners milling doll at Mill-Doll sang 'the most lewd songs men or devils invented'.

MILLING-COVE: A pugilist.

In 1817, a record number of spectators gathered to watch pugilists William Daniels and Robert Lee compete in a prizefight. Colonists wagered money on the outcome of prizefights, but they also wagered property such as farms, pigsties and livestock—Daniels and Lee competed for a prize of sixty ewes. But Daniels forfeited the fight because, after eighty punishing rounds, his eyes were so swollen that he was 'totally blind'. Daniels, a celebrated 'milling *cove*' transported from London, spent approximately thirty-four years in Van Diemonian prisons.

MITTS: Gloves.

Mitts is an abbreviation of mittens. Fourteen-year-old John Westbrook and sixteen-year-old Daniel Murphy were sentenced to seven years' transportation for stealing 'six pair of glove mitts'.

MITTENS: The hands.

Mitten comes from *mitaine*, Old French for half-glove. In 1854, Margaret Williams was accused of robbing a drunken sailor after she 'decoyed' him into her 'den'. But Williams swore to her innocence, claiming the sailor had given her his valuables because she'd saved him from 'the mittens of the *traps*'. By the time the case went to trial the sailor had shipped out, so Williams was acquitted.

MIZZLE: To quit or go away from any place or company; to elope, or run away.

Mizzle may derive from *misli*, a Shelta word that means 'to go'. In 1835, Sarah 'Kitty Clover' Barnes was prosecuted for stealing a watch from a drunken sailor. But Barnes insisted that she was entrusted with the watch for safekeeping. Because the sailor couldn't remember what he had said, he offered to drop the charge if Barnes returned the watch. She agreed so the case was dismissed, and, arm in arm, 'they mizzled off together'. Barnes may have been nicknamed after Kitty Clover, the 'plump and round' protagonist of a popular ballad.

MOLLISHER: A woman.

Edward Jones, eyewitness to a jewellery robbery, alleged that one of the suspects referred to the shopkeeper as a 'monisher', a 'cant word' that Jones believed meant 'woman'. Sometimes spelt mollesher and mollisker, mollisher may derive from *monishi*, Romani for woman. But the term also has been attributed to moll, a slang word for woman derived from Mary. Mary Bowater, a convict mollisher nicknamed 'Moll Smith', prospered as a horse breeder. A ford outside Campbell Town, Van Diemen's Land, was dubbed 'Moll Smith's Bottom' in her honour.

MONKEY: A padlock.

Monkey may come from monkey, meaning 'tamper'. The New South Wales press declared that Van Diemonian absconders William Smith and John Adams were 'gambling monkeys'. In 1845, they were arrested for conning a farmhand using the 'padlock trick'. At their trial a policeman informed the court that 'monkey' is a '*flash* name' for 'padlock' and explained the trick to the jury: a conman exhibits a padlock that can be effortlessly unlocked then passes it to his accomplice who secretly switches it with a padlock that cannot be  unlocked. A '*flat*' is encouraged to wager that he can unlock the padlock but is duped out of his money. Both men were charged with stealing and sentenced to ten years' transportation to Van Diemen's Land.

MONKERY: The country parts of England are called *The Monkery*.

Monkery may stem from *munk'ri*, a Shelta word that means 'the country'. But because many tramps led a simple, peaceful life not dissimilar to practising monks, the term is also attributed to monkery, meaning 'monastic lifestyle'. Numerous areas in Australia were referred to as the Monkery. Frederick Ward, more famously known as Captain Thunderbolt, roamed 'the Monkery' of New South Wales.

MONTRA: A watch.

Montre is French for watch. In 1794, Louisa Le Sage was charged with stealing a montra from her mistress in Buckingham Gate, London. Because Le Sage was French, the jury comprised French and English jurors, and an interpreter translated the proceedings. Le Sage was sentenced to seven years' transportation to New South Wales. There, she married Gabriel Louis Marie Huon de Kerilleau, a Frenchman in the New South Wales Corp. Convicts transported to Australia came from all over the world, including Canada, New Zealand, Africa, Spain, Russia, Jamaica and America. Indigenous Australians were also subject to British law.

MORNING-SNEAK: Going out early to rob private houses or shops by slipping in at the door unperceived, while the servant or shopman is employed in cleaning the steps, windows, etc.

Catherine Evans was such a notorious thief in the Holborn district of London that local law enforcement dubbed her 'a regular morning sneak'. When, in 1825, a shopkeeper charged Evans with stealing his cat, police searched her and discovered 'a large bloody knife' and six 'quite warm' cat skins. Evans, it transpired, had taken to skinning Holborn's 'favourite tabbies' and selling their pelts. During her trial, police expressed 'disgust and horror'  as they described the piles of flayed cats they'd discovered heaped in Holburn streets. Locals were outraged. But because there was no law for the protection of cats, Holburn's alderman was 'at a loss' as to how Evans could be punished.

MOTT: A *blowen*, or woman of the town.

Mott may come from *mot*, Dutch for woman. Prostitution, or 'mott-ism' as it was termed in the *Swell's Night Guide* to London, was commonplace. An estimated one in three female convicts engaged in prostitution. Elizabeth Carlisle's record states that she was '10 years a Prostitute' and 'a Woman of the Town of the lowest class'. When she was sentenced to fourteen years' transportation for pickpocketing, the judge remarked that he was 'doing her a service' by granting her the 'opportunity of reforming her life'. In 1835, she married Van Diemonian convict Michael Hoadley. But a few days after they were wed, a man was discovered in their marital bed and Carlisle was sentenced to three months in second class at the Cascades Female Factory. Carlisle may have continued her career as a mott despite her marriage. According to contemporaneous historian John West, many convict marriages 'were a disguise for licentiousness, and of a very temporary character.'

MOUNT: To swear, or give evidence falsely for the sake of a gratuity. To *mount* for a person is also synonymous with *bonnetting for* him.

MOUNTER: A man who lives by *mounting*, or perjury, who is always ready for a guinea or two to swear whatever is proposed to him.

Men hired to provide false testimony were mounted in elegant wigs and coats so that when they mounted the witness box they appeared to be a credible witness. According to author George Parker, 'mounters' charged five shillings. Mounters risked harsh punishments—mounter William Millner was sentenced to stand for one hour in the pillory situated outside Newgate Prison, and to seven years' transportation.

MOUTH: A foolish silly person; a man who does a very imprudent act, is said to be a *rank mouth.*

In 1877, West Australian convict Michael Brady was woken by a 'sharp pang' on his mouth. To his horror, he discovered his lower lip had been cleaved away 'leaving only the corners.' Looming above him, with the lip clenched between his teeth, was rank mouth Patrick Gibbons, also a convict. Gibbons, who had bickered with Brady earlier that day, committed the 'cannibal act' as a brutal form of retribution. He was sentenced to twelve months' hard labour at Fremantle Prison.

MOVE: Any action or operation in life; the secret spring by which any project is conducted, as, There is a *move* in that business which you are not *down to*. To be *flash to every move upon the board*, is to have a general knowledge of the world, and all its numerous deceptions.

Thomas Bowler, a one-legged shoemaker from Oxford, was one of the many *'downey'* convicts infamous for pulling crooked 'moves' in Van Diemen's Land. When, in 1847, he was arrested for passing counterfeit money,  police discovered a letter stashed in his wooden leg. Because the letter was written in cant, the attorney-general offered to translate it. He concluded the letter outlined a plan for Bowler's wife, also a convict, to persuade the prosecutor to drop the charges. Bowler was sentenced to two years' hard labour, with one months' solitary confinement.

MR. KNAP. See KNAP.
MR. NASH. See NASH.
MR. PALMER. See PALM.
MR. PULLEN. See PULL or PULL UP.

MUFF: An epithet synonymous with mouth.

MUG: The face; a *queer mug* is an ugly face.

Mug may come from eighteenth-century mugs that featured ugly faces. When Sophia Hunter Naylor was sentenced to one month in the Parramatta Female Factory for 'continually running after the men', she vowed to assault her master in his 'ugly mug'. But Naylor may not have been in a position to trade insults. The reporter who attended her trial described her as 'five feet ten without shoes', as 'thin as a hard run greyhound', with a face resembling a 'battle axe'. However, according to Naylor's physical description in the Black Books, she was four feet nine and a quarter inches tall, her complexion was 'ruddy', her nose was 'short & a little cocked', and she was devoid of 'front upper teeth'.

MURPHY'S COUNTENANCE: A pig's face.

Murphy's countenance may have originated as an insult for Irish people—Murphy, a surname common in Ireand, is slang for Irishman. Irishman John Tooney, for '*prigging*' his master's smoked murphy's countenances, was punished with seventy-five lashes.

NAIL: To *nail* a person, is to over-reach, or take advantage of him in the course of trade or traffic; also, to rob, or steal; as, I *nail'd* him *for* (or *of*) his *reader*, I robbed him of his pocket-book; I *nail'd the swell's mantra in the push,* I picked the gentleman's pocket of his watch in the crowd, etc. A person of an over-reaching, imposing disposition, is called a *nail*, a *dead nail*, a *nailing rascal*, a *rank needle*, or a *needle pointer*.

In 1840, the New South Wales press reported that William 'Billy the Nailer' Reeves 'nailed' Ann Reed with a marriage proposal. But because Reeves also nailed women's clothing and jewellery to provide Reed with bridal attire, he was nailed with two years' hard labour in leg irons. Reeves, a convict transported for stealing clothes, acquired his nickname because he was a nailer by profession.

NANCY: The posteriors.

Convict children who misbehaved could be whipped or caned across their bottom and thighs, an area of the body termed 'posteriors' and 'breach'. At the Point Puer Boys' Prison, fifteen-year-old Isaac Bailey drew 'improper figures' at school and was punished with twenty strokes across his 'breech', or, as he may have termed it, his nancy.

NAP the BIB: To cry; as, the *mollisher nap'd* her *bib*, the woman fell a crying.

Nap may derive from *nappa*, Swedish for take. Bib, meaning 'weep' or 'flow', may come from *bibben*, a Middle English word that means 'to drink'. Some convicts denied their captors the satisfaction of seeing them nap the bib. In New South Wales, James Clayton, a so-called '*flash*' convict, bit his lips so he wouldn't nap the bib when undergoing a flogging. An observer noted that Clayton's 'body and mind had been hard-

ened by former punishments' and that his skin was 'thick to an uncommon degree'. Despite Clayton's tough exterior, his back bled after the fifth stroke from the cat-o'-nine-tails. In Van Diemen's Land, a convict sentenced to a flogging bit on a lead musket ball, and, according to convict William Gates, the man did not utter a 'groan or word' even though his back was 'a raw, mangled piece of flesh from which the blood had run in such quantities as to fill his shoes till they gushed over'.

NASH: To go away from, or **quit**, any place or company; speaking of a person who is gone, they say, he is *nash'd*, or *Mr. Nash is concerned.*

Nash and *nasher* are Romani words for run. When, in 1835, Constable Thomas Nash arrested a man for drunkenness, the man refused to nash. Nash commandeered a wheelbarrow to cart the drunk to gaol but his friends came to his rescue and bashed Nash unconscious. The brawlers were arrested and sentenced to one month in Sydney Gaol.

NE-DASH: Nothing.

Ne-dash may derive from *nastis*, Romani for 'I cannot'. English play-wright William Thomas Moncrieff, who wrote the operatic drama *Van Diemen's Land*, based his characters on well-known convicts, including James Hardy Vaux. The characters' dialogue, which includes the term 'ne-dash', was probably sourced from Vaux's lexicon.

NEEDLE: (see: NAIL) To *needle* a person is to haggle with him in making a bargain, and, if possible, take advantage of him, though in the most trifling article.
NEEDLE-POINTER. See: NAIL.

During the voyage of the *Maitland* to Van Diemen's Land in 1843, convict John Hill, who 'worked all and every day with his needle', tattooed his shipmates to needle them out of contraband goodies, such as tobacco.

NEEDY-MIZZLER: A poor ragged object of either sex; a shabby-looking person.

Ann Sill, a sixty-year-old 'antiquated lump of depravity' with a pock-pitted face and a 'diseased' right forefinger, '*mizzled*' out of a butcher's shop after purchasing meat with counterfeit coins. Charged with '*smashing*', the needy-mizzler was sentenced to three months in Sydney Gaol.

NIB: A gentleman, or person of the higher order. People who affect gentility or consequence, without any real pretensions thereto, are from hence vulgarly called *Half-nibs* or *Half-swells*; and, indeed, persons of low minds, who conceive money to be the only criterion of gentility, are too apt to stigmatize with the before-mentioned epithets any man, who, however well-bred and educated, may be reduced to a shabby external, but still preserves a sense of decorum in his manners, and avoids associating with the vagabonds among whom he may unfortunately be doomed to exist.

Bushranger Matthew Brady, a nib renowned for his fashionable dress and gallantry to women, was described as 'a good looking man'. But his contemporary, cannibalistic baby-murdering half-nib, Thomas Jeffries, was 'a monster in countenance'. When, in 1826, Brady was arrested, he was inundated with 'baskets of fruit, bouquets of flowers, and dishes of confectionary prepared by his fair admirers'. But when Jeffries was arrested an elderly woman attempted to stab him with a fork.

NIBB'D: Taken in custody.

Nibb'd, an abbreviation of nibbed, derives from nabbed. But criminals were also nippered, nicked, nibbled and napped. When, in 1843, Timothy Bryan was carrying a stolen bolt of cloth, his accomplice remarked that if they did not keep out of sight they would be 'nibbled'. They were caught and Bryan was transported to Van Diemen's Land for a ten-year term.

NIBBLE: To pilfer trifling articles, not having spirit to touch any thing of consequence.

NIBBLER: A pilferer or petty thief.

Samuel Rathbone, who felt hands 'nibbling' at his watch, seized a nibbler named Mark Benjamin. Benjamin, who was notorious for teaching 'poor unprotected children' how to nibble, was sentenced to ten years' transportation.

NIX, or NIX MY DOLL: Nothing.

Nix is probably derived from *nichts*, German for nothing. 'Nix My Dolly, Pals, Fake Away,' is a song from a hit theatre production inspired by infamous thief Jack Sheppard. So popular was the song that 'every dirty guttersnipe' sung, hummed and whistled the tune until it was 'deafening in the streets'. The first verse is: 'In a box of the stone jug I was born, of a hempen widow the kid forlorn, fake away!' This translates as: 'In a cell of Newgate Prison I was born, of a woman whose husband had been hanged, the child criminal forlorn, commit crime!' Lord Chamberlain, fearing that such plays incited criminal behaviour, banned plays featuring 'Jack Sheppard' in their title.

NOB IT: To act with such prudence and knowledge of the world, as to prosper and become independent without any labour or bodily exertion; this is termed *nobbing it*, or *fighting* *nob work*. To effect any purpose, or obtain any thing, by means of good judgment and sagacity, is called *nabbing it* for such a thing.

In 1832, the *Tasmanian* printed a series of letters that drew colonists' attention to dubious goings-on in Van Diemen's Land. According to one  letter, the colony's finest farmland had been acquired by *'swells'* who 'nobbed it' to leaseholders. The letters were signed 'Timothy Boniface', a publican newly arrived from England. But because Boniface is slang for innkeeper, it's likely the name was a pseudonym. The colonial government, to reward its administrators and encourage growth, granted land to colonists, politicians, civil servants, religious leaders and military personnel, some of whom became extremely wealthy.

NOB-PITCHERS: A general term for those sharpers who attend at fairs, races, etc., to take in the *flats* at prick in the garter, cups and balls, and other similar artifices.

In the game of cups and balls, three identical cups are placed upside down and a ball is positioned beneath one of the cups. The cups are shuffled about and punters lay bets on which cup contains the ball. The game was also played with a pea and half-walnut shells, or with thimbles—termed 'thimblerig'. Practitioners of the game were so skilled in deception that finding the ball was a virtual impossibility. In prick-in-the-garter, a garter, belt or piece of material was doubled over then tightly rolled. Punters were invited to insert a bodkin into the centre of the loop to win a prize. But because the loop was folded in a deceptively simple manner, finding the centre was extremely difficult. In 1833, Michael Burke, a New South Wales nob-pitcher, was gaoled for perpetrating thimblerig, and, in 1857, Melbournian Thomas Nicholls was gaoled for perpetrating prick-the-garter.

NO DOWN. See: FAKE AWAY, etc.

NOSE: A thief who becomes an evidence against his accomplices; also, a person who seeing one or more suspicious characters in the streets, makes a point of watching them in order to frustrate any attempt they may make, or to cause their apprehension; also, a spy or informer of any description.

NOSE: To *nose*, is to pry into any person's proceedings in an impertinent manner. To *nose upon* anyone, is to tell of any thing he has said or done with a view to injure him, or to benefit yourself.

Surgeon Superintendent Peter Cunningham noted that convicts caught 'nosing' were beaten and bullied but could also have their noses bitten off. Because convict informants were nicknamed 'dogs,' biting off a nose was called 'a mouthful of dog's nose'. Thomas 'Nosey' Barrett, who was said to have 'a most unprepossessing countenance' because he  had 'little or no nose at all,' may have been a nose. But in 1839, a wharfinger nosed on him—he was sent to Sydney Gaol for stealing cloth.

NULLING-COVE: A pugilist.

Nulling may derive from annul, meaning 'cancel'. John Perry, known as 'Perry the Black', was a black nulling-cove born in Ireland in 1819. Perry, who trained under renowned pugilist Jem Ward, soon found fame and fortune. But in 1846, he was convicted of passing forged notes and sentenced to seven years' transportation. In 1849, Perry fought George Hough for the Australian championship and won. But after repeated run-ins with the law, he died a drunken and penniless drifter in 1867.

NUT: To please a person by any little act of assiduity, by a present, or by flattering words, is called *nutting* him; as the present, etc., by which you have gratified them, is termed a *nut*.

Nut may stem from the sweetness of a nut. When, in 1896, the Wiffen children returned home from school and discovered 'peanut candy' on their dining table, they assumed it was a nut left by their loving parents. But after they devoured the candy and became violently ill, a doctor discovered they'd been poisoned with arsenic. The culprit, who police suspected was the jilted lover of their philandering father, was never caught.

NUTS UPON IT: To be very much pleased or gratified with any object, adventure, or overture; so a person who conceives a strong inclination for another of the opposite sex, is said to be quite *nutty*, or nuts *upon him* or her.

Harry Sharney was nuts upon it when he cheated a punter with the 'bounding pea' game. But Sharney was caught and in his pockets police

170

discovered a trove of incriminating paraphernalia: three half-walnut shells, balls, a dicebox and 'bent, cut and trimmed' playing cards prepared for the three-card trick. Sharney and his two card-sharp companions copped one month in Bunbury Gaol in Western Australia.

NUTS UPON YOURSELF: A man who is much gratified with any bargain he has made, narrow escape he has had, or other event in which he is interested, will express his self-satisfaction or gladness by declaring that he is, or was, quite *nuts upon himself.*

Convict William Angus Watt, a clerk in the offices of the colonial secretary, sheriff and archdeacon, was nuts upon himself—he was awarded a ticket-of-leave for good behaviour and scored a job as editor of the *Sydney Gazette*. But because he published articles condemning the convict system, his detractors called him a 'nut brown'—a derogatory name for a convict that comes from the tan they acquired from working in the sun.

OFFICE: A hint, signal, or private intimation, from one person to another; this is termed *officeing* him, or *giving* him *the office*; to *take the office*, is to understand and profit by the hint given.

Dennis McCarthy was notorious for 'the office'—when his convict '*pals*' were on the '*job*' gambling at cards, he sat behind their opponents to relay the result of their cards.

OLD LAG: A man or woman who has been transported, is so called on returning home, by those who are acquainted with the secret. See: LAG.

In January 1838, Hobart Town police noticed an 'old lag' Henry James Witton 'genteely' dressed and 'flourishing' a cane. He was '*lumbered*' with a caution 'not to put on airs and manners unbecoming his station in life'. Witton was a graduate of London's Royal Academy of Music. When he completed his seven-year term of transportation the following January, he advertised his services as an instrumentalist. But a few days after posting his ad, he was charged with forgery and sentenced to life on Norfolk Island.

OLIVER: The moon.

OLIVER IS IN TOWN: A phrase signifying that the nights are moonlight, and consequently unfavourable to depredation.

The moon was nicknamed Oliver because of the likeness it bears to the letter 'O'. Preacher-turned-bank-robber Andrew George Scott, more commonly known as 'Captain Moonlite,' is alleged to have adopted the moniker because Oliver was in town on the night of his first robbery. But according to a contemporaneous lunar calendar, the robbery was committed under a waning crescent moon. Scott was the inspiration for Thomas Alexander Browne's acclaimed novel *Robbery Under Arms*.

OLIVER'S UP: The moon has risen.

Convicts newly arrived in Australia were typically disembarked from their transport ships at five o'clock in the morning. Because the journey was made after Oliver was up, some convicts went 'moon blind', a form of blindness called nyctalopia, which is caused by vitamin A deficiency.

OLIVER WHIDDLES: The moon shines.

According to his physical description in the Black Books, Oliver whiddled on Hugh Smith's left arm. Tattooed next to Smith's moon were a sun, stars and the initials of family members. Smith's right arm was tattooed with hearts pierced by darts, more initials, and a jug, pipe and glass. The tattoos probably commemorated Smith's homeland and his love of sharing a smoke and a drink with his family. Tattoos were popular—Smith was just eleven years old. Approximately forty per cent of male convicts were tattooed.

ONE UPON YOUR TAW: A person who takes offence at the conduct of another, or conceives himself injured by the latter, will say, never mind, I'll be *one upon your taw*; or, I'll *be a marble on your taw*; meaning, I'll be even with you some time.

Taw was slang for hide. During a heated game of ring taw at Gloucester in 1827, twelve-year-old John Baldwin was one upon the taw when he stabbed fifteen-year-old James Carpenter. Baldwin was charged with attempted murder—a crime punishable by death. But the judge released Baldwin with a warning to 'keep a guard over his passions'. Ring taw, more commonly known as marbles, is a game in which players attempt to knock their opponent's marbles out of a ring.

ONION: A watch-seal, a *bunch of onions*, is several seals worn upon one ring.

A watch seal is a small stamp attached to a watch chain. Seals were pressed into melted wax to seal or authenticate a document. Because

seals were made from gold, brass and copper, they resembled onions. In 1834, at the Vulcan's Head pub, coalminer Robert White commissioned itinerant artist Signor Benesontagi to paint his portrait for one '*bob*'. White, to impress his wife, instructed Benesontagi to incorporate blue velvet '*kicksies*'. But when he was presented with the finished painting, he was furious to discover that Benesontagi had added a dandyish 'bunch of onions'. White refused to pay, so Benesontagi took him to court. He was awarded fifteen pence compensation.

ORDER-RACKET: Obtaining goods from a shopkeeper, by means of a forged order or false pretence.

In 1815, a gang of '*smashers*' perpetrated a spate of order-rackets in New South Wales. According to the *Sydney Gazette*, shopkeepers were 'deluged with forged bills'. Meticulously drawn by hand with designs painstakingly impressed into the paper to give them the appearance of having been printed, the notes were traced to Joseph Lycett, a convict serving a fourteen-year sentence for forging English banknotes. An artist of 'extraordinary ingenuity', Lycett is alleged to have been granted freedom for his contribution to the Australian arts. But in 1827, he was caught forging banknotes and cut his own throat in an attempted suicide. He died the following year as a result of his injury.

OUT-AND-OUT: Quite; completely; effectually. See: SERVE, and: FAKE.

The British press dubbed Joseph Lawrence an 'out-and-out swindler'. He was sentenced to seven years' transportation twice on the same day, making for a total term of fourteen years. Lawrence was transported to Van Diemen's Land, but after he was caught passing a forged cheque he received a third seven-year sentence and was sent to Port Arthur Penal Station.

OUT-AND-OUTER: A person of a resolute determined spirit, who pursues his object without regard to danger or difficulties; also an incorrigible depredator, who will rob friend or stranger indiscriminately, being possessed of neither honour nor principle.

At Hobart Town in 1827, George Lacey was hanged for murdering an overseer at the Sarah Island Penal Station. When Lacey stood on the scaffold he leaned into the crowd as far as the rope would allow and said: 'You may think it strange that a character like me, who used to boast of being what you call a regular out and outer say this, but I make no bravado here, and I tell you if it was not for the blood of the blessed Jesus, I should not now have the least hope for mercy. You see the miserable state to which I have brought myself and I hope you will all take warning.'

OUT OF FLASH. See: FLASH.

OUT OF THE WAY: A thief who knows that he is sought after by the *traps* on some information, and consequently goes out of town, or otherwise conceals himself, is said by his *palls* to be *out of the way for* so and so, naming the particular offence he stands charged with. See: WANTED.

In 1823, convict Henry Bayne was arrested on suspicion of burglary. Bayne denied the allegation but the authorities did not believe him, and he was sentenced to receive twenty-five lashes every day until he confessed. On the sixth morning, flagellator James Walton, for fear of killing Bayne, 'got out of the way all day'. But when Walton reappeared he was instructed to inflict a final batch of twenty-five lashes. Bayne survived the ordeal, maintaining his innocence. When the torturous punishment was detailed in Sydney newspapers, Walton was ambushed and beaten. His attacker escaped detection because he got out of the way.

OUT OF TWIG: To *put* yourself *out of twig*, is to disguise your dress and appearance, to avoid being recognised, on some particular account; a man reduced by poverty to wear a shabby dress is said by his acquaintance to be *out of twig*; to *put* any article *out of twig*, as a stolen coat, cloak, etc., is to alter it in such a way that it cannot be identified.

Absconder Patrick McGuire put himself out of twig, but a *'trap'* saw through his *'prime twig'* disguise and arrested him. McGuire was punished with a seven-day stint on 'Murray's anti-roaming machine'— the treadmill at Carters' Barracks, superintended by Andrew Murray.

PALL: A partner; companion; associate; or accomplice.

In 1848, Melbourne police were on the lookout for a 'gang of scoundrels' who looted vessels moored to Queen's Wharf. When a patrolling policeman observed a man purloin a jacket from the deck of a schooner and pass it to his 'pall,' he followed them. But the two thieves spotted the policeman and made a '*bolt*' into a nearby hostel. There, police discovered the jacket draped on the end of a bed occupied by a man named Francis Moore. Moore's roommates refused to assist with police enquiries, however, and so the jacket could not be conclusively linked to Moore. He was let off with a warning to keep '*square*'.

PALM: To bribe, or give money, for the attainment of any object or indulgence; and it is then said that the party who receives it is *palmed*, or that *Mr. Palmer is concerned.*

In 1843, nineteen-year-old James Spelman informed the police that fourteen-year-old Thomas Nicholls was carrying counterfeit coins. The police apprehended Nicholls, but soon discovered that Spelman 'palmed the money' to him to get him arrested and score a reward. Nicholls was acquitted, but Spelman, a 'well known *smasher*', was sentenced to nine months' gaol.

PALMING-RACKET: Secreting money in the palm of the hand, *a game* at which some are very expert.

Mary Callaghan perpetrated the palming-racket. In 1832, she was caught rifling through her master's till with a halfpenny 'sticking to the palm' of her hand. She was punished with six months' third class at the Parramatta Female Factory. Palmers, as they were called, held their fingers out straight to allay suspicion. To ensure the coins stuck, they smeared their palms with a sticky residue made from boiled-down beer.

PANNY: A house.

Panny may derive from pantry, meaning 'a place filled with items'. When, in 1786, George Lyons, Thomas Hopkins and John Farrell were arrested for burglary, Farrell informed on his accomplices to save himself. According to his confession, the trio spotted Thomas Bowers at the pub with his mistress, so put his wife '*flash*' to his infidelity and then burgled the 'panney' after she left to confront him. Because the judge did not understand cant language, Farrell explained that 'panney is the meaning of the house'. Lyons and Hopkins were executed.

PANNUM: Bread.

Panem is Latin for bread. Convicts appointed to bake the daily bread were carefully monitored, as durable foods such as flour were often stockpiled to provision absconders. Convict-baker Richard Bruin was notorious for absconding, stealing flour and baking underweight bread called 'short pannum'.

PARK. See BUSHY-PARK.

PATTER: To talk; as, *He patters good flash*, etc.

Patter comes from *paternoster*, meaning prayer. James Owen was known to 'patter *flash* a *rum'n'*. When, in 1848, he was caught passing forged cheques, he convinced the judge that his accomplice, Alexander Fraser, was innocent. Fraser escaped punishment and Owen copped two years in Melbourne Gaol.

PATTER'D: Tried in a court of justice; a man who has undergone this ordeal, is said to have *stood the patter*.

In 1833, 'ragged urchin' Michael Smith was arrested for stealing a bottle of ginger beer. Smith was so young that when he stood the patter he could barely 'peep over the bar'. In gaol he scrawled a cant rhyme on the cell wall ('he who takes what isn't his, when he's caught will go to prison'):

> *Him as prigs wot isn't hisn,*
> *Wen his cothced vil go to pris'n'.*

PEAR-MAKING: Enlisting in various regiments, taking the bounty, and then deserting.

Because pear-making soldiers were known to make an appearance and then a disappearance, pear-making may come from pear (as in disappear) and make. Soldiers charged with desertion were tattooed with a 'D' for deserter below their left armpit. The tattoo was designed to prevent the soldier from re-enlisting or remaining at large undetected. Thomas Carey, transported for pear-making, was branded with a 'D' three times.

PENSIONER: A mean-spirited fellow who lives with a woman of the town, and suffers her to maintain him in idleness in the character of her *fancy-man*.

John Walsh, a vicious pensioner and brothel keeper in Adelaide, struck prostitute Catherine Driscoll with an axe and stole her money. When he was sentenced to seven years' gaol, Driscoll opened a brothel in his absence—she was charged with keeping a 'house of ill-fame' and fined £10.

PETER: A parcel or bundle, whether large or small; but most properly it signifies a trunk or box.

Peter is probably derived from *portmanteau*, French for a large travel bag. William Burnside, paroled from Fremantle Prison in 1885, absconded from Western Australia by mailing himself to South Australia. Burnside, who stood six feet tall, squeezed himself into a peter that measured just three feet six inches long, two feet wide and two feet deep. When a customs officer discovered Burnside eight days into his ordeal, he was dehydrated to the point of death. Burnside was nursed back to health, fined for not paying for his fare and returned to Fremantle.

PETER-HUNTING: Traversing the streets or roads for the purpose of cutting away trunks, etc., from travelling carriages; persons who follow this *game*, are from thence called *peter-hunters*, whereas *the drag* more properly applies to robbing carts or wagons.

Peter Cunningham, a surgeon-superintendent who served on several convict transports, noted that convicts kept '*slang* journals'. According to Cunningham, a common entry was 'peters *cracked* and *frisked*'. Because cargo was stored in their quarters, some convicts couldn't resist stealing tasty treats. In 1834, when sailing to Port Arthur Penal Station, a group of peter-hunting boys drank themselves senseless after they broke into a case of wine.

PETER-HUNTING-JEMMY: A small iron crow, particularly adapted for breaking the patent chain, with which the luggage is of late years secured to gentlemen's carriages;  and which, being of steel, case-hardened, is fallaciously supposed to be proof against the attempts of thieves.

John 'Jockey Jack' Southton, an 'indefatigable *peterman*' armed with the 'best' peter-hunting jemmy that 'could possibly be made', was caught robbing a coach and sentenced to seven years' transportation.

PETER-THAT: synonymous with *Stow-that*. See: STOW THAT.

PICK-UP: To accost, or enter into conversation with any person, for the purpose of executing some design upon his personal property; thus, among gamblers, it is called *Picking up a flat*, or a *mouth*: sharpers, who are daily on the look-out for some unwary countryman or stranger, use the same phrase; and among *drop-coves*, and others who act in concert, this task is allotted to one of the gang, duly qualified, who is thence termed *the picker-up*; and he having performed his part, his associates proceed systematically in *cleaning out the*  *flat*. To *pick up a cull*, is a term used by *blowens* in their vocation of street-walking. To *pick* a person *up*, in a general sense, is to impose upon, or take advantage of him, in a contract or bargain.

In 1860, Arthur Hibbett was strolling through Sydney when James Murrell introduced himself and insisted on buying him a beer. When they were seated at a nearby bar, James Davis, a patron, suggested they play chalks, a coin-tossing game. Davis, a self-professed coin-tossing expert, boasted that he could correctly guess the result of five coin tosses before Hibbett could correctly guess three coin tosses. With a piece of chalk, Davis drew a line down the bar and scrawled five strokes on one side of the line and three stokes on the other side. One stroke, he explained, would be rubbed out for each correct guess. To prevent the men seeing the result of their coin toss, a hat was positioned over the coin. Murrell urged Hibbett to play and Hibbett, liking the odds, agreed. But Murrell was a picker-up—when Hibbett flipped the coin, Murrell saw it land beneath the hat and he relayed the result to Davis by signaling 'heads' with his fist and 'tails' with an open hand. The duo bilked Hibbett out of more than £5, but were caught and sentenced to five years in a road gang.

PIGS, or GRUNTERS: Police runners.

 England's first official police force, the Bow Street Runners, was established in 1749. They may have been nicknamed pigs because they searched for criminals in the manner of pigs rooting for food. When, in 1828, a patrol was passing the New Inn, John Jennings and William Page yelled, 'There go the pigs!' A fight broke out and Jennings and Page, who beat the policemen senseless, were charged with assault. But because they claimed to have been calling to a sounder of swine, they avoided serious punishment and were bound to keep the peace.

PINCH: To purloin small articles of value in the shops of jewellers, etc., while pretending to purchase or bespeak some trinket. This *game* is called *the pinch*—I *pinch'd* him *for a fawney*, signifies I purloined a ring from him; Did you *pinch* any thing in that *crib*? Did you succeed in secreting any thing in that shop? This *game* is a branch of shoplifting; but when *the hoist* is spoken of, it commonly applies to stealing articles of a larger, though less valuable, kind, as pieces of muslin, or silk handkerchiefs, printed cotton, etc. See: HOIST.

John Black, Thomas Smith and Henry Williams perpetrated the pinch at a draper's shop in Ballarat. While Smith distracted the draper, Black pinched a coat and passed it to Williams. But Williams was caught and the coat returned to the draper. However, when the draper was returning to his shop he was tripped up from behind and the coat was stolen a second time. Black and Smith were suspected of the crime and, after they were overheard discussing the robbery at a pub, they were arrested. Smith remarked

that it was a 'jolly *lark*' to steal the coat in plain view of a policeman, but lamented that Williams had been 'pinched'—pinch was also slang for arrested. Black and Smith were released with a caution but Williams was sentenced to twelve months' gaol.

PINCH-GLOAK: A man who *works upon the pinch*.

Convict John Hansell was a pinch-gloak. He pretended to be a stockist selecting articles to purchase from shopkeepers, but then, after requesting the bill of sale to take to the bank, fled with his pockets stuffed with stolen goods. In 1839, he was charged with stealing from 'nearly all the large shopkeepers' in Hobart Town and sentenced to two years in leg irons at Port Arthur Penal Station. Hansell had a long history of working upon the pinch—for pinching clothing nine years earlier he was punished with fifty lashes and a stint on the treadmill.

PINS: The legs.

When, in 1833, two *'charlies'* discovered Ann Guerdian asleep in George Street, Sydney, she 'sprung on her pins' and challenged them to a fight. She was punished with two hours with 'the wooden professor'—the stocks.

PIPES: Boots.

Boots were nicknamed pipes because the shape and texture of a clay-covered boot is similar to a clay tobacco pipe. Catherine McWey was arrested for *'bolting'* with a pair of 'mud pipes'.

PIT: The bosom pocket in a coat.

Captain George Laval Chesterton, Governor of Coldbath Fields Prison, studied the prison inmates and published his findings. He advised the public to securely carry their valuables in their 'pits'. But for pickpockets such as Sarah Brown, a person's inner pocket was not an impediment. She greeted her victims with an affectionate hug and slipped her hands inside their coat to steal their belongings.

PIT-MAN: A pocket-book worn in the bosom-pocket.

Ellen O'Neill was a seventeen-year-old pit-worker—a pickpocket who specialises in stealing pit-mans. To safeguard against getting caught with stolen pit-mans, O'Neill emptied them of cash and slipped them into the pockets of unsuspecting strangers. But in 1850, she was caught and sentenced to seven years' transportation to Van Diemen's Land.

PITCHER: Newgate in London is called by various names, as *the pitcher, the stone Pitcher, the start,* and *the stone jug,* according to the humour of the speaker.

Because a pitcher is a large jug, nicknames for Newgate Prison may stem from joug—an iron collar used to punish criminals. Slang names for people confined in Newgate Prison included Knights of the Jug and Gentlemen of the Stone Pitcher. In 1843, Mary Hudson stole a pitcher and was sent to the pitcher. According to her testimony, she committed the crime to 'get herself sent out of the country' because she was 'starving' and without 'a friend in the world'.

PLANT: To hide, or conceal any person or thing, is termed *planting* him, or it; and any thing hid is called, *the plant*, when alluded to in conversation; such article is said to be in *plant*; the place of concealment is sometimes called *the plant*, as, I know of a fine *plant*; that is, a secure hiding-place. To *spring a plant*, is to find any thing that has been concealed by another. To *rise the plant*, is to take up and remove any thing that has been hid, whether by yourself or another. A person's money, or valuables, secreted about his house, or person, is called his *plant*. To *plant upon* a man, is to set somebody to

watch his motions; also to place any thing purposely in his way, that he may steal it and be immediately detected.

When, in 1843, a '*swag*' of stolen goods was discovered 'planted' in a pub courtyard, police planted themselves in the pub to plant upon the culprit. John Williams, caught 'raising the plant', was sentenced to seven years' transportation, with a recommendation he be clapped in leg irons and sent to Port Arthur Penal Station.

PLAY A-CROSS: What is commonly termed playing booty, that is, purposely losing the game, or match, in order to take in the *flats* who have backed you, (see BRIDGE) while the *sharps* divide the spoil, in which you have a share. This sort of treachery extends to boxing, racing, and every other species of sport, on which bets are laid; sometimes a sham match is made for the purpose of inducing strangers to bet, which is decided in such a manner that the latter will inevitably lose. *A-cross* signifies generally any collusion or unfair dealing between several parties.

Samuel Norton perpetrated a play a-cross—he performed the three-card trick and his accomplices pretended to be participants to give the trick an air of legitimacy. But working in groups had other benefits; when Norton was arrested, his accomplices attempted to bribe witnesses. The trio was sentenced to one months' gaol with hard labour.

PLUMMY: Right; very good; as it should be; expressing your approbation of any act, or event, you will say, *That's plummy,* or *It's all plummy*; meaning it is all right.

Plummy convicts were rewarded with sugar, rum, tobacco, vegetables and fresh fruit. Inmates at Fremantle Prison celebrated Christmas with a

giant plum pudding made from ninety kilograms of flour, thirty kilograms of currents, thirty kilograms of suet and twenty-three kilograms of raisins. Alcohol confiscated from the inmates was added to the mix.

POGUE: A bag

Pogue derives from *poke*, Scottish for bag. Cornelius Sullivan was sentenced to eighteen months' gaol for stealing a 'poge'. Convicts, as a  rule, were not permitted items to store or transport goods. But William Argent crafted pogues from an eel skin and a pig bladder. He was shot dead attempting to fill the bags with booze syphoned from barrels stored in the commissariat on Sarah Island.

POPS: Pistols; an obsolete term.

Henry Holden, after a three-day spree in the Emu Inn, South Australia, demanded 'pops', cried 'hoist the red flag, and bring out the pistols' and attempted to shoot his employer. Holden was arrested and restrained in a straightjacket, but he burst its seams and so, under the charge of nine men, was lashed to a cart and wheeled into town. There, he was charged with being a 'dangerous lunatic' and sentenced to a weeks' gaol where he would be 'treated kindly'.

POST, or POST THE PONEY: To stake, or lay down the money, as on laying a bet, or concluding a bargain.

Pony may be a pun on money. In 1849, in New South Wales, a prize-fight between John Perry and George Hough was set at £50 a side. According to news of the day, 'Mine Host of the Gas Hotel' posted money on behalf of

Perry, and 'My Uncle posted the poney' for Hough. 'Mine host' is slang for publican, while my uncle is a slang name for a pawnbroker.

POUNDABLE: Any event which is considered certain or inevitable, is declared to be poundable, as the issue of a game, the success of a bet, etc.

In 1805, soldiers of the New South Wales Corps were summoned to quash a cockfight. To prevent a pound-able rematch, the two cockerels, 'Bone-a-part' and 'Sir Sidney', were dished up to children in the town orphanage. Bone-a-part is a pun on Napoleon *Bonaparte*, the French emperor and military leader, and Sir Sidney refers to Sydney, but also Sir William Sidney Smith, a Royal Navy Officer who fought in the Napoleonic Wars.

POUND IT: To ensure or make a certainty of any thing; thus, a man will say, I'll *pound it* to be so; taken, probably from the custom of laying, or rather offering ten pounds to a crown at a cock-match, in which case, if no person takes this extravagant odds, the battle is at an end. This is termed pounding a cock.

In 1835, Sydney chimneysweep Benjamin Franklin was arrested for hawking his services without a license. To prevent the proliferation of 'sneaking pedlars' who undercut established trade rates, a law requiring hawkers to be licensed was introduced in 1834. Hawkers without a license risked a forty-shilling fine. Franklin promised to purchase a license if the judge agreed to leniency. The fine was reduced to one shilling, so Franklin promised to 'pound it'.

PRAD: A horse.

Prad is derived from *paraveredus*, Latin for horse. In 1824, William Macrae was arrested when he stripped a horse of its saddle, bridle, collar, hames, traces and reins. At the local lockup a policeman asked Macrae why he didn't steal the horse. He replied that he 'never took the prad because that would touch his life'. Until 1832, horse theft was a crime punishable by death. Macrae was charged with grand larceny and sentenced to seven years' transportation to Van Diemen's Land. But he never arrived—during the voyage he succumbed to scurvy. The ship's surgeon documented Macrae's worsening condition: 'teeth loose frequently Bleeding from the Gums which are soft and Spongy', and 'a very strong Cadaverous Smell issues from his person'. Scurvy, characterised by swollen bleeding gums, loss of teeth and open suppurating wounds, is a disease resulting from vitamin C deficiency.

PRADBACK: Horseback.

Brothers Thomas and John Clarke, bushrangers notorious for daring horse riding, taunted police perusing them on 'government prads'. The law eventually caught up with the Clarkes, however, and in 1867 they were sentenced to death by hanging. But their pradback days did not end until they dropped beneath the scaffold—a gallows was nicknamed a wooden horse and a three-legged mare.

PRIG: A thief.

PRIG: To steal; to *go out a-prigging,* is to go a-thieving.

Because sting is slang for steal, prig may derive from prick. But prig may also have come from *preguntar,* Spanish for demand, and from *pregare,* Latin for entreat. At Hobart Town Theatre in 1846, John Findlater interrupted

a performance of *Jack Sheppard* by bellowing: 'Constables, why don't you do your duty? Don't you see a fellow a-prigging a man on the stage?!' Findlater's quip did not amuse the police on duty, so they attempted to evict him from the theatre. But Findlater challenged

them to a fight and caused such bedlam that the play was abandoned. Findlater, a 'regular fighting *cove*' and prig transported from London, was punished with a stint on the treadmill.

PRIME: In a general sense, synonymous with plummy; any thing very good of its kind, is called a prime article. Any thing executed in a stylish or masterly manner, is said to be done in prime twig. See FAKEMENT, and GAMMON THE TWELVE.

John Macintosh was charged with neglect of duty when he was discovered smoking in bed exclaiming, 'isn't this prime'. But Macintosh insisted that it was his right to relax after a hard day's work and that his master had 'a *down* upon him'. Macintosh was sentenced to twenty-eight days on the Launceston treadmill.

PULL: An important advantage possessed by one party over another; as in gaming, you may by some slight, unknown to your adversary, or by a knowledge of the cards, etc., have the odds of winning considerably on your side; you are then said to have a great *pull*. To have the power of injuring a person, by the knowledge of any thing erroneous in his conduct, which leaves his character or personal safety at your mercy, is also termed having *a pull upon him*, that is (to use a vulgar phrase) that you have him under your thumb. A person speaking of any intricate affair, or feat of ingenuity, which he cannot comprehend, will say, There is some *pull* at the bottom of it, that I'm not *fly* to.

In 1838, Caroline '*Flash* Carry' Lucas, a nineteen-year-old 'unfortunate,' was suspected of 'hocussing and robbery'— hocussing was slang for administering drugs to a person without their knowledge. The victim, who police suspected had over-  dosed on a potent concoction of alcohol and opium known as laudanum, died. Due to a lack of evidence, Lucas was not charged with murder. But when a witness testified that Lucas boasted about 'a pull of £4', she was convicted of stealing and transported to Van Diemen's Land for a fifteen-year term. The term 'unfortunate' was synonymous with prostitute.

PULL, or PULL UP: to accost; stop; apprehend; or take into custody; as to pull up a *Jack*, is to stop a post-chaise on the highway. To *pull* a man, or have him *pulled*, is to cause his apprehension for some offence; and it is then said, that *Mr. Pullen is concerned.*

PULLED, PULLED UP, or IN PULL: Taken in custody; in confinement.

According to the memoirs of convict James Porter, he was 'pulled' for looting a ship anchored off Hobart Town. But he talked his way out of trouble and his master, who had accused him of the crime, received a 'severe reprimand'.

PUSH: A crowd or concourse of people, either in the streets, or at any public place of amusement, etc., when any particular scene of crowding is alluded to, they say, *the push*, as *the push*, at the *spell* doors; *the push* at the *stooping-match*, etc.

Pickpockets such as Francis Smith targeted people gathered in 'a push'. For picking pockets at a crowded execution, Smith copped three months' gaol. Executions in Australia were conducted in public until the mid-1850s. The grisly spectacle was intended to deter criminal behaviour and the condemned were encouraged to repent their sins and make a remorseful speech. But when New South Wales hangman Alexander Green interrupted John Tiernan while he was praying, the seventeen-year-old pushed Green off the scaffold.

PUT DOWN. See DOWN.
PUT FLASH. See FLASH.
PUT FLY. See FLY.

PUT UP: To suggest to another, the means of committing a depredation, or effecting any other business, is termed, *putting* him *up* to it.

John Paradise, a 'diminutive imp' between nine and thirteen years old, committed burglaries considered beyond the bounds of possibility. He conducted surveillance for up to thirty-six hours straight and squeezed through barred windows with six-and-a-half-inch gaps. But in 1834, he was charged with burglary and confessed to the '*job*' because he was furious that his teenaged accomplice 'put him up' to the '*crack*' but did not pay him a fair share of the proceeds. Paradise was reprimanded and returned to the care of family. A few months later, however, he was prosecuted for burglary and sentenced to seven years' transportation to Van Diemen's Land.

PUT UP AFFAIR: Any preconcerted plan or scheme to effect a robbery, etc., undertaken at the suggestion of another person, who possessing a knowledge of the premises, is competent to advise the principal how best to proceed.

PUTTER UP: The projector or planner of a *put-up affair,* as a servant in a gentleman's family, who proposes to a gang of housebreakers the robbery of his master's house, and informs them where the plate, etc., is deposited, (instances of which are frequent in London) is termed the *putter up,* and usually shares equally in the booty with the parties executing, although the former may lie dormant, and take no part in the actual commission of the fact.

James Lee Farmer, identified as 'the putter up' of a put up affair in New South Wales, advised a gang of burglars to steal cash from strongboxes stashed beneath his master's bed. The burglars were caught and transported to Van Diemen's Land for seven-year terms. But because police could not place Farmer at the scene of the crime, he received a lesser sentence of two years' hard labour in leg irons.

PUZZLING-STICKS: The triangles to which culprits are tied up, for the purpose of undergoing flagellation.

Puzzling-sticks may come from puzzle, meaning confound. A flogging frame, commonly called a 'triangle,' was constructed from three slender pieces of timber joined at the top to form a tripod. Victims were stripped to the waist and securely tied to the frame. The triangles were a dreaded object—convict William Day incinerated puzzling-sticks in a kiln.

QUEER: Bad; counterfeit; false; unwell in health.
QUEER, or QUEER-BIT: Base money.

Carl Weber was caught with queer-bit, so he swallowed the evidence—eighteen gilded shillings. When he appeared in court he was 'very ill' and in 'great pain' but because the coins were not forthcoming, the queer counterfeiter was acquitted for lack of evidence.

QUEER SCREENS: Forged Bank-notes.

When Ann Woodman was tried for forgery in 1816, she explained to the court that 'screens' was cant for 'forged banknotes'. Forgery was punishable by death—Ann's husband, Thomas, was executed for his part in their forgery operation. But Ann was granted a stay of execution because she was pregnant, a point of law known colloquially as a 'belly plea'. To safeguard against execution, some women on death row fell pregnant to men within the prison system, termed 'child-getters'. When the child of a condemned mother was born, the mother could be executed, transported, imprisoned or released. Ten months after Woodman's arrest she was released from prison, which suggests that the ruling was made within the weeks following the birth of her baby, and that Thomas may not have been the father.

QUEER IT: To SPOIL IT, which see.

QUEER-BAIL. Persons of no repute, hired to bail a prisoner in any bailable case; these men are to be had in London for a trifling sum, and are called *Broomsticks*.

According to a report in the *Evening Mail*, a 'queer bail' charged a flat rate or a percentage of the accused's debt. Professional perjurers—'broomsticks' and 'men of straw'—loitered outside courthouses and slyly advertised their services with a piece of straw stuck in their shoe. Jeremiah Mather was identified as a 'straw bail'. In 1828, he was convicted of perjury and sentenced to seven years' transportation.

QUID: A guinea.

Quid, a gold coin, is Latin for 'how much'. The Humane Society of England donated a quid to poverty-stricken people saved from suicide by drowning. Some recipients, however, were not disconsolate paupers but *'queer* plungers'—reckless con artists who risked their lives to obtain the money. Harriet Greaves was a notorious queer plunger, but she also was known to fake suicide by poisoning and hanging. When, in 1809, she consumed a near-fatal dose of opium and collapsed outside London's Doctors' Commons, the 'incorrigible vagabond and imposter' narrowly avoided a sentence of transportation to Australia.

QUOD: A gaol. To *quod* a person is to send him to gaol. *In quod*, is in gaol.

Quod comes from quadrangle, a square or rectangular space or court-yard enclosed by buildings. When Frances Stewart was charged with drunkenness in 1840, the *Sydney Monitor and Commercial Advertiser* described her as 'an old and multitudinous offender, with face as red as scarlet, and nose blue as bilberry'. Stewart explained to the judge that she drank to cope with the loss of her lover, and, in summing up her sorry plight, stated 'I expects you won't send me to quod'. But Stewart was 'ordered to study Zimmerman for 120 hours, in Mr Keck's library'— five days' solitary confinement in Sydney Gaol, supervised by gaoler Henry Keck. Zimmerman refers to *Solitude*, a book written by John George Zimmerman.

QUOD-COVE: The keeper of a gaol.

William John Speed, a disgraced army lieutenant transported to New South Wales in 1809 to complete a seven-year sentence for bigamy, was appointed keeper of Richmond Gaol in Van Diemen's Land. A quod-cove lived on site, recorded the daily goings-on in a journal, inspected inmates at least once every twelve hours, and maintained cleanliness and order. But in 1830, convicts complained that they were freezing, starving and filthy because Speed did not supply adequate firewood, rations and soap. He was dismissed.

QUODDING-DUES. See DUES.

RACKET: Some particular kinds of fraud and robbery are so termed, when called by their *flash* titles, and others *Rig*; as, *the Letter-racket, the Order-racket; the Kid-rig; the Cat and Kitten-rig*, etc., but all these terms depend upon the fancy of the speaker. In fact, any *game* may be termed a *rig, racket, suit, slum*, etc., by prefixing thereto the particular branch of depredation or fraud in question, many examples of which occur in this work.

Convicts desperate to escape the rigours of transportation entered into pacts whereby one murdered another in front of witnesses, ensuring the death penalty for the murderer and time to repent his crime. Witnesses called to court scored a *'slant'*—an exemption from labour. In 1835, the *Tasmanian* reported on the murder-suicide racket at Port Arthur Penal Station: John Bennett did 'what he considered a kind act' and slayed James Stephens. Three convict witnesses were transferred from the 'earthly hell' to Hobart Town to testify. Bennett was convicted of murder and executed. To stop the murder-suicide racket, Chief Police Magistrate Matthew Forster suggested that convicts be tried at the station. But Judge Algernon Montague opposed the idea, so Lieutenant-Governor George Arthur ordered that convict witnesses called to Hobart Town were returned to the station 'immediately' after their testimony.

RAG: Money.

A sum of money was called rag because it was a piece or scrap. When

John Templeton, a 'small boy' with a 'pug-nose', was fined for detonating fireworks in Sydney, his mother paid the 'rag'—ten shillings.

RAG-GORGY: A rich or monied man, but generally used in conversation when a particular gentleman, or person high in office, is hinted at; instead of mentioning his name, they say, the *Rag-gorgy*, knowing themselves to be understood by those they are addressing. See: COVE, and SWELL.

William 'Jackey Jackey' Westwood, a 'gentleman bushranger,' was infamous for stealing the fastest racehorses and the finest clothes and then venturing into Sydney to party with the proceeds of his robberies. In 1841, a rag-gorgy walking through Sydney was mistaken for Westwood and thrown in gaol. But Westwood himself was eventually caught and sentenced to death for leading a bloody rebellion on Norfolk Island. While on death row, the twenty-six-year-old wrote to Reverend Thomas Beagley Naylor, condemning the transportation system as 'refined cruelty'. Jackey Jackey, a derogatory name for an Indigenous Australian, may have been applied to Westwood because of his affinity with the Australian bush. Gentleman bushrangers were renowned for their chivalry and fashionable attire.

RAMP: To rob any person or place by open violence or suddenly snatching at something and running off with it, as, I *ramp'd* him of his *montra*; why did you not *ramp* his *castor?* etc. A man convicted of this offence, is said to have been *done for a ramp.* This audacious *game,* is called by *prigs, the ramp,* and is nearly similar to the RUSH, which see.

Ramp comes from criminals who 'ramped up' their assault. At Kirkdale Gaol, England, George Metham stabbed and killed William Hudson. Metham claimed self-defence because Hudson and his two accomplices, one of whom was armed with a towel, were 'going to ramp him or rifle him of his money'. Metham was acquitted of murder but convicted of manslaughter and sentenced to life in Van Diemen's Land. To overpower a convict or prevent him witnessing a theft, other convicts, in a crime termed 'blanketing', smothered him

in a blanket. In 1826, Peter Aylward was blanketed by four convicts who stole his cash, comb and knife. They were punished with life sentences.

RANK: Complete; absolute, downright, an emphatical manner of describing persons or characters, as *a rank nose, a rank swell*, etc. etc.

In 1853, Convict-Constable Charles Wilson was confined to Hobart Town Prisoners' Barracks for placing a 'rank *flat*' under false arrest and charging a '*tip*' to let him go.

RATTLER: A coach.

Coaches were nicknamed ratters because they rattled. When, in 1821, Henry Elkins was arrested for burglary, he informed on his accomplices to save himself—Samuel Hayward, for transporting stolen goods in a *'cross* rattler' to a *'crib'*, was executed.

READER: A pocket-book.

To avoid paying gambling debts, John Thurtell turned to murder. He shot his moneylender in the face then slit his throat and beat his brains out. But Thurtell also stole his victim's 'reader', which according to coverage in the *Morning Chronicle*, was a *'flash'* name for 'note case'. Thurtell was executed in 1824.

READER-HUNTERS. See: DUMMY-HUNTERS.

REGULARS: One's due share of a booty, etc. on a division taking place. Give me my *regulars*, that is, give me my dividend.

Ten-year-old Edward Lock overheard two men discussing a robbery—their accomplice was threatening to *'split* if they did not give him his regulars'—so he informed Sydney Police. But the two 'ugly looking ruffians' were released due to a lack of evidence.

REIGN: The length or continuance of a man's career in a system of wickedness, which when he is ultimately *bowled* *out*, is said to have been a long, or a short *reign*, according to its duration.

In 1818, Constables Joseph Fryer and James Baker arrested Michael Fox for dealing counterfeit shillings. According to Baker's testimony Fox 'had reigned long enough.' But Fox swore to his innocence, stating the police tricked him into delivering a package containing counterfeit coins to score a reward. When Fox was transferred to gaol, Baker paid the one-shilling transfer fee to the gaoler, who was shocked to discover the coin was counterfeit. But Baker and Fryer escaped punishment and Fox, a fifty-six-year-old impoverished father of five, was sentenced to one years'  gaol. Newspapers reporting on the incident decried the 'villainous practices' of corrupt police who reigned throughout England.

RESURRECTION-COVE: A stealer of dead bodies.

 Human bodies were required for anatomical research. Because demand for legally obtained cadavers greatly exceeded supply, resurrection-coves robbed graves and committed murder. James May, nicknamed 'Black Eyed Jack', was charged with accessory to murder and transported to Van Diemen's Land for life. When he arrived the authorities noted that he was 'many years a resurrection man'. 'Black eye' was slang for a person with 'a bad reputation'. But May may also have been nicknamed after his 'sallow' skin and 'light hazel' eyes.

RIBBAND: Money in general.

Ribband may derive from ribbon, as cash was often bound in fabric to keep it secure. Convicts who acquired ribband risked having it confiscated or stolen. John Frederick Mortlock kept hold of a half-sovereign for nearly five years before it was stolen. To prevent the theft of more cash, he tailored a leather money belt and wore it night and day.

RIDGE: Gold, whether in coin or any other shape, as a *ridge montra*, a gold watch; a *cly*-full of *ridge*, a pocket full of gold.

Ridge may be a corruption of rich. In 1841, thieves burgled an English optician and stole spectacles, eyeglasses and telescopes valued at approximately £300. When John Thompson Woode and Charles Tibbs attempted to sell several such items to a local jeweller, they were arrested. Found in their possession were two notes written in cant. Constable James Ainsworth transcribed the notes, informing the court that 'ridge quiz' referred to the stolen gold eyeglasses and '*wedge*' described items made of silver. But the court stenographer warned the jury that it was 'dangerous' to convict on theoretical evidence, so the duo was acquitted.

RIG. See: RACKET.

RINGING, or **RINGING-IN:** To *ring* is to exchange; *ringing the changes*, is a fraud practised by *smashers*, who when they receive good money in change of a guinea, etc., *ring-in* one or more pieces of base with great dexterity, and then request the party to change them.

Michael Duffey was notorious for ringing. When, in 1817, he was arrested for stealing clothing, jewellery, cash and a tea caddy, he offered twelve shillings in exchange for the stolen items. But he was prosecuted for stealing and transported to New South Wales for a seven-year term. There, he worked as a costermonger. But in 1845, he was literally caught 'ringing the changes'. He advertised his wares with a stolen bell and doled out counterfeit coins to his customers. He was punished with six months' hard labour in leg irons. To check if they'd been dealt a counterfeit coin, people scrutinised the colour of the coin, bit it to assess its texture, and weighed it to check if it was the correct weight. But coins were also appraised by the sound they made when they were dropped on a hard surface, which may have inspired the term 'ringing'.

RINGING CASTORS: Signifies frequenting churches and other public assemblies, for the purpose of changing hats, by taking away a good, and leaving a shabby one in its place; a petty *game* now seldom practiced. See: CASTOR.

In 1831, William Ward was gaoled for ringing castors in Sydney—he *'floored'* a man and switched his 'caster' for a 'greasy old tile'. Ward may have been a 'cabbagite' and a member of the 'cabbage-tree hat mob'—a group of unruly youths nicknamed after the hats they wore made from cabbage palm. A hat was called a tile because it was worn on the top of a person's head, similar to a roofing tile positioned on the top of a house.

RISE THE PLANT. See: PLANT.

ROCK'D: Superannuated, forgetful, absent in mind; *old lags* are commonly said to be thus affected, probably caused by the sufferings they have undergone.

Rock'd may be an abbreviation of 'rocked in a stone kitchen', a punning phrase that attributes a person's forgetfulness to the rough treatment they experienced as a baby in its cradle. John Quigley, a convict who fractured his skull during a fight on Norfolk Island, was rumoured to

have used his injury as an excuse for his bad behaviour. Quigley's gaolers accused him of feigning madness and pretending to be mute or rock'd to avoid punishment for a multitude of offences that included absconding and bushranging, but also biting, stabbing and shooting people. In 1856, a board of inquiry concluded Quigley was 'insane' and a 'dangerous lunatic'. At Port Arthur Penal Station, he was confined to a padded cell and a palisaded yard known as 'Quigley's cage.'

ROLLERS: Horse and foot patrole, who parade the roads round about London during the night, for the prevention of robberies.

Roller may derive from patrol. In colonial Australia, many rollers were serving convicts. Convict rollers provided the government with an inexpensive police force. Horse patrols, termed 'field police', were established in New South Wales and Van Diemen's Land in 1825. Trustworthy convicts with policing experience were especially sought after. William Allensby, an English policeman transported for pickpocketing, was appointed to the foot patrol in Van Diemen's Land. But for

boozing with convicts and allowing them to escape custody, he was dismissed and sentenced to twelve months in leg irons. Allensby then joined the field police, but was dismissed and sentenced to twelve more months in leg irons for carousing with a female convict. He was then appointed as flagellator.

ROMANY: A gypsy; to *patter romany,* is to talk the gypsy *flash.*

Romani were stereotypically viewed as vagabonds who spoke cant and committed crime. They were subjected to brutal and oppressive laws implemented to suppress their culture and itinerant lifestyle. Romani clan leader Ann Graham, née Brown, was transported to New South Wales for a seven-year term. Though she prospered in Sydney, she eventually returned to her home in Scotland. When asked why she left Australia, she replied: 'It was just to let them see I could come home again.' But if she answered in Romani, she may have said something similar to: *Ke mook len dik man sástis av keré apópli*.

ROOK: A small iron crow.

A crowbar garnered its nickname from the resemblance its blackened flukes bear to the feet and beak of a rook—a small type of crow. But rook is also slang for 'cheat' and 'swindler'. Edward Coleman, a burglar who used a 'rook' to lever open a grocer's cellar window, was a rook—he informed on his three accomplices to save himself. They were transported to New South Wales for life.

ROUGH-FAM, or ROUGH-FAMMY: The waistcoat pocket.

Rough may allude to the rough texture of a well-worn pocket. Tier rangers, robbers who looted moored vessels, wore specialised clothes such as flared trousers that concealed long bags strapped to their legs, and undercoats with deep rough-fams sewn into the front and back. In 1818, Officer Thomas Walker arrested tier ranger William Petch. He was wearing three coats, two waistcoats, two pairs of pantaloons and carrying an array of items stuffed in his pockets, including in his rough-fam. Police reunited the items with the crew of three separate vessels, and charged Petch with grand larceny. He was transported to New South Wales for a seven-year term.

ROW IN THE BOAT: To go snacks, or have a share in the benefit arising from any transaction to which you are privy. To let a person *row* with you, is to admit him to a share.

In 1792, a gang of masked burglars clad in black and armed with pistols and cutlasses committed a violent home invasion in Blackwall, England. Police investigating the robbery discov-ered the missing items in the house of Mary Randall. But she accused her lodger, Elizabeth Payne, of the crime. According to Randall's testimony, Payne boasted that she had 'plenty of *plants*' because 'she knew of a good *speak*' and would 'row in it'. But further investigation revealed Randall was lying. Her brother, a notorious river pirate, was executed for his part in the robbery and she was transported to New South Wales for a fourteen-year term.

RUFFLES. Handcuffs.

Handcuffs may have been nicknamed after the frilled *ruffles* worn on the end of shirtsleeves. After escaping from Berrima Gaol in 1840, bushrangers Mark Wood and Thomas Brett were sentenced to life imprisonment and locked in St James Watchhouse. Because they were notorious gaolbreakers, their gaolers took the extra precaution of hand-cuffing them. Soon after they were locked in a cell, however, a gaoler was astonished to discover they'd cut through the handcuffs. A 'fresh pair of ruffles' was called for and the 'inveterate *bolters*' were relayed to Sydney Gaol.

RUGGINS'S: To go to bed, is called going to Ruggins's.

Ruggins's derives from rug. Seventeen-year-old Patrick Campbell, an inmate of Braidwood Gaol, requested to go to Ruggins's to facilitate his escape. When locked in his cell he crept out of bed, pried the ventilation grate off the wall, squeezed through the shaft and lowered himself to the ground with his bedding. But in his haste to escape, he forgot his trousers, jacket and hat. Because the weather was 'bitter cold', when police caught up with Campbell he was asleep by a fire, cloaked in bushel bags.

RUM: Good, in opposition to *queer*.

Rum may derive from Rome, a city synonymous with 'splendour'. In 1832, 'regular rum old joker' Patrick Reynolds snuck out a '*jump*', absconded from his master's house and got drunk. But a '*charley*' arrested him and he was punished with a three-day stint on the Sydney treadmill.

RUMBLE-TUMBLE: A stage-coach.

Coaches were nicknamed after the loud noise they made and the movement they caused among their passengers and cargo. In 1829, a rumble-tumble conveying seventeen female convicts to their transport ship was upended in a traffic accident. Seven women chained to each other and seated on the carriage roof were catapulted into the air. Mary Williams' leg irons cut a three-inch gash in her right leg.

RUMP'D: Flogged or scourged.

Rump refers to a person's 'lower back'. Convicts sentenced to be 'rumped' typically received twenty-five or fifty strokes from a cat-o'-nine-tails. But Thomas Halford, for stealing potatoes when provisions were scarce, was sentenced to  two thousand lashes. Joseph Mansbury was flogged so severely that his back was said to be 'quite bare of flesh' and that his collarbones were like 'two ivory Polished horns.' A medical practitioner attended each flogging and could stop the procedure if the victim was deemed close to death. But at the Sarah Island Penal Station, it was rumoured that John Ollery died on the triangles and the flagellator lashed his lifeless corpse.

RUMPUS: A masquerade.

On January 25, 1839, 'a great rumpus' drew police to a building in Elizabeth Street, Sydney. There, in a hayloft, they discovered 'prostitutes, reputed thieves, and young men of debauched appearance' celebrating the 50th anniversary of the founding of the colony. Isaac Solomon was dressed as 'Jim Crow', the alter ego of Thomas D. Rice, an English performer infamous for popularising blackface. Mary Underwood was dressed as Don Giovanni or Don Juan, a fictional libertine and seducer. And John O'Neil was Massaroni, an Italian bandit. The magistrate residing over the case wryly declared that the three convicts 'had no character' and dismissed them without charge.

RUSH: *The rush,* is nearly synonymous with *the ramp*; but the latter often applies to snatching at a single article, as a silk cloak, for instance, from a milliner's shop-door; whereas *a rush* may signify a forcible entry by several men into a detached dwelling-house for the purpose of robbing its owners of their money, etc. A sudden and violent effort to get into any place, or vice-versa to effect your exit, as from a place of confinement, etc., is called *rushing them,* or *giving it to 'em upon the rush.*

Thomas Ryan perpetrated the rush in Sydney. When, in 1825, Ann Wheeler was ironing her laundry, he 'rushed into the house' and snatched a bundle of clothing. But he was caught, and, at his trial, 'in a most

hardened and depraved manner', he declared that 'he would continue the same course of depredation so long as he had his hands to use, and could fasten them on to any property within his reach'. He was sentenced to one hundred lashes and banished from Sydney.

RUSSIAN COFFEE-HOUSE: A name given by some punster of the *family*, to the Brown Bear public-house in Bow-street, Covent-garden.

The Brown Bear pub may have acquired its nickname because a brown bear is both symbolic of Russia and rhyming slang for brown beer. When, in 1822, Joseph Fowler stole a hat and handkerchief from a Russian Coffee-House patron, he was sentenced to seven years' transportation. Nineteenth-century pubs, including the Brown Bear, were hotspots for thieves who targeted drunks. But pubs also catered to police detaining or imprisoning criminals, and medical practitioners who performed inquests.

SACK: A pocket; to sack any thing is to pocket it.

Police investigating a spate of robberies in Wolumla, New South Wales, were drawn by the sound of gunfire to a remote region of the Black Range. There, they discovered a hermitage comprising hollow logs stuffed with stolen goods. The occupant, Thomas Jones, a hermit described by the press as a 'wild man' and 'dilapidated specimen of humanity', filled his sacks with items sacked from local farmsteads—at the time of his arrest he was dressed in a 'sack' that was 'sewn up in the middle with laces' and had two holes cut for his legs.

SALT-BOXES: The condemned cells in Newgate are so called.

A saltbox is a style of building that is multistorey at the front and single-storey at the back with a steeply pitched roof, named after a type of box with a sloping lid that stored salt. According to author Charles Dickens, the cells at Newgate Prison were arranged 'one above the other' in a style similar to a saltbox building. Michael Connor escaped from Newgate Prison in 1788. When the police caught up with Connor, he was hard at work—he confessed to escaping to support his impoverished family of four. For 'feloniously returning from transportation and being found at large', Connor was condemned to death and sent to the salt-boxes, but he received a stay of execution and was transported to New South Wales.

SALT-BOX-CLY: the outside coat-pocket, with a flap.

A pocket flap was nicknamed after the sloped lid of a saltbox. Pocket flaps safeguarded against theft. Isaac Greenslade held his jacket to shield his accomplice, John Asbury, while he raised their victim's salt-box-cly flap. But they were caught—Greenslade was sentenced to ten years' transportation to Van Diemen's Land, but Asbury, on account of a good character reference, got off with three months' gaol.

SAND: Moist sugar.

William 'Billy' Blue worked as a lumper unloading cargo from vessels moored in the River Thames. Because lumping was exhausting work, lumpers drank energising drinks, and Blue brewed a beverage made from cocoa, spice and sand. But in 1801, he was arrested for embezzling sugar and transported to New South Wales. There, he married convict Elizabeth Williams and fathered six children. Blue worked as a waterman, constable and watchman, and, in later years, served as New South Wales' unofficial 'commodore'. Blue died in 1834. Numerous landmarks in Sydney bear his name, such as Blues Point in Sydney Harbour.

Blue, whose true name is not known, may have been named after the colour of his skin—blue is slang for black. But it's also possible that his name refers to his military service—soldiers, due to their blue uniforms, were called blueskins.

SAWNEY: Bacon.

Sawney may come from *sani*, Romani for pork. But the term is also attributed to rashes sawn from a side of bacon, and to Sawney Beane, a Scottish cannibal who smoked the flesh of his victims—Sawney is slang for Scotsman. Mary Moriarty and her sister, Nelly, were notorious for 'sawney hunting', which, according to the newspaper detailing their crimes, was slang for 'bacon stealing'. In 1844, Mary was transported to Van Diemen's Land for a seven-year term for stealing. She probably got sick of eating preserved pork. Known as 'grunting peck' and 'cag mag,' pork dolled out to convicts was packed with salt and preserved in barrels to keep it from spoiling. Notoriously unpleasant, the meat had to be soaked in fresh water for at least twenty-four hours before it was cooked and eaten. Rendered salt pork was also used to dress convicts' wounds, and the leftover bones were carved into gaming pieces, tools and weaponry—condemned convict William Harvery attempted to cut his own throat with a sharpened dinner bone.

SCAMP: The *game* of highway robbery is called *the scamp*. To *scamp* a person is to rob him on the highway. *Done for a scamp* signifies convicted of a highway robbery.
SCAMP, or SCAMPSMAN: A highwayman.

Scamp may come from *scamp*, a Scottish word that means 'to wander' and 'to shirk'. At an English boarding house packed to capacity, Abraham Abbott agreed to share his bed with a 'creditable young man' who was in desperate need of accommodation. But Abbot's bedfellow was Mary Piles—'the female highwayman'—a sixteen-year-old scamp who roamed the countryside disguised as a male postilion. When Piles scamped Abbott she was done for a scamp, and, in 1787, she was transported to Australia with the First Fleet.

SCHOOL: A party of persons met together for the purpose of gambling.

Elijah Molineux, an ex-convict and *'sharp'* notorious for swindling his opponents at gambling games, was also infamous for deceiving the authorities. When, in 1859, he was charged with attending a 'school' gathered at the Sydney docks, he declared  that he was an innocent fishmonger. The arresting officer wryly replied: 'I don't know if you're a fisherman, but you were there on Monday catching *flats*'. Molineux, however, provided such 'elaborate defence' that he escaped prosecution. Flat is slang for an 'honest or naïve person,' but also for flathead, a type of fish with a flattened head.

SCOT: A person of an irritable temper, who is easily put in a passion, which is often done by the company he is with, to create fun; such a one is declared to be a fine *scot*. This diversion is called *getting* him *out*, or *getting* him *round the corner*, from these terms being used by *bull-hankers*, with whom also a *scot* is a bullock of a particular breed, which affords superior diversion when hunted.

SCOTTISH: Fiery, irritable, easily provoked.

According to Captain John Henderson of the 78th Highlanders, Scottish convicts worked harder than convicts born in England and Ireland, but they also were 'the most vicious and depraved'. Approximately eight thousand Scots were transported to Australia. John Julius McDonald, a Scottish schoolteacher convicted of 'willful fire raising', was sentenced to life transportation. During the voyage to Van Diemen's Land, Surgeon-Superintendent John Wilson noted that McDonald was 'a man of most ungovernable and unhappy Temper'. For refusing to bathe, McDonald was handcuffed and placed in solitary confinement. But when Wilson released McDonald with a warning to 'curb his violent temper', the

Scot clambered up the ship's rigging, taunted his captors, threw his cap to his fellow convicts and leapt into the ocean. Though he was hauled on board 'without exhibiting the slightest motion' he was revived with tea and brandy. Because of his scottish behaviour he spent the remainder of the voyage confined to the infirmary with his wrists bound together each night.

SCOUT: A watchman.
SCOUT-KEN: A watch-house. See: KEN.

Scout comes from scout, meaning search or examine. In 1822, three men, for barging into a private function, were '*lumbered*' in a London 'scout *ken*'. But offenders also were appointed as scouts. Edward Rainsford, transported to Van Diemen's Land for stealing tobacco, was the Bothwell Chief District Constable. But in 1854, he exited the watchhouse and plummeted twenty-five feet to his death. Watchhouses—buildings where offenders were held under temporary arrest—were typically situated in areas with a commanding view.

SCRAG'D: Hang'd.
SCRAGGING-POST: The gallows.

On Christmas Eve in 1849, fourteen-year-old Alfred Dancey pulled a brass-barreled pistol from his pocket and shot nineteen-year-old William Braud through the chest, severing an artery in his throat. Dancey fled, but he was caught and arrested. When police searched him they discovered bullets, a mould for making bullets, percussion caps, cash, a picklock and playing cards. Dancey remarked, 'I suppose I shall get scragged for this,' but he was not sent to the scragging-post. Instead, he was charged with manslaughter and transported to Van Diemen's Land for a ten-year term. Because people were hanged from a rope fastened around their neck, scrag may derive from *crag*, a Teutonic word for neck.

SCREEN: A bank-note. See: QUEER SCREENS.

Banknotes may have been called screens because they screened people from poverty. William Atkinson, caught with '*prigg'd* screens,' was charged with forgery and executed. But convict Thomas Bock was celebrated for dealing banknotes. He was an award-winning artist appointed as engraver to the Bank of Van Diemen's Land. In 1824, he produced 'beautiful' banknotes on special paper imported from England to prevent forgeries.

SCREEVE: A letter, or writing paper.

Screeve may come from *scrieve*, a Scottish word that means 'to read' and 'to write quickly or continuously'. In the early days of the colony of New South Wales, a rumour persisted among the convicts that an area south-west of Sydney had been colonised by an unidentified group of Europeans who enjoyed 'all the comforts of life without the necessity of labour.' In 1798, approximately sixty convicts prepared to leave

Sydney equipped with a compass drawn on a screeve to guide them to their fabled land. But Governor John Hunter got wind of their 'deluded' plan and so sentenced them to 'severe corporal punishment'. Convicts were not permitted to travel unless issued with a pass—a document detailing their destination, the duration of their journey and their physical description, such as their eye colour and height. A convict issued with a pass was a passholder. For good behaviour convicts were issued a ticket-of-leave—a document that granted the recipient the right to earn wages, own property and live in lodgings of their choosing located within a stipulated area. A convict issued with a ticket-of-leave was a paper man.

SCREW: A skeleton or false key. To *screw* a place is to enter it by false keys; this *game* is called the *screw*. Any robbery effected by such means is termed *a screw*.

A key was called a screw because it unscrewed a lock. Keys filed down to fit locks may have been called skeleton keys because of their skeletal framework. Seventeen-year-olds James Summers and John Knight were charged with burglary after a witness testified that the duo asked him to inspect several 'skeleton keys' and 'screws'. They were sentenced to life in New South Wales.

SCREWSMAN: A thief who *goes out a screwing*.

Thomas Smith, a 'screwsman' and 'very bad character,' was 'one of the most dangerous burglars' in Ballarat. Smith was also a braggart—he boasted about his uncanny ability to commit crime without detection. But in 1866, police sentenced him to seven days' gaol for vagrancy. A person could be charged with vagrancy if they had 'no visible means of support but had the ability to work'—a common means of ridding the streets of suspected criminals.

SCURF'D: Taken in custody.

Scurfed may derive from scruff, meaning apprehend. In 1805, sixteen-year-old John Leach, a pickpocket and 'master of the *slang* language', mistook undercover policeman Edward Crocker for a criminal after hearing him speak slang. Leach boasted that he'd been to a '*gaff*' and stolen twenty-two '*fogills*' and £20 worth of '*screens*', and that he was saving to buy a '*prad*' to go '*dragging*'. Leach then invited Crocker to join his gang and '*shake* some *dummies* to get some *thimbles*,' but Crocker 'scurft' him.

SEEDY: Poor, ragged in appearance, shabby.

Seedy may stem from the phrase *to go to seed*, meaning to 'deteriorate through neglect'. When Inspector James Singleton observed 'seedy' John Lawson '*frisking*' pockets at Sydney Police Court, he arrested him. Lawson was charged with two counts of pickpocketing but the jury, perhaps because they couldn't believe that anyone would pick pockets in a police station, found him not guilty.

SELL: To *sell* a man is to betray him, by giving information against him, or otherwise to injure him clandestinely for the sake of interest, nearly the same as *bridgeing* him. (See: BRIDGE.) A man who falls a victim to any treachery of this kind, is said to have been *sold like a bullock in Smithfield*.

George Growsett, when sentenced to fifteen years in Launceston Gaol for armed robbery, complained that Judge Thomas Horne 'sold him like a bullock in Smithfield'. But Horne declared the trial was 'fair and impartial' and that Growsett was guilty of a crime punishable by death, to which Growsett bullheadedly replied: 'I would rather be hanged.' Smithfield, a locality in England, functioned as a cattle market and slaughter yard for nine centuries. Other phrases attributed to the market include: *A Smithfield Bargain*—'a transaction in which the purchaser is duped' and 'a marriage of convenience where the fair sex are bought and sold like cattle'.

SERVE: To *serve* a person, or place, is to rob them; as, I *serv'd* him *for* his *thimble*, I rob'd him of his watch; that *crib* has been *served* before, that shop has been already robbed, etc. To *serve* a man, also sometimes signifies to maim, wound, or do him some bodily hurt; and to *serve* him *out and out*, is to kill him.

In 1839, William Harding was sentenced to three years' hard labour in leg irons for bludgeoning Mary Griffiths with a frying pan. But as he was leaving court he shook his fist in the face of the arresting officer and swore 'to serve him out' in three years' time and 'make it all *square* with his head'. Harding was returned to court and sentenced to fifteen years.

SHAKE: To steal, or rob; as, I *shook* a chest of *slop*, I stole a chest of tea; I've been *shook* of my *skin*, I have been robbed of my purse. A thief, whose *pall* has been into any place for the purpose of robbery, will say on his coming out, Well, is it all right, have you *shook?* meaning, did you succeed in getting any thing? When two persons rob in company, it is generally the province, or part, of one to *shake*, (that is, obtain *the swagg*), and the other to carry, (that is, bear it to a place of safety).

In 1847, John Edwards, a notorious pickpocket arrested on at least seventeen separate occasions, was sentenced to two months in Sydney Gaol after a '*trap*' caught him '*gammoning*' a drunken man to 'shake' his money.

SHALLOW: A hat.

A hat was nicknamed a shallow because
of its shallow crown. Female convicts
were issued with cotton bonnets and straw
sunhats, and male convicts with hats made
of wool, straw and leather. Losing, trading

or damaging a hat could result in severe punishment. When the *Lady
of the Lake* departed England in 1829, eighteen-year-old Christiana
McDonald's shallow blew away in gust of wind. She attempted to catch
it but fell overboard and drowned in the depths of the English Channel.

SHAN: Counterfeit money in general.

Shan may derive from sham, meaning 'something that it is not what it
purports to be'. In 1828, Robert White suggested that innkeeper George
Watts purchase some of his counterfeit coins to turn a profit by palming
them off on his patrons. But because Watts was not the type of person
who 'speculated in shans,' he contacted the police. When a patrol burst
into White's house, he produced a knife and threatened to 'tear open the
body of the first that advanced'. White was taken without incident and
sentenced to seven years' transportation to New South Wales.

SHARP: A gambler, or person, professed in all the arts of
play; a cheat, or swindler; any *cross-cove*, in general, is called
a *sharp*, in opposition to *a flat*, or *square-cove*; but this is only
in a comparative sense in the course of conversation.

In 1865, a quarrel between Emanuel Jacobs and Joseph Brown, 'sharpers' notorious in Melbourne for 'card-sharping,' turned deadly. Brown stabbed Jacob in his throat with a sharp object, thought to be a tobacco knife. Brown died and Jacobs was executed.

SHARPING: Swindling and cheating in all their various forms, including the arts of fraud at play.

In 1859, at the Melbourne Magistrates' Court, an elderly man named Bartholomew Donnelley was accused of swindling a prospector in a game of 'chalks'. Donnelley, at the time of his arrest, was dressed in the style of a farmer and carrying a large amount of money. He claimed he was a respectable veteran of the Indian War who'd struck it rich at the Rockhampton goldfields. But the money was deemed to be ill-gotten gains gleaned from punters deceived by his innocent appearance, so he was sentenced to four months' hard labour in gaol. A few days after his sentencing two men dressed as farmers were identified as his cardsharp companions and also sent to gaol. Donnelley, nicknamed 'The ex-Indian Warrior,' was infamous for 'sharping' Melbournians at thimblerig, chalks and cards but, had his true life story been known, he might have served serious gaol time—Donnelley was transported to Van Diemen's Land in 1835 for duping a man out of one hundred shillings.

SHIFTER: An alarm, or intimation, given by a thief to his *pall*, signifying that there is *a down*, or that some one is approaching, and that he had, therefore, better desist from what he is about.

Shifter may come from shift, meaning move. Criminals raised a shifter with whatever means was available: Daniel Sullivan whistled; Reuben Winstanley coughed; John Coffee lifted his hat; and Henry Smith rattled coins. But  bushranger Ned Kelly rapped on his armour to get the attention of his dying comrade Joe Byrne.

SHINER: A looking-glass.

Shiner comes from *shine*, meaning 'reflected light'. According to an 1827 edition of the *London Evening Standard*, a thief would '*prig*' a 'shiner' then take it to '*fences*' who replaced the frame so it could be on-sold without  alerting suspicion. Flora McInnes was charged with stealing a 'looking glass'. She copped seven years' bad luck—transportation to Van Diemen's Land for a seven-year term. But after completing her sentence, she stole another 'looking glass' and was sent back to prison.

SHOOK: Synonymous with *rock'd*. See: ROCK'D.

SHOVE-UP: Nothing.

While sailing the Queensland coast in 1893, sailors aboard the *Star of Hope* rescued a man they discovered floating on pieces of driftwood bound together with clothing. The castaway identified himself as Dean Mahmin, a cook from the *Taka Chita*, who'd been robbed by his crewmates and shoved overboard with shove-up. Seamen who robbed people and tossed them into the ocean were called 'ark ruffians'. But according to Mahmin, he swam to Thursday Island, where, after sixteen days' starvation, he built his raft in desperation. However, a board of inquiry concluded that Mahmin had jumped ship after pocketing his pay, then made the near-fatal mistake of decamping to a desolate island.

SHUTTER-RACKET: The practice of robbing houses, or shops, by boring a hole in the window shutter, and taking out a pane of glass.

When, in 1839, Officer William Kent was patrolling Westminster, he spotted a house that had been broken into by means of the shutter-racket. Kent searched the residence and discovered James Brady and Henry Tyrrell hiding in a coal store. But he also unearthed their burglary tools: a lanthorn, a box of matches and a knife—thieves who perpetrated the shutter-racket used a 'round about,' a tool that cut a hole approximately five inches in diameter. The two teens were charged with burglary and sentenced to seven years' transportation.

SINGLE-HANDED: Robbery by yourself, without a pall.

David Leyshon, a one-armed thief who stole a horse single-handed, was sentenced to ten years' transportation to Van Diemen's Land. Leyshon

proved to be something of a loner—he did stints in solitary confinement for hitting and kicking his fellow convicts. In 1847, for 'assaulting a fellow prisoner,' Leyshon was sentenced to thirty days in solitary, the maximum period that a convict could be sentenced to. Convicts in solitary confinement typically subsisted on bread and water and had no interaction with the outside world. The psychological effects of solitary confinement were considered greater than those of corporal punishment and by the mid-nineteenth century solitary confinement was the prevalent form of punishment.

SIR SYDNEY: A clasp knife.

Notorious bushrangers James Whitehead and Michael Howe swore a blood oath that if one was mortally wounded, the other would cut off his head to prevent headhunters claiming a reward. When Whitehead was shot during a raid on a Van Diemonian farmhouse, Howe decapitated him using a Sir Sydney. Sir Sydney may originate in the criminal under-world of Sydney, or stem from Sir William Sidney Smith, a naval officer and member of the Order of the Sword renowned for his knife-fighting expertise.

SKIN: A purse, or money bag.

At a Punch and Judy puppet show in London, fourteen-year-old Isaac Levy was arrested for stealing a purse when he was overheard bragging about 'a bloody good skin'.

SKIN: To strip a man of all his money at play, is termed *skinning* him.

Edward Oakes, a 'well-known magsman' notorious for skinning his opponents at gambling games, was arrested after he 'skinned' George Fitzgerald, an American newly arrived in England. In a trick so old that news coverage referred to it as 'stale,' Oakes stole Fitzgerald's cash after schooling him on how to carry his wallet to prevent it being stolen. Oakes was sentenced to seven years' transportation but escaped. A £50 reward was advertised for his recapture, and, in 1840, he was apprehended and sentenced to transportation for life. Magsman—a swindler who preys on gullible people—may stem from mag, meaning 'to talk persuasively'.

SLANG: A watch chain, a chain of any kind; also a warrant, license to travel, or other official instrument.

A watch-wearer, to prevent the loss of his watch, attached it to his clothing with a chain or ribbon. Because a length of chain has the appearance of a snake, slang may come from *slang*, Dutch for snake.

But it may also come from sling, meaning carry. John Williams and James Ryan, accused of stealing a drunken man's watch at London's Red Lion Pub, refuted the allegation until a barman testified that he overheard them discussing whether to break or cut the man's 'slang'. They were sentenced to ten years' transportation.

SLANG: To defraud a person of any part of his due, is called *slanging* him; also to cheat by false weights or measures, or other unfair means.
SLANG WEIGHTS, or MEASURES: Unjust, or defective ones.
SLANGING-DUES: When a man suspects that he has been curtailed, or cheated, of any portion of his just right, he will say, there has been *slanging-dues concerned.*

Goods and equipment, whether sold commercially or dispensed from government stores, were scrupulously weighed and measured. Weights were calculated in pounds, ounces and drams, while volume was measured in bushels, pecks, gallons, quarts, pints and gills. Inspectors armed with scales and imperial standards roamed the streets of Australia performing spot checks, and vendors caught with deficient weights and measures were penalised. Their prosecutor was rewarded with a percentage of their fines. When Chief Constable George Jilks was appointed as New South Wales' Inspector of Weights and Measures in 1833, he blitzed the Sydney markets, prosecuting forty-three vendors for slanging-dues and confiscating three cartloads of slang weights and measures. Jilks, whose handiwork netted him £27, was well acquainted with weights and measures—he was transported to New South Wales for slanging a copper basin.

SLANG'D: Fettered.

Leg irons were riveted around convicts' ankles to impede their movement and make their life miserable. A standard set of leg irons weighed approximately two kilograms. But 'heavy slangs' could weigh as much twenty-five kilo-  grams, making walking 'almost impossible'. Convicts were also slang'd to wooden logs. When bathing in the ocean, nineteen-year-old George Wiggins' leg irons, chain and log, estimated to have weighed fifteen kilograms, became entangled in kelp and he drowned.

SLANGS: Fetters, or chains of any kind used about prisoners; *body-slangs* are body-irons used on some occasions.

In 1826, two privates of the 57th regiment, Joseph Sudds and Patrick Thompson, concluded that convict life was preferable to life in the military. A well-behaved convict was awarded a ticket-of-leave enabling him to procure paying work and score an early release, while soldiers could be stuck on low pay serving in dismal or dangerous conditions for decades. Things went according to plan for Sudds and Thompson when they stole cloth, were charged with petty larceny and sentenced to seven years' transportation. But Governor Ralph Darling was livid. He re-sentenced the two men to seven years' hard labour in slangs. A spiked collar was riveted around their necks, which was connected to two chains that ran to their waists and then to their leg irons. Unable to walk, sit or lay down comfortably, Sudds died. Thompson was released from his body-slangs and Darling was criticised for his illegal and inhumane sentencing.

SLAVEY: A servant of either sex.

John Brown, a 'miserable looking wreck of humanity', was charged with vagrancy in 1852. The 'emaciated and unclean' sixty-seven-year-old

admitted to sleeping in the 'nooks and cavities' of Sydney Domain and eating scraps that townsfolk tossed 'into the streets to the dogs'. But when Magistrate James Sheen Dowling offered to arrange a bed for Brown in Sydney Benevolent Asylum, he refused the offer for fear that asylum staff would treat him like their 'slavey'. He was sentenced to two weeks in Sydney Gaol.

SLIP: The slash pocket in the skirt of a coat behind.

Because a slash pocket typically has a diagonal slit for an opening, slip may be a pun on slit. But the term may also come from slip, meaning 'glide' and 'pass'. Pickpockets slipped stolen items in their 'slip' for safe-keeping. Edward Strudd wore a jacket with slash pockets in each coat tail where he stored the cash he stole from his victims along with two knives that he used to steal with. For stealing a woman's purse after slicing his way into her pocket, Strudd was transported to New South Wales for a seven-year term.

SLOP: Tea.

In an 1827 edition of the *London Evening Standard*, an exposé on crime revealed

that a '*fence*' typically paid '*buzzes*' £15 per stolen 'chest of slop', and £20 for a chest of 'tip-top slop'. Tip-top, meaning the top of the top, is slang for 'the very best'.

SLOP-FEEDER: A tea-spoon.

Thomas Jones stole a slop-feeder valued at one shilling, the minimum amount required to convict a person of grand larceny. He was sentenced to seven years' transportation.

SLOUR: To lock, secure, or fasten; to *slour up* is also to button up; as one's coat, pocket, etc.
SLOUR'D, or SLOUR'D UP: Locked, fastened, buttoned, etc.

Slour may come from slore, slang for 'grasp' and 'hold fast'. In 1891, nineteen-year-old Anne Smith, an inmate at Melbourne Gaol and servant to gaol governor Colonel Frederick William Bull, slour'd up in Bull's wife's fur-trimmed cape, pulled the satin-lined hood over her head, donned a white straw hat trimmed with blue and white ribbon, and walked out a back door that Bull had neglected to slour. Smith was caught and slour'd in gaol with a three-month extension on her prison term.

SLUM: A room.
SLUM. See RACKET and LODGING-SLUM.

Slum may derive from slumber. Slums in the female factories and male convict barracks located in New South Wales and Van Diemen's Land were, at times, overcrowded, dirty, leaking and infested with vermin. Convicts, as a reward for good behaviour, were permitted to build their own accommodation—typically inexpensive one-slum huts constructed  of split timber and sheets of bark. When Sydney police raided James Hamilton's one-slum hut, he had nowhere to hide so he clambered up the chimney, even though the fire beneath was still burning.

SLY: Any business transacted, or intimation given, privately, or under the rose, is said to be *done upon the sly*.

'Under the rose' meant something said or done in confidence—the rose is sacred to Harpocrates, the Greek god of silence. 'The Grand Conversation under the Rose' was a ballad popular with sailors—when convicts at Sarah Island Penal Station seized a ship, James Porter sang the song to distract the guards on duty. Ex-convict Samuel Terry also operated under the rose—he ran a 'slye grog and pawnbroker's shop' in Sydney. A sly grog shop was an unlicensed pub and liquor store that catered to convicts. So sly was Terry, that, living by the axiom 'never give value without obtaining value for it, and, moreover, as much, as only to keep his neck out of the halter, or his legs out of chains,' he amassed great wealth. At the time of his death, in 1838, he was worth 3.39 per cent of the colony's gross domestic product—the twenty-first century equivalent of more than twenty-four billion dollars.

SMASHER: A man or woman who follows the *game* of *smashing*.

SMASHING: Uttering counterfeit money; *smashing* of *queer screens*, signifies uttering forged bank notes. To *smash* a guinea, note, or other money, is, in a common sense, to procure, or give, change for it.

Smasher may derive from smashing, meaning 'well done'. In 1837, London police received a tipoff that a '*flash*' gang of smashers was producing counterfeit coins in a building located in Westminster. When police stormed the building, Thomas Oliver barricaded the door while

his two accomplices, Harriet Wood and James Birch, crushed incriminating plaster moulds and liquefied counterfeit coins. But police broke down the door and arrested them. Among the items recovered were crucibles filled with molten metal and three counterfeit '*bulls*'. Birch snatched up the coins, mashed them in his mouth, spat out the gobs and remarked to his accomplices, 'It is all right, that has saved the *bellowsing.*' According to police, the gang spoke enough '*flash*' words to fill 'eight or ten foolscap sheets'. The trio was convicted of 'smashing' but as the evidence had been destroyed, they were not sentenced to transportation but three years' imprisonment.

SMISH: A shirt.

Smish derives from *camicia*, Italian for 'shirt'. Male convicts were issued with two smish per year. Clothing issued to convicts remained government property, but according to government storekeeper Thomas Lempriere, convicts altered, dyed and did

what they pleased with their clothes. At Port Arthur Penal Station, convicts constructed small boats from wattle branches lined with their shirts. But absconders also used shirts to dress their wounds, carry their provisions and equipment, and to start fires—scorched cloth, known as 'charcloth', was ideal tinder in wet weather.

SMUT: A copper boiler, or furnace.

A boiler was probably nicknamed after the smut that coated its surface. Nineteen-year-old Matthew Berry stole a smut from a washhouse in Fulham, London. But Constable Isaac Hawkins, who followed a trail of 'smut' that led from the washhouse to Berry's outhouse, discovered the smut and arrested Berry. He was sentenced to fourteen years' transportation to Van Diemen's Land. To safeguard against getting caught with incriminating metalwork, thieves melted stolen items into unidentifiable slag, also called smut.

SNEAK: *The sneak* is the practice of robbing houses or shops, by slipping in unperceived, and taking whatever may lay most convenient; this is commonly the first branch of thieving, in which young boys are initiated, who, from their size and activity, appear well adapted for it. To *sneak* a place, is to rob it *upon the sneak*. A *sneak is* a robbery effected in the above manner. One or more prisoners having escaped from their confinement by stealth, without using any violence, or alarming their keepers, are said to have *sneak'd 'em, or given it to 'em upon the sneak*. See: RUSH.

In 1833, Constables Francis Keys and Philip Webster were patrolling London when they spotted Joseph Pearce and George Gordon loitering suspiciously in the marketplace. When Pearce snuck into a bakery, reached over the counter  and groped around for the cash till, Keys arrested him 'for being on the sneak'. Gordon, who was collared by Webster, was carrying a pair of stolen spectacles. The two seventeen-year-olds were charged with theft and sentenced to seven years' transportation. Pearce was transported to Van Diemen's Land, while Gordon was sent to New South Wales.

SNEAKSMAN: A man or boy *who goes upon the sneak.*

John Pepper was an infamous 'sneaksman' arrested in 1851 for 'sneaking' into a Sydney pub and stealing seven shillings from the till.

SNEEZER, or SNEEZING-COFER: A snuff-box.

Because snuff is powdered tobacco inhaled through the nose, snuffboxes were nick-named *sneezers*. A coffer is a chest that stored valuables. George Barrington, Australia's most infamous 'stook *buzzer*'—a pickpocket who preys on wealthy people with valuable 'sneezers', '*skins*' and '*dummies*'—is alleged to have stolen a gold diamond-encrusted sneezing-cofer valued at £30,000.

SNITCH: To impeach, or betray your accomplices, is termed snitching upon them. A person who becomes king's evidence on such an occasion, is said to have turned snitch; an informer, or talebearer, in general, is called a snitch, or a snitching rascal, in which sense snitching is synonymous with nosing, or coming it.

In 1797, Henry Ellis checked into a lodging house after an arduous day trekking through the English countryside. Before crawling into

bed, Ellis ejected Ann Crocker, a prostitute determined to sleep with him. Because Ellis was suspicious of Crocker's intentions, he stashed his valuables beneath the mattress. When he woke, however, the valuables were missing. Ellis contacted police who interrogated Crocker but also Sarah Crutchley, the housekeeper. Crutchley broke under questioning and confessed their guilt, so Crocker snapped, 'You snitching bitch, if I am the thief, you are the receiver.' At their trial, the arresting officer explained the meaning of snitch: 'Them that turn evidence they call them snitches.' Crocker was charged with stealing and sentenced to seven years' transportation to New South Wales, but Crutchley, charged with receiving, copped fourteen years. Because *nose* is slang for 'informer,' snitch may derive from snitchel, slang for 'a nose fillip' or 'stimulant'.

SNIPES: Scissors.

Snipes may be a pun on snip. But the name may also refer to scissors with long beak-shaped blades and handles shaped like the body of a snipe (a kind of bird). In 1831, police connected a pair of stolen gold-handled snipes to John Broach, a caretaker who pawned stolen goods to fund vacations with his sweetheart. He was charged with theft and executed. His death, as reported in the press, was intended to quell the increasing number of servants stealing from their masters.

SNIV: An expression synonymous with *bender*, and used in the same manner. See: BENDER.

SNOOZE: To sleep; *a snooze* some-times means a lodging; as, Where can I get a *snooze* for this *darky* instead of saying a bed.

Snooze may be a confluence of *snore* and *doze*. John Brown was discovered 'snoozing in a horse trough half full of water'. He was charged with drunkenness and punished with a three-hour stint in the Sydney stocks.

SNOW: Clean linen from the washerwoman's hands, whether it be wet or dry, is termed *snow*.

Because linen was white and draped over foliage to dry, it has the appear-ance of fallen snow. Peter Doyle, a clothier transported to New South Wales for stealing clothes, completed his seven-year sentence in 1843. But in 1846, when convicts spotted him hanging women's clothing on a bush to dry, he was charged with 'snow-dropping'—stealing washing—and sentenced to twelve months' hard labour in leg irons.

SNUFFING: Going into a shop on some pretence, watching an opportunity to throw a handful of snuff in the eyes of the shopkeeper, and then running off with any valuable article you can lay hands on; this is called *snuffing* him, or *giving it to him upon the snuff racket.*

In 1834, John Jones stepped into Joseph Behrens' jewellery shop and asked for directions. But when Behren commenced talking, Jones threw snuff in his face, snatched a pair of earrings from the counter and raced out the door. Because Behrens was blinded and powerless to pursue Jones, he yelled 'stop thief'. Jones was caught, charged with snuffing, and sentenced to seven years' transportation.

SOLD. See: SELL.

SOUND: To *sound* a person, means generally to draw from him, in an artful manner, any particulars you want to be acquainted with; as, to *sound* a *kid*, porter, etc., is to pump out of him the purport of his errand, the contents of his bundle, or load, etc., that your *pall* may know how to accost him, in order to *draw the swag*. See: DRAW and: KID-RIG. To *sound* *a cly*, is to touch a person's pocket gently on the outside, in order to ascertain the nature of its contents.

In a pub situated in Sydney's notorious Rocks, Thomas Davis became acquainted with Robert Bayles, a thief infamous for his 'marvelous' but disarming conversation. Davis, who failed to notice Bayles 'taking soundings in his pocket', eventually discovered he'd been robbed of thirty-two 'ring dollars'. But because Bayles had stashed the booty, there was no evidence to connect him to the crime. Ring dollars were coins with a hole in the centre, minted by convict William Henshall.

SPANGLE: A seven-shilling piece.

A seven-shilling piece was called a spangle because its gold lustre spangled. In 1810, William Stafford was gaoled for deserting the East Middlesex Militia. To ingratiate himself with his superiors, he informed on a gang who were '*down* on the *queer*'. According to his testimony, Robert Butt produced 'spangles', '*bobs*' and '*tanners*' that were processed

by his accomplices: Mary Watson and Sarah Slater trimmed and filed them to size, and Joseph Cope painted them to appear as though they were made of gold or silver. The authorities suspected that Stafford was in cahoots with the gang but he insisted that, although he shirked military duty, he was doing 'his duty' in assisting the Royal Mint to catch counterfeiters. Butt was transported to New South Wales for life and Cope was executed.

SPANK: To *spank a glaze,* is to break a pane of glass in a shop window, and make a sudden snatch at some article of value within your reach, having previously tied the shop-door with a strong cord on the outside, so as to prevent the shopman from getting out, till you have had full time to escape with your booty; to *spank* a place, is to rob it *upon the spank, a spank* is a robbery effected by the above means.

Thomas Wilcox and John Newgent robbed Mary Wanion's haberdashery upon the spank: they lashed her shop door with 'strong cord,' smashed a window and grabbed eleven pairs of stockings. Police collared Wilcox and Newgent, but because Wanion was trapped inside her shop she did not see their faces and could not swear to their identities in court.

Newgent was acquitted but Wilcox, for committing a separate spank on a haberdasher, was charged with grand larceny and sentenced to seven years' transportation. According to barrister and author John Frederick Archbold, 'spanking the glaze' was also perpetrated by thieves in plain view of the shopkeeper: a man pretending to be a drunken vagabond bumps into his well-dressed accomplice who falls against the shop window and breaks a pane of glass. The *'swell'* rebukes the drunk, pays for the damage and the duo depart. They then return to the shop after the window has been repaired to remove the pane while the putty is still malleable and steal items within arm's reach.

SPEAK: Committing any robbery; is called *making a speak;* and if it has been productive, you are said to have *made a rum speak.*

SPEAK TO: To *speak to* a person or place is to rob them, and to *speak to* any article, is to steal it; as, I *spoke to the cove for his montra*; I robb'd the gentleman of his watch. I *spoke to* that *crib for* all the *wedge*; I robb'd that house of all the plate. I *spoke* to a chest of *slop*; I stole a chest of tea. A thief will say to his pall who has been attempting any robbery, "Well, did you *speak*? or, have you *spoke*?" meaning, did you get any thing?

Deliveryman Robert Daniel stole a trunk from his employer then celebrated at the pub. But when the publican overheard him boast that he'd 'made a good speak to a box', he was arrested and sentenced to seven years' trans-  portation to New South Wales. Daniel never left England—he died in Newgate Prison.

SPELL: The play-house. See: BREAKING UP OF THE SPELL.

Convicts built the first Australian spell at New South Wales in 1796. The proprietor, Robert Sidaway, was a convict transported for stealing. But Governor John Hunter ordered the theatre be closed, believing it to be a corruptive influence. It was rumoured, however, that the closure was due to the number of burglaries occurring on nights that colonists attended the theatre.

SPICE: *The spice* is the *game* of footpad robbery; describing an exploit of this nature; a rogue will say, I *spiced* a *swell of* so much, naming the booty obtained. *A spice* is a footpad robbery.

In 1787, a gang of thieves looted a sloop moored in the River Thames. But according to witness testimony, they also 'spiced' the crew. Though the thieves tied handkerchiefs around their heads to conceal their faces, James Cunningham was identified by his 'squinted' eyes. He was convicted and executed. Footpad robbery—committed by criminals who travel by foot—may have been called spice because it was 'lively' and 'exciting'.

SPICE GLOAK: A footpad robber.

Van Diemonian spice gloaks Michael Cody and James Murphy wore shoes with heels attached to the front of the soles. But their specialised footwear failed to throw off the soldiers tracking them and they were caught. Murphy was shot to death and Cody was beaten so badly that he died from his injuries.

SPIN A YARN. See: YARN.

SPLIT: To *split upon* a person, or *turn split*, is synonymous with *nosing*, *snitching*, or *turning nose*. To *split* signifies generally to tell of any thing you hear, or see transacted.

When police interrupted a burglary in Shoreditch, England, Edmund Miller was caught but his three accomplices fled the crime scene. Because they '*put him in a hole*', Miller 'split upon them'. Henry Hutchinson was caught  and sentenced to life in Van Diemen's Land, while Miller was sentenced to life in New South Wales. The two burglars may have been sent to different colonies to prevent reprisals. Informing was called splitting because informants split from their accomplices.

SPOIL IT: To throw some obstacle in the way of any project or undertaking, so as to cause its failure, is termed *spoiling it*. In like manner, to prevent another person from succeeding in his object, either by a wilful obstruction, or by some act of imprudence on your part, subjects you to the charge of having *spoiled him*. Speaking of some particular species of fraud or robbery, which after a long series of success, is now become stale or impracticable from the public being guarded against it, *the family* will say, that *game* is *spoiled* at last. So having attempted the robbery of any particular house or shop, and by miscarrying caused such an alarm as to render a second attempt dangerous or impolitic, they will say, that place is *spoil'd*, it is useless to *try it on* any more.

Samuel Taylor was arrested on suspicion of committing a burglary in Bethnal Green, London, on Christmas Day in 1825. A witness alleged that Taylor and his gang were spotted scoping the house, so they declared 'the place was spoiled' and went to the pub, but returned to commit the robbery after the coast was clear. A shoe print left at the crime scene corresponded with the iron toe attached to one of Taylor's shoes, but he removed the toe, spoiling the police investigation.

SPOKE TO: Alluding to any person or place that has been already robbed, they say, that place, or person, has been *spoke to* before. A *family man* on discovering that he has been robbed, will exclaim, I have been *spoke to*, and perhaps will add, *for* such a thing, naming what he has lost. *Spoke to upon the screw, crack, sneak, hoist, buz,* etc. etc., means robbed *upon* either of those particular *suits* or *games.* Upon any great misfortune befalling a man, as being apprehended on a very serious charge, receiving a wound supposed to be mortal, etc., his friends will say, Poor fellow, I believe he's *spoke to,* meaning it is all over with him.

Landlady Mary Roberts leased rooms to prostitutes who robbed their clientele and paid her a percentage of the proceeds. Roberts charged five shillings for every pound the women stole, and three pence per shilling. But when her tenants carried in a drunken man and bungled the robbery, she stole his money and demanded 'half snacks' instead of her usual percentage. The women, however, were caught, and after one of them testified that Roberts 'had spoke', she was sentenced to death. But because she 'pleaded her belly', she was granted a stay of execution.

SPOONY: Foolish, half-witted, nonsensical; a man who has been drinking till he becomes disgusting by his very ridiculous behaviour, is said to be *spoony* drunk; and, from hence it is usual to call a very prating shallow fellow, *a rank spoon.*

Foolish people may have been called spoony because, like the bowl of a spoon, they are shallow and lack depth. When, in 1857, William Graham was robbed in a Melbourne brothel, he ran through the streets calling for police assistance. But police dismissed his complaint because he was a 'spooney' who was 'too drunk to know what he was doing'. Graham, however, made his way to a police station where he persuaded a constable to assist him in recovering his property. Graham's purse and cash were discovered wedged in a stack of five mattresses in the bedroom of prostitute Mary Jane Reily. Reily was arrested and sentenced to eight months' gaol.

SPOUT: To pledge any property at a pawnbroker's is termed *spouting* it, or *shoving* it *up the spout.*

Spout refers to a spout-like duct that pawnbrokers used to convey items to storerooms situated above or below their shopfront. Thomas Campbell, after spending the night with prostitute Martha McLaren, was informed that his jacket was 'up the spout'. Campbell prosecuted McLaren to recover his jacket, but she alleged that Campbell instructed her to pawn it so he could afford to buy her breakfast. McLaren was sentenced to ten years' transportation to Van Diemen's Land.

SPREAD: Butter.

Butter was called spread because it was spread on food. George Rivers stole his master's spread and was punished with two years' hard labour. But John Drew, for purchasing the spread and knowing it was stolen, was charged with receiving and sentenced to seven years' transportation.

SPRING THE PLANT. See: PLANT.

SQUARE: All fair, upright, and honest practices, are called *the square*, in opposition to *the cross*. Any thing you have bought, or acquired honestly, is termed *a square article*; and any transaction which is fairly and equitably conducted, is

said to be *a square concern*. A tradesman or other person who is considered by the world to be an honest man, and who is unacquainted with *family people*, and their system of operations, is by the latter emphatically styled *a square cove*, whereas an old thief who has acquired an independence, and now confines himself to *square* practices, is still called by his old *palls* a *flash cove*, who has *tyed up prigging*. See: GROSS and FLAT.

In making a bargain or contract, any overture considered to be really fair and reasonable, is declared to be *a square thing,* or to be *upon the square.* To be *upon the square* with any person, is to have mutually settled all accompts between you both up to that moment. To threaten another that you will *be upon the square with him,* some time, signifies that you'll be even with him for some supposed injury, etc.

Square, meaning 'fair and honest', may originate in *s*quare dealing, a respected method of dealing playing cards. When Police Magistrate John Forster was mistaken for an absconder and arrested, he explained the situation to arresting officer Convict-Constable William Birch. But because Birch insisted that Forster 'give him a glass of grog to square it', he was arrested, charged with drunkenness and false arrest, dismissed from the police force and sentenced to nine months' hard labour.

SQUARE-COVE. See: SQUARE.

In 1845, Ambrose Kreeley was walking through Sydney when William Knight, a 'well known thief,' asked him to keep a lookout for *'traps'* so he could engage in *'snow* dropping'. But Kreeley alerted a passing policeman and Knight was arrested fleeing the scene with a bundle of wet linen. At Knight's court appearance he swore the linen was his property but did admit to mistaking Kreeley—a 'square cove'—for a 'crooked' (slang for a dishonest person). Despite Knight's incriminating testimony, he was acquitted because police could not locate the owner of the linen to lay charges.

SQUARE-CRIB: A respectable house, of good repute, whose inmates, their mode of life and connexions, are all perfectly *on the square.* See: CROSS-CRIB.

Edward Bulwer-Lytton, a nineteenth-century politician and best-selling novelist, coined phrases such as 'the great unwashed' and 'the pen is mightier than the sword'. But he is also credited with helping introduce cant into popular literature. Lytton's breakthrough novel, *Pelham,* includes a multitude of cant terms such as *'square crib'.* Lytton probably sourced the terms from Vaux's dictionary—*Pelham* includes a footnote referring the reader to Vaux's memoirs.

SQUEEZE: The neck.

According to a report in the *Sydney Herald,* a *'charley'* discovered Salina Harding at the Sydney Domain tying a 'true lover's knot' around her lover's 'squeeze'. She was punished with a one-month stint in the Female Factory, third class. But Alice Blackstone, for attempting to  reunite with her lover, was ordered to wear an iron collar. Female convicts could be punished with a heavy iron collar that was riveted around their neck. Some collars were fitted with two long prongs that prevented the wearer from sitting or lying comfortably. Squeeze, meaning neck, may stem from tightly tied neckerchiefs. But it's also possible that the term comes from the noose that tightened around the neck of a person executed by hanging. A 'true lover's knot' is a knot tied to symbolise unending devotion—the farther the ends of the knot are pulled apart, the tighter the knot becomes, strengthening the bond.

STAG: To *turn stag* was formerly synonymous with *turning nose*, or *snitching*, but the phrase is now exploded.

STAG: To *stag* any object or person, is to look at, observe, or take notice of them.

To turn stag is a phrase based on a belief that herds of deer 'turn their horns against any of their number who is hunted.' Irishman Thomas Beckham, a notorious thief, murderer and transported convict, was sentenced to death for assassinating a magistrate. At the time of his execution, he proudly declared: 'I want you to know that I never was turncoat or stag.' Among the thousands of people gathered to stag the execution was Beckham's son, who yelled, 'Bravo, father! I knew you would die true.'

STAINES: A man who is in pecuniary distress is said to be *at Staines*, or *at the Bush*, alluding to the Bush inn at that town. See: BUSH'D.

The Bush Inn was situated at Staines-upon-Thames in Surrey, England. Because homeless or impoverished people subsisted in the bush, Staines may be a pun on *bush*, slang for 'poor'. When, in 1833, county officials ordered that the Bush Inn be demolished to make way for a bridge, licensee Richard King was at staines.

STAKE: A booty acquired by robbery, or a sum of money won at play, is called *a stake*, and if considerable, *a prime stake*, or a *heavy stake*. A person alluding to any thing difficult to be procured, or which he obtains as a great favour, and is therefore comparatively invaluable, would say, I consider it a *stake* to get it at all; a valuable or acceptable acquisition of any kind, is emphatically called a *stake*, meaning a great prize.

Escaped convicts who subsisted in the bush on their stake were called bushrangers. In 1826, the Jeffries Gang exhausted their supplies so ate their comrade, Edward Russel. According to Jeffries, Russel was 'cut into steaks'.

STALL: A violent pressure in a crowd, made by pick-pockets for the more easily effecting their depredatory purposes; this is called *making a rum stall in the push*.

Stall may allude to animals confined in a stall. But because stall is also slang for 'a pick-pocket's accomplice', the term may come from stall, a decoy bird used in hunting. In 1841, John Griffiths, 'a vagrant-looking rascal', was charged with 'creating a fight' to 'examine the contents of the pockets of the parties assembled'. Constable William O'Neil testified that he prevented Griffiths committing a similar robbery on a previous occasion: in a Melbourne pub O'Neil overheard Griffiths whisper to his accomplice '*stash* the *glim*, give us a stall, and I'll cop the gilt'. Griffiths was fined ten shillings.

STALL OFF: A term variously applied; generally it means a pretence, excuse, or prevarication——as a person charged with any fault, entering into some plausible story, to excuse himself, his hearers or accusers would say, O yes, that's a good *stall off*, or, Aye, aye, *stall it off* that way if you can. To extricate a person from any dilemma, or save him from disgrace, is called *stalling* him *off*; as an accomplice of your's being detected in a robbery, etc., and about to be given up to justice, you will step up as a stranger, interfere in his behalf, and either by vouching for his innocence, recommending lenity, or some other artifice, persuade his accusers to forego their intention, and let the prisoner escape; you will then boast of having *stalled him off in prime twig*. To avoid or escape any impending evil or punishment by means of artifice, submission, bribe, or otherwise, is also called *stalling* it *off*. A man walking the streets, and passing a particular shop, or encountering a certain person, which or whom he has reasons for wishing to avoid, will say to any friend who may be with him, I wish you'd *stall* me *off from* that *crib*, (or *from* that *cove*, as the case may be) meaning, walk in such a way as to cover or obscure me from notice, until we are past the shop or person in question.

In 1848, Van Diemonian pastoralist Jonathan Ives overheard his convict servant Peter Curtis plotting to steal his booze. Curtis was persuading a boy to fetch him a key that unlocked Ive's larder. But because the boy was worried they'd be caught, Curtis assured him that if anyone interrupted them he'd 'stall them off'. Ives prosecuted the two would-be thieves but Curtis, as was reported in the press, attempted to 'stall it off' in court by lying to the jury. Curtis, who was transported for perjury, was severely punished with six months' hard labour in leg irons. Ives, however, was no stranger to theft—he was an ex-convict transported for burglary.

STALL UP: To *stall* a person up, (a term used by pick-pockets,) is to surround him in a crowd, or violent pressure, and even sometimes in the open street, while walking along, and by violence force his arms up, and keep them in that position while others of the gang rifle his pockets at plea-sure, *the cove* being unable to help or defend himself; this is what the newspapers denominate hustling, and is universally practised at the doors of public theatres, at boxing matches, ship-launches, and other places where the general anxiety of all ranks, either to push forward, or to obtain a view of the scene before them, forms a pretext for jostling, and every other advantage which the strength or numbers of one party gives them over a weaker one, or a single person. It is not unusual for the *buz-coves*, on particular occasions, to procure a formidable squad of stout fellows of the lower class, who, though not expert at *knuckling*, render essential service by violently pushing and squeezing in the crowd, and, in the confusion excited by this conduct, the unconcerned *prigs* reap a plentiful harvest, and the *stallers up* are gratified with such part of the gains acquired, as the liberality of the *knuckling* gentlemen may prompt them to bestow. This coup *de guerre* is termed *making a regular stall* at such a place, naming the scene of their operations. See STALL.

John Bland was robbed in a stall up in Covent Garden, England, in 1819.

According to his testimony, he was 'hustled by a gang of pickpockets'. To prevent the gang stealing his watch, he covered his fob with his hand. But gang members  wrenched his arms in the air and ransacked his pockets. A passerby tackled one of the pickpockets, Edward Hawkins, who was transported to New South Wales for life.

STAMPS: Shoes.

Shoes were called stamps because people stamped the ground with their feet. When, in 1835, Samuel Whitaker and John Smith were gaoled for burglary, police overhead them discussing their crime: the two young thieves wore wet stockings over their 'stampers' to muffle the sound of their footsteps. They were sentenced to life transportation to New South Wales.

STAND THE PATTER. See: PATTER'D.

STAR. *The star* is a *game* chiefly practised by young boys, often under ten years of age, although the offence is capital. It consists of cutting a pane of glass in a shop-window, by a peculiar operation I called *starring the glaze,* which is performed very effectually by a common penknife; the depredators then take out such articles of value as lie within reach of their arm, which if they are not interrupted, sometimes includes half the contents of the window. A person convicted of this offence is said to have been *done for a star*.

The star probably acquired its nickname because fractured glass resembles a star. In 1809, Michael Connelly and Richard Evans, both aged fourteen, and Charles Evans, aged twelve, were spotted cutting a hole in a cutler's shop  window. They were charged with stealing five knives and, according to police testimony, they used an especially sharp knife to 'star the *glaze*'. The trio was charged with breaking and entering and sentenced to seven years' transportation.

START. See: PITCHER.

STASH. To *stash* any practice, habit, or proceeding, signifies to put an end to, relinquish, or quash the same; thus, a thief determined to leave off his vicious courses will declare that he means to *stash* (or *stow*) *prigging*. A man in custody for felony, will endeavour, by offering money, or other means, to induce his prosecutor's forbearance, and compromise the matter, so as to obtain his liberation; this is called *stashing the business*. To *stash* drinking, card-playing, or any other employment you may be engaged in, for the time present, signifies to *stow* it, *knife* it, *cheese* it, or *cut* it, which are all synonymous, that is, to desist or leave off. See: WANTED.

STASH IT. See: STOW IT, which has the same meaning.

At Whitechapel, London, in 1821, Watchman Thomas Brown caught Abraham Myers and Robert Day stashing stolen goods. Myers offered Brown £2 and a 'share in the *swag*' to 'stash it', but he refused the bribe and the two thieves were charged with grand larceny and transported to New South Wales for seven-year terms.

STAUNCH: A resolute faithful associate, in whom one may place implicit confidence, is said by his *palls* to be a *staunch* cover.

In 1843, convict William Francis was awarded his freedom for apprehending two bushrangers. Francis, who then commenced bushranging, declared his accomplices not 'staunch enough' so roamed the bush solo. Because he was Jewish and bailed up travellers in the region of Den Hill in central Van Diemen's Land, he was known as 'Billy the Jew' and 'Billy of the Den'. But, in 1847, after a two-week drinking spree in Whittaker's Tavern, he was caught and sentenced to life imprisonment.

STEAMER: A tobacco-pipe.

Pipes were nicknamed steamers because they emitted steam-like smoke. Tobacco, as a general rule, was forbidden and so, too, were steamers. When Margaret Gordon was discovered smoking and breastfeeding in the nursery at the Cascades Female Factory, she

refused to relinquish her pipe. Because Gordon was a nursing mother her punishment was delayed until her baby was 'old enough to be weaned'.

STEVEN: Money.

Steven may derive from *stivver*, Dutch for 'a low-valued coin'. When Brisbane pickpocket Martin Brennen stole a man's pocketbook, he was disappointed to discover it contained 'not a stiver'.

STICK: A pistol.

Pistols were called sticks because of their stick-like appearance. Edward Wakefield, a well-to-do Englishman sentenced to three years in Newgate Prison for abducting and marrying a fifteen-year-old heiress, became fascinated with the lives of Newgate inmates, which led him to study punishment, transportation and colonisation. When Wakefield was released from prison he travelled extensively, becoming a key figure in the colonisation of South Australia and New Zealand. But he also wrote about his adventures and recorded *'flash'* language, such as 'shooting sticks' (pistols) and 'dust' (gunpowder).

STICKS: Household furniture.

Because furniture was made of wood, it was called sticks. When Henry Keck, govenor of Sydney Gaol, was charged with misconduct and dismissed, his wife, Theresa, prosecuted him for alimony. According to her testimony she received 'a

few sticks' but required 'a pound a week'. Keck agreed to pay the sum on condition that Theresa 'moderate the rancor of her tongue'.

STING: To rob or defraud a person or place is called *stinging* them, as, that cove is too *fly*; he has been *stung* before; meaning that man is upon his guard; he has already been trick'd.

Mark Jeffrey, after '*sounding* the *crib*,' robbed his friend's master's house. But Jeffrey, for stinging his friend, was imprisoned in Ely Gaol. There, he assaulted a gaoler. To calm his 'rugged nature,' a prisoner was placed in his cell to read him passages from the bible, but Jeffrey dismissed the scripture as 'nonsensical twaddle' that 'stung to madness' and assaulted his cellmate.

STINK: When any robbery of moment has been committed, which causes much alarm, or of which much is said in the daily papers, the family people will say, there is a great stink about it. See: WANTED.

In 1832, police arrested convict Isaac Simpson when they discovered a bundle of stolen clothes stashed in the loft of his house. But Simpson accused his neighbour, Philip Thomas, of the crime. Thomas, also a convict, oper-  ated a 'grog shop' and brothel that shared a roof with Simpson's house. A trapdoor that led to Simpson's loft was discovered in Thomas's ceiling, but three prostitutes came to his defence claiming they heard Simpson say it was his '*cross* property' and that if there was 'any stink about it' he would 'burn it'. They were not believed, so Simpson was acquitted.

STONE-JUG; STONE-PITCHER: See: PITCHER.

STOOP: The pillory is called *the stoop*; to be *stoop'd*, is to be set on the pillory.
STOOPING-MATCH: The exhibition of one or more persons on the pillory. See: PUSH.

A pillory is a wooden framework with holes for securing the head and hands of a person charged with an offence. Offenders stood stooped, exposed to public ridicule. But they also could have their crimes scrawled across their face or written on a placard suspended from their neck. The stoop in New South Wales, situated in the Sydney marketplace, stood ten feet from the ground and revolved horizontally under the weight of its victims, creating the impression that they were chasing each other. In 1825, Elizabeth Charlton and John Creswell were branded with their crimes and sentenced to a stooping-match. But they also were sentenced to seven years' transportation. Other offenders were sentenced to multiple stints, a flogging, or to have the ears nailed to the framework—Convict-Constable Thomas Green suffered a nailing and later received 1200 lashes. Pillory may come from *pilori*, French for peephole. But a pillory was also known as a penance board, picture frame, nutcracker, whirligig, wooden ruff and Norway Neckcloth, so named after a type of Nordic timber. Slang names for people locked in a pillory include stoop-nappers and overseers of the new pavement.

STOW: To *stow* any business, employment, or mode of life, is the same as to *stash* it, etc. See: STASH.

STOW, STOW IT; or STOW FAKING: An intimation from a thief to his *pall*, to desist from what he is about, on the occasion of some alarm, etc. See: AWAKE.

STOW, or STOW-MANGING: An intimation from one *flash-cove* to another in a mixed company to be silent, or drop the subject, he was upon. See: MANG.

At Covent Garden in 1792, twelve-year-old Charles Jones stole an unattended horse-drawn carriage. But when coachman George Smith hopped aboard for a ride and noticed the suspiciously youthful driver, he called for the police. Jones pleaded with Smith to 'stow it',  which Smith supposed meant 'let him go', but he refused and Smith was charged with horse theft and sentenced to death. Because of his young age the sentence was commuted to service in the army.

STOW THAT. When a person advances any assertion which his auditor believes to be false, or spoken in jest, or wishes the former to recant, the latter will say, *stow that*, if you please, or, *cheese that*, meaning don't say so, or that's out of the question.

263

When, in 1843, William Hilton Rainbow was drinking in the Coach and Horses Inn, he spotted pickpocket Catherine Lowrie purloin his friend's handkerchief. Rainbow rebuked Lowrie, saying, 'that won't do, stow that,' so Lowrie returned the handkerchief. But when she stole it a second time, and Rainbow threatened to have her arrested, she bellowed, 'You damned old bugger, I will bury this glass in your skull,' and lobbed a tumbler at Rainbow's head. Rainbow was hospitalised and Lowrie was sentenced to one months' gaol.

STRETCH. Five or ten *stretch*, signifies five or ten yards, etc.; so in dealing for any article, as linen, etc., I will give you *three hog a stretch*, means, I'll give three shillings a yard. See: HOG.

A yard of fabric was called a stretch because the material was stretched and then measured. Officer George Dudley arrested George Holmes for stealing an array of items including 383 stretch of twill. But when Holmes struggled futilely to escape his clutches, Dudley asked him, 'What do

you struggle for?' Holmes replied, 'Would you not struggle if you saw seven stretch staring you in the face?' Stretch was also slang for 'a prison term'—seven stretch meant 'seven years,' stretch singularly was one year, half a stretch was six months, and a quarter stretch was three months. Convicts sentenced to a 'stretching match'—execution by hanging—were said to 'stretch hemp' or 'stretch rope'.

STRING. See: LINE.

STRUMMEL: The hair of the head. To get your *strummel faked in twig*, is to have your hair dressed in style.

Female convicts who misbehaved could be sentenced to have their strummel cut off or their heads shaved. But for some convicts, having their strummel faked in twig by the authorities was of little concern. Ann Wilson, for throwing stones at her superintendent's window, had her head shaved. She remarked: 'I do not care if it is cut off fifty times!' Strummel, also slang for 'straw', may derive from *estramaille*, Old French for 'straw bedding'.

STUBBS: Nothing.

Stubbs probably comes from stub, the end piece or remnant of an article. But it may also be back slang, derived from *butt*. A person who pawned an item received a ticket, or stub, listing the particulars of the loan. But when Sarah Simpson pawned stolen clothing, she burned the ticket so there was stubbs to connect her to the crime. She was caught and sentenced to one years' gaol.

SUIT: In general synonymous with *game*; as, what *suit* did you *give it to 'em upon?* in what manner did you rob them, or upon what

pretence, etc., did you defraud them? **One** species of imposition is said to be a *prime suit,* another *a queer suit*: a man describing the pretext he used to obtain money from another, would say, *I draw'd* him *of a quid upon the suit* of so and so, naming the ground of his application. See: DRAW. A person having engaged with another on very advantageous terms to serve or work for him, will declare that he is *upon a good suit.* To use great submission and respect in asking any favour of another, is called *giving it to him upon the humble suit.*

Suit may derive from *pursuit,* meaning 'an activity'. In 1840, sixteen-year-old Francis McCallum was literally caught in a suit—he tailored clothing out of another convict's bedding. McCallum was sentenced to ten days' solitary confinement with bread and water.

SWAG: A bundle, parcel, or package; as a *swag* of *snow,* etc. *The swag,* is a term used in speaking of any booty you have lately obtained, be it of what kind it may, except money, as Where did you *lumber the swag?* That is, where did you deposit the stolen property? To carry *the swag* is to be the bearer of the stolen goods to a place of safety. *A swag* of any thing, signifies emphatically a great deal. To have *knap'd* a good *swag,* is to have got a good booty.
SWAG. Wearing-apparel, linen, piece-goods, etc., are all comprehended under the name of *swag,* when describing any *speak* lately *made,* etc., in order to distinguish them from plate, jewellery, or other more portable articles.

Swag may originate in bags that sway and sag. Burglar Mark Jeffery was convicted of stealing swag and transported to Norfolk Island for a fifteen-year term. But before he turned to crime he earned his living hawking goods purchased from London 'swag shops'. Other convicts transported to Australia, such as John Frederick Mortlock, hawked swag when they acquired their freedom. Swagmen, as they became known, were commonplace. In the ballad 'Waltzing Matilda'—the tale of a suicidal sheep-stealing swagman—Andrew  Barton 'Banjo' Paterson spun the rebellious swagman spirit into a national identity. Paterson's ballad is recognised as Australia's unofficial national anthem.

SWELL: A gentleman; but any well-dressed person is emphatically termed a *swell*, or a *rank swell*. A *family man* who appears to have plenty of money, and makes a genteel figure, is said by his associates to be in *swell street*. Any thing remarkable for its beauty or elegance, is called a *swell article*; so *a swell crib*, is a genteel house; *a swell mollisher*, an elegantly-dressed woman, etc. Sometimes, in alluding to a particular gentleman, whose name is not requisite, he is styled, *the swell*, meaning the person who is the object of your discourse, or attention; and whether he is called *the swell, the cove*, or *the gory*, is immaterial, as in the following (in addition to many other) examples: I was *turned up at China-street*, because *the swell* would not appear; meaning, of course, the prosecutor: again, speaking of a person whom you were on the point of robbing, but who has taken the alarm, and is therefore on his guard, you will say to your *pall*, It's of no use, *the cove* is as *down as a hammer*; or, We may as well *stow it, the gory's leary*. See: COVE and: DOWN.

Henry Byron and John Leach, transported to Van Diemen's Land for life, were 'active members of the Swell Mob'—a gang of English pickpockets infamous for dressing in fancy clothes so they could mingle with

the upper class to perpetrate lucrative crimes. When they arrived in Hobart Town, they joined an even larger mob of swell characters—the police force. In 1840, the two convict-constables were reprimanded for attempting to break into a woman's house in the middle of the night.

SWIMMER: A guard-ship, or tender; a thief who escapes prosecution, when before a magistrate, on condition of being sent on board the receiving-ship, to serve His Majesty, is said by his *palls* to be *swimmered*.

At the Bow Street Police Court in 1805, John Leach, his younger brother, James, and friend, Richard Danvers, were charged with pickpocketing. To 'do them a service in preventing them from being hanged', the Bow Street Magistrates appointed the trio as swimmers on a swimmer—a small boat that tenders to a larger vessel. Tenders ferried convicts to and from their transport ships.

SWISH'D: Married.

Swish'd may be a corruption of switched, meaning 'to change from unmarried to married'. Because men outnumbered women in colonial Australia, female convicts were 'speedily swished'. Marriage was one way for a convict to improve her situation, and some women married into wealth, security and ultimately freedom. Ellen Heath, transported for attempting to poison her husband with arsenic-laced pudding, was married the year after she arrived in Van Diemen's Land. Later, having served less than five years of a life sentence, she was pardoned.

SWODDY, or SWOD-GILL: A soldier.

When, in 1845, William Dean called James McGuggan a 'swaddy', and his regiment 'damned cowardly dastardly villains', he narrowly avoided a charge of 'inciting a private of the 96th Regiment to commit a breach of the peace'. But Dean, a Launceston baker, had good reason to slander the regiment. A few weeks prior, fifty soldiers armed with 'heavy bludgeons, palings and other weapons' stormed the town and assaulted men, women and children, who suffered broken bones, cuts and contusions. Other members of the 96th quelled the uprising and the offending soldiers were banished from Launceston. Swoddy may derive from shoddy, a slang name for inexpensive wool used to darn military coatees. But the term may also come from swad, slang for 'country bumpkin'.

TANNER: A sixpence. Three and a tanner, is three and sixpence, etc.

Tanner may come from the New Testament—according to *Acts of the Apostles*, Simon the Tanner provided St Peter with free room and board. In 1858, Anne 'The Dumpling' Bourke fell on hard times. With her remaining money—'three *bobs* and a tanner'—she arranged room and board at a lodging house in the slums of Sydney. When the money ran out she did odd jobs for her landlord, James Barry. But one morning while making Barry's bed she discovered a purse stashed beneath his pillow, so stole sixteen sovereigns, rented a room in an upmarket lodging house and went on a spending spree. Barry, however, had marked the coins with a black stroke to safeguard against theft. When the police caught up with Bourke, they discovered three blackened sovereigns in her possession but, despite the incriminating evidence, the coins could not be definitively attributed to Barry, so Bourke was acquitted. She may have acquired her nickname because of her stout appearance.

TAT: To flog or scourge.

Tat, meaning 'to cut,' may come from tatters, meaning 'shreds' and 'scraps'. Alexander Green stole fabric and was transported to New South Wales for life. At Hyde Park Barracks, he was appointed flagellator to tat his fellow convicts. In 1828, Green graduated  to executioner—he is credited with the executions of 490 people. But in 1830, a convict attacked Green with an axe, cutting his face to tatters and scarring him for life.

TATTS: Dice.

TATT-BOX: A dice-box.

 Tatts may be a pun on *rattle*. Because gambling was illegal, gamblers gathered at covert locations, such as an innocuous looking tailor shop in Druitt Street, Sydney. In 1859, police raided the shop and arrested six men in the midst of a game of tatts. But police also discovered that the proprietor, John 'Jackey' Johnson, 'a sly looking little old snip,' cheated his clientele with a tatts-box that was 'so cleverly contrived that a *sharp* when playing with a *flat* could turn the dice out nearly to any figure'. Snip is slang for tailor, because tailors *snipped* fabric with scissors. But the term also meant 'cheat,' possibly derived from snipe, meaning 'a sly attack'.

TATS AND ALL: An expression used *out of flash*, in the same manner as the word *bender*; and has a similar meaning. See: BENDER.

TEAZE: To flog, or whip.

Teaze probably derives from tease, meaning 'to separate strands'. Convicts were teazed with a cat-o'-nine-tails—a nine-tailed whipping device that

lacerated a man's back in the manner of a cat's claws. Flagellators—men responsible for delivering a flogging—were selected from serving convicts. Those of solid build with experience in the armed forces were given preference. Thomas Jeffries, who served in the army and navy, was appointed as a flagellator at Launceston, in 1825. He was reputed to be a 'very strong man' but also a 'diabolical villain' and a 'monster in human shape'. When meting out fifty lashes, Jeffries would teaze for 'twenty luxuriating minutes, curling his lash around the torso so that the victim's breast as well as back might be torn and bloodied'.

THIMBLE: A watch.
THIMBLED: Having, or wearing a watch.

When Benjamin Batt passed out thimbled in a London pub and woke to discover his pockets inside out and his money and watch missing, he called for the police. James Churcher, a waiter, overheard patron Thomas Cordwell boast he '*napped* the bloody thimble'. Cordwell accused Churcher of allowing the theft to transpire but Churcher claimed that he did not understand cant, so he could not have known the meaning of Cordwell's words. Churcher was absolved of any wrongdoing but Cordwell was transported to New South Wales for life. Because a watch is disc-shaped, it may have been nicknamed after a thimble—'a circular metal ring, around which a loop of rope is spliced'.

THROUGH IT, or THROUGH THE PIECE: Getting acquitted on an indictment, or surmounting any other trouble, or difficulty, is called *getting through it*, or *thro' the piece*; so, to *get* a man *through it*, etc., is to extricate him by virtue of your counsel and friendly assistance; sometimes called *pulling* him *through it.*

In 1827, the *Colonial Times* alerted the public to the great number of unauthorised liquor shops trading in Van Diemen's Land. According to  the report, unlicensed vendors catered to convicts who traded 'grog' for items they stole from their masters. But the 'notorious grog-sellers' operated with impunity because they bribed police and, if taken to court, they hired a quick-witted barrister named Joseph Gellibrand, to 'pull us through it'. Grog, slang for alcohol, comes from *Old Grog*, the nickname of Admiral Edward Vernon who wore a grogram cloak and ordered diluted rum be served to sailors.

THRUMS, THRUMBUSKINS, or a THRUM-MOP: Three pence.

Thrums may originate in the compound value of a threepenny piece—thrum refers to loose thread, such as the strands that protrude from a mop. Constable David Hartley arrested William Mallet on suspicion of *'glazing'* and stealing cash, but because the only *'blunt'* found on Hartley was *'thrums'*, he was absolved of any wrongdoing.

THROW OFF: To talk in a sarcastical strain, so as to convey offensive allusions under the mask of pleasantry, or innocent freedom; but, perhaps, secretly venting that abuse which you would not dare to give in direct terms; this is called *throwing off*, a practice at which the *flash* ladies are very expert, when any little jealousies arise among them. To begin to talk *flash*, and speak freely of robberies past, or in contemplation, when in company with *family people*, is also termed *throwing off*; meaning to banish all reserve, none but friends being present; also, to sing when called on by the company present. See: CHAUNT.

During a heated argument at the White Swan Hotel in Hobart Town, Mary Watson told Louisa Thompson 'she ought to get a new set of teeth', then punched her twice in the face. Thompson refused to '*square* the matter' and so prosecuted Watson for 'throwing off at her'. Watson was fined five shillings and ordered to pay court costs or spend seven days in gaol with hard labour.

———————— ————

TILBURY: A sixpence.

A sixpence was nicknamed a tilbury because of the sixpence fare that ferrymen charged commuters to cross the River Thames between Gravesend and Tilbury Fort. In 1840, brothers and ferrymen Henry and Thomas Marshall attempted to rob a group of churchgoing 'ladies and gentlemen'. The party escaped their clutches, so the Marshall boys splashed then with water and heckled them with 'very offensive language' including wordplay: 'They are Sunday *swells*; they only come out once a week.' The Marshalls were fined £5.

———————— ————————

TINNY: A fire; a conflagration.

TINNY-HUNTERS: Persons whose practice it is to attend fires, for the purpose of plundering the unfortunate sufferers, under pretence of assisting them to remove their property.

Tinny may derive from *tini*, a Shelta word for 'fire', or from tinder—'flammable material used for lighting a fire'. In 1892, a tinny tore though the township of Broken Hill, threatening to engulf Sayers Crown Hotel. But as fire-fighters rallied to save the pub, tinny-hunters Arthur Wallace and James Stevens stole some booze. Stevens was punished with three months' hard labour at Silverton Gaol, but because Wallace 'helped to remove and take back furniture' from the pub, he escaped with a lighter sentence of two months' gaol without hard labour.

TIP: To give, pay, or bribe. To *take the tip*, is to receive a bribe in any shape; and they say of a person who is known to be corruptible, that he will *stand the tip*. *The tip* is a term frequently used to signify the money concerned in any dealings or contract existing between parties; synonymous with *the dues*. See: DUES.

According to convict Linus Miller, everyone accepted 'tip,' from 'the governor down to scavenger'. John Stack, a convict-overseer at Carters' Barracks, embezzled  convict rations to sell at a profit, recruited convicts to work for him, and accepted bribes allowing convicts to abscond or skip work. When Stack was caught, he seized a pistol and threatened to shoot gaol governor

Henry Keck. But gaol personnel wrestled Stack to the ground and he was arrested and sentenced to twelve months' gaol. Keck, however, was also accused of accepting tip, and, after several lengthy investigations, he was dismissed. Tip may come from tip, meaning 'to touch lightly'.

TITTER: A young woman or girl.

Young women may have been called titters because they tittered, or because they developed tits, slang for breasts. Seventeen-year-old Mary Ann Lucas, for singing 'obscene songs' at the Cascades Female Factory, was confined to a ward for three days. But according to an exposé in the *True Colonist*, some titters enjoyed confinement in the wards because they were 'more lively' and 'more fun' than other parts of the factory. A board of inquiry determined that factory women spent their free time dancing, singing, performing plays, dressing up and playing cards.

TOBY: To *toby* a man, is to rob him on the highway; a person convicted of this offence, is said to be *done* for *a toby*. *The toby* applies exclusively to robbing on horseback; the practice of footpad robbery being properly called *the spice*, though it is common to distinguish the former by the title of *high-toby*, and the latter of *low-toby*.
TOBY-GILL, or **TOBY-MAN:** Properly signifies a highwayman.

Toby, meaning road, may derive from *tober*, which means road in both Shelta and Romani. In one of the largest gold heists in Australian history, a gang of toby-men, disguised in crimson hats and jumpers and with their

faces blackened, stole approximately £14,000 in gold from an armed
escort in New South Wales. One of the
bushrangers, Francis 'Frank' Gardiner,
was recognised by the sound of his voice.
When police caught up with Gardiner in
Queensland, he was done for a toby and
sentenced to thirty-two years' hard
labour. But due to a technicality, he was
released subject to exile from Australia.
Gardiner spent time in Hong Kong and America and went by several
aliases, but he also was known as the 'Prince of Tobymen'.

TODDLE: To walk slowly, either from infirmity or choice.
Come, let us *toddle*, is a familiar phrase, signifying, let us be
going.

Daniel McDonald stole a '*peter*' containing '*toggery*' then 'toddled' through
Pitt Street in Sydney. He was caught and sentenced to eighteen months'
hard labour in leg irons. Leg irons could cause irreparable damage to
a convict's legs—because of the many years Mark Jeffrey spent in leg
irons, he was crippled and required two canes to toddle.

TODDLER: An infirm elderly person, or a child not yet
perfect in walking.

Female Factories catered to 'toddlers' young and old. Convicts who fell
pregnant while assigned to colonists were usually returned to a Female
Factory. After their baby was born the mother was transferred to the

nursery to care for her child. Three months later she was supplied with an additional child, and then another child after another three months. When her own child was weaned at nine months old, the woman was removed to the crime class for six months' punishment and her child was placed under the care of another convict to continue the cycle. Many mothers never saw their children again. But elderly or infirm convicts were also returned to the factory, some of whom ended their days in the hospital infirmary.

TOG: A coat; to *tog*, is to dress or put on clothes; to *tog* a person, is also to supply them with apparel, and they are said to be well or *queerly tog'd*, according to their appearance.

Tog is derived from *toga*, Latin for gown. Burglar Mark Jeffrey togged as a ghost—he wore white gloves, white leggings, a long white jumper and a white mask with 'eyelet holes'. But he was caught and transported to Van Diemen's Land. There, in the 1860s, he was imprisoned in Port Arthur's Separate Prison, where convicts were confined to individual cells for nearly twenty-four hours a day. When they were let out of their cells they

were queerly tog'd to prevent them communicating to each other, wearing hooded masks similar to Jeffrey's ghost mask. Inmates were not referred to by their names, but by a number that was printed on a badge that hung from a button sewn onto their tog. The 'separate system', as it was termed, was designed to prevent criminal contamination, and to compel inmates to reflect upon and repent their crimes.

TOG'D OUT TO THE NINES: A fanciful phrase, meaning simply, that a person is well or gaily dressed.

When Harriet Nixon, a so-called 'rowdy Cyprian', faced court on a charge of assault, a newsman attending her trial reported that she was 'togged to the nines'. The origin of 'to the nines' is not known, but the term may derive from *up to the eyen*, an archaic phrase that means 'to the satisfaction of one's eyes'. Cyprian, slang for prostitute, refers to the denizens of Cyprus who revered Aphrodite, the Greek Goddess of beauty, love, pleasure and procreation.

TOGS, or TOGGERY: Wearing-apparel in general.

When, in 1836, a convict in a New South Wales road gang was spotted wearing 'beautiful toggery', William Foster, the superintendent of Hyde Park Barracks, immediately branded the man's clothes with 'P.B.', an abbreviation of Prisoners' Barracks. According to a local reporter, the convict was 'crestfallen'. Convicts under sentence, ganged convicts especially, were, as a rule, compelled to wear distinctive and humiliating uniforms.

TOM BRAY'S BILK: Laying out ace and deuce at cribbage.
TOM BROWN: Twelve in hand, or crib.

In the card game cribbage, players compete for points and record their score on a cribbage board. But how Tom Bray and Tom Brown came to be associated with cribbage is not known. Cribbage was popular— William 'Milky' Jones was transported to New South Wales for life after he stole an array of items including a cribbage board. He was probably nicknamed after his pale appearance. According to his physical description in the Black Books, his complexion was 'sallow' and his eyes were 'grey'.

TOOLS: Implements for house-breaking, picklocks, pistols, etc., are indiscriminately called *the tools*. A thief, convicted on the police act, of having illegal instruments or weapons about him, is said to be *fined for the tools*.

The frontispiece of George Barrington's biography depicts an array of innocuous items, such as a house key and finger ring, which conceal tiny retractable hooks. But it's unlikely that Barrington was armed with gadgetry to assist him picking pockets, and more probable that the publisher printed the illustration to cash in on the public's fascination with criminals and their 'tools'. In the early 1840s, theatregoers attending a production based on the life of infamous thief Jack Sheppard, were sold 'Sheppard-bags'; goody bags containing 'a screw driver, and iron lever'. But when William 'the little *cracksman*' Giles and his teenage accom-

plice were discovered carrying 'house-breaking implements' they were arrested and sentenced to three months' gaol with hard labour. People caught with burglary equipment could be charged with 'intent to commit a felony'. John Starkey was fined for the tools even though the tools he was carrying were in the form of an illustration. He was gaoled for two months when police discovered him carrying a love token that bore pictures of pistols, a crowbar, a picklock, two skeleton keys, a dark lanthorn, a phosphorus box and matches.

TOP: To *top* a *clout* or other article (among pickpockets) is to draw the corner or end of it to the top of a person's pocket, in readiness for *shaking* or *drawing*, that is, taking out, when a favourable moment occurs, which latter operation is frequently done by a second person.

In 1812, Constable Joseph Martin observed two boys top a handkerchief: one boy 'drew the handkerchief half out' of a man's pocket, then, when the man walked away, the boy 'drew the handkerchief clean out' and passed it to his accomplice. Martin pounced and the boys were arrested. They were convicted of theft but released from gaol because of their young age.

TOP'D: Hanged.

In 1828, Henry Jones and William Rice were arrested fleeing the scene of a burglary in Tottenham, London. Jones remarked that he 'might get *lagged*', but Rice said 'he did not mind if he was not topped'. The two men were charged with the '*job*', but they also were suspected of perpetrating other '*jobs*' in the area. Jones, as he predicted, was sentenced to seven years' transportation to Van Diemen's Land, but Rice was sentenced to death. Topped, meaning 'hanged,' may originate in the manner in which executed people were suspended from the top part of the body. When Rice dropped beneath the gallows he 'struggled violently' so the hangman grasped his body to weigh him down and accelerate asphyxiation.

TO THE NINES; or, TO THE RUFFIAN: These terms are synonymous, and imply an extreme of any kind, or the superlative degree.

Ruffian, meaning 'very' and 'extremely,' is slang for devil, as demonstrated in the saying *devilishly good*. Peter Kelly was so obsessed with his landlady, Mary Ann Sheedy, that he was said to be 'shook to the ruffin'. But because Sheedy spurned his advances the 'brutal scoundrel' bludgeoned her with a 'life-preserver'. Sheedy recovered and Kelly was charged with assault and sentenced to three months' hard labour in Darlinghurst Gaol. A life-preserver is a small club typically carried for protection.

TOUT: To *tout* a person, is to watch his motions; to *keep tout*, is to look out, or watch, while your *pall* is effecting any private purpose. *A strong tout*, is a strict observation, or eye, upon any proceedings, or person.

The proprietors of unlawful gaming houses employed 'touts and *bonnets*' to keep watch and update them with information. Hawk Tong operated a gaming house in Diamond Gully, Victoria. He positioned a sentry on the top of a nearby hill. When, in 1869, a posse of police descended on the gaming-house the sentry raised the alarm and fifty gamblers fled the building. But Tong needn't have worried. Because Chinese gambling games were not stipulated in gaming legislation, they were not illegal. When the case went to trial it was dismissed. Tout may come from *pushing toute*, a slang name for 'a thief's watchman' who was employed to *scout* and *lookout*.

TOW; or, TOWLINE. See: LINE. To *tow* a person *out*; that is, from his premises, or post: is to decoy him therefrom by some fictitious story, or other artifice, while your *pall* seizes the opportunity of his absence, to rob the place he has imprudently quitted.

According to Alexander Harris, an army deserter who fled to Australia, convict-shepherds kept their masters 'in a tow-line'—if sheep strayed from the flock under the convict's care, he borrowed sheep from another convict-shepherd to  make up the difference. The convict-shepherds were also known to bolster their rations with mutton acquired on '*on the cross*'.

TRAPS: Police officers, or runners, are properly so called; but it is common to include constables of any description under this title.

Policemen were traps because they trapped criminals. When Constable William Roach encountered three convicts exiting the Bull's Head pub, the publican urged the convicts to '*give it to* the trap'. Roach was bludgeoned with fence palings and the convicts also  'tore off his hair by handfuls'. Constable Robert Shanahan, who came to Roach's assistance, was also beaten but managed to escape and raise the alarm. The convicts were arrested and tried for assault, but the jury found them not guilty. Roach and Shanahan, however, were charged with neglect of duty and sentenced to solitary confinement. They were convicts under sentence who, according to witness testimony, were drunk at the time of the fracas because they'd been drinking in pubs throughout Hobart Town. Convicts were often recruited into Australia's first police forces. Some convict-constables accepted bribes, perpetrated thefts and entrapped colonists to acquire fines and rewards. But other policemen, such as Henry Byron, who helped extinguish a house fire, were praised for their meritorious conduct—he was rewarded with an early release.

TRICK. See **DO THE TRICK**.

TRIG: A bit of stick, paper, etc., placed by thieves in the keyhole of, or elsewhere about, the door of a house, which they suspect to be uninhabited; if the trig remains unmoved the following day, it is a proof that no person sleeps in the house, on which the gang enter it the ensuing night upon the screw, and frequently meet with a good booty, such as beds, carpets, etc., the family being probably out of town. This operation is called trigging the jigger.

Trig may come from trigger, meaning 'set in motion'. In 1836, Joseph Keegan, Michael Askin and William Byrne were charged with stealing teeth from corpses interred at St Andrew's Church in Dublin, Ireland. The church sexton alleged that the boys placed a trig in the keyhole of the churchyard gates so that they could determine when the cemetery was deserted. For committing the 'indecent and revolting outrage', the trio copped twelve months' imprisonment with hard labour. Because the judge was so appalled by their crime, he stated his desire to transport them to Australia.

TRY IT ON: To make all attempt, or essay, where success is doubtful. So to try it on with a woman, signifies to attempt her chastity.

In 1835, James Coleman was discovered naked, drunk and creeping into the bedroom of his master's wife. Coleman, for trying it on, was punished with seventy-five lashes of the cat-o'-nine-tails and sent to Port Arthur Penal Station for 'severe discipline'. According to colonial commentator Gordon Forbes Davidson, 'the cat' was the ideal remedy for convicts caught 'trying it on'.

TURN UP: To desist from, or relinquish, any particular habit or mode of life, or the further pursuit of any object you had in view, is called *turning it up*. To *turn up* a mistress, or a male acquaintance, is to drop all intercourse, or correspondence, with them. To *turn up* a particular house, or shop, you have been accustomed to use, or deal at, signifies to withdraw your patronage, or custom, and visit it no more. To quit a person suddenly in the street, whether secretly or openly, is called *turning him up*. To *turn* a man *up sweet*, is to get rid of him effectually, but yet to leave him in perfect good humour, and free from any suspicion or discontent; this piece of *finesse* often affords a field for the exercise of consummate address, as in the case of *turning up a flat*, after having stript him of all his money at play, or a shopkeeper, whom you have just robbed before his face of something valuable, *upon the pinch*, or *the hoist*.

TURNED UP: A person acquitted by a jury, or discharged by a magistrate for want of evidence, etc., is said to be turned up. See SWELL.

William 'Scotchy Hand' Campbell was charged with impersonating a policeman, robbing a '*lushy*' sailor and 'turning him up'. Campbell swore he'd been wrongfully accused but police proved he was an ex-convict who served time on Cockatoo Island and in the '*Stone Jug*' at Parramatta. However, because the police used 'unnecessary violence' when arresting Campbell, the judge turned up the case and penalised him £5. Campbell may have been nicknamed Scotchy because of his *Scottish* heritage and vicious disposition.

TURNIPS: To *give* any body *turnips* signifies to *turn* him or her *up*, and the party so *turned up*, is said to have *knap'd turnips*.

Turnips is probably a pun on *turn up*, meaning 'acquit' and 'discharge'. When 'old hand' Peter Duddy was arrested for stealing vegetables, he knap'd turnips—the prosecutor felt sorry for him and dropped the charges. Duddy was a sixty-five-year-old ex-convict who lived in bushland at Brown's River in Van Diemen's

Land. According to historian James Backhouse Walker, 'old hand' was a term applied to 'prisoners who have been long in the Colony; and especially those of notoriously bad character'.

TURN UP A TRUMP: To be fortunate in getting a good *stake*, or by any other means improving your finances.

Trump, meaning triumph, is a winning card in some card games. In 1838, William Trump charged his convict servant, Mary Smith, with stealing three gowns belonging to his wife. Smith claimed that the gowns were a gift because she'd been sleeping with Trump since his wife had been sent to a Female Factory. But Smith, as was reported in the press, did not 'turn up a trump'. She was sentenced to twelve months in a Female Factory, third class.

TWIG: Any thing accomplished cleverly, or as it should be, is said to be done *in twig, in good twig*, or *in prime twig*. A person well dress'd is said to be *in twig*. See: DROP, GAMMON THE TWELVE, and: OUT OF TWIG.

In 1835, pipeclay peddler Samuel 'Sammy Jumbo' White was arrested for public intoxication. But White, 'in rare twig,' scooped a glob from his wheelbarrow and threatened to lob it at the '*beak*'. The policeman '*gammoned*' White with a sudden lunge, dodged his clay projectile and arrested him. White was fined five shillings. Pipeclay is a type of clay used to make tobacco pipes. Because *jumbo* is slang for 'a clumsy person', White may have been nicknamed after the way he drunkenly plodded through Sydney.

TWISTED: Hanged.

A person who was hanged twisted suspended at the end of the rope. When, in 1829, Charles Goodland was arrested for stealing, he lamented that he would be 'twisted'. At Goodland's execution, the twenty-two-year-old stood with three other criminals, one of whom was twenty-one-year-old Thomas Birmingham. But according to news of the day, Birmingham's noose accidently 'twisted' under his chin and he dropped beneath the gallows writhing in agony. The hangman, spurred on by the screams of the horrified crowd, rushed beneath the scaffold and, with all his weight, clung to Birmingham's legs. For five harrowing minutes Birmingham struggled as the rope slowly tightened around his neck and strangled him to death.

TWO POLL ONE. See: BRIDGE.

TYE IT UP: To *tye up* any particular custom, practice, or habit, is synonymous with *knifeing, stowing, turning it up,* or *stashing* it. To *tye it up* is a phrase, which, used emphatically, is generally understood to mean quitting a course of depredation and wickedness. See: SQUARE, and: DO THE TRICK.

Bushranger Charles Routley, to tye it up, confessed to his crimes from the gallows and prayed to God for forgiveness. Because his crimes were so barbaric, the press declared him 'one of the most horrid, and blood-thirsty monsters that have yet disgraced the annals of humanity'. John 'Pretty Jack' Buckley, one of Routley's victims, was beaten, tied in bullock hide and burned alive in a campfire. Buckley was nicknamed because of his 'pockpitted' and 'very disagreeable face'.

UNBETTY: To unlock. See: BETTY.

In 1879, Ernest Geoffrey broke out of his cell in Brisbane Gaol, crept into the prison yard, threaded rope from bits of oakum and, using a bucket handle as a grappling hook, scaled the gaol wall. When he was caught the authorities demanded to know how he'd accomplished the seemingly impossible feat of breaking out of a padlocked cell. So, with a scrap of iron, a rusty old knife, two nails, two bits of timber and a piece of thread, Geoffrey constructed a hook and picklock, reached through the grating on his cell door, blindly unbettied the padlock, hoisted it through the grating and strode out the door. Because Geoffrey revealed how he escaped, his punishment was mitigated to a weeks' imprisonment.

UNDUB: To unlock, unfasten, etc. See: DUB UP.

In 1858, Thomas Munroe and his four friends stopped at a 'refreshment tent' pitched by the Ballarat roadside. But, after requesting 'nobblers,' they demanded the proprietor *'turn up the plant'*. The gang stole £2 and a bundle of clothing but was soon caught. Munroe, however, escaped. Using a piece of wire for a picklock, he was able to undub his handcuffs. When he was recaptured he was sentenced to fourteen years' hard labour. Nobbler is slang for 'a small measure of liquor'.

UNPALLED: A thief whose associates are all apprehended, or taken from him by other means, is said to be *unpalled*, and he is then obliged to *work single-handed*.

290

In 1870, bushwalkers traipsing the wilds of Mount Ben Lomond bumped into an old man with 'long curved toe and finger nails' and a 'grizzly beard hanging down to the middle of his body'. The man struggled to speak, but eventually explained that he'd lived in a hollow tree for twelve years and hadn't spoken to another person for six years. But the bushwalkers noticed vents drilled in the side of the tree that concealed smoke billowing out of the hermit's campfire, so they alerted the police. Robberies perpetrated at local farmsteads were attributed to the hermit, who was arrested. He was identified as Robert James

McKay, a New South Wales bushranger unpalled from his associates and transported to Van Diemen's Land. He was sentenced to four years' gaol.

UNSLOUR: To unlock, unfasten, or unbutton. See: SLOUR. Speaking of a person whose coat is buttoned, so as to obstruct the access to his pockets, the *knucks* will say to each other, the *cove* is *slour'd up*, we must *unslour* him to get at his *kickseys*.

In 1800, William Jeary woke in a strange room and discovered Esther Lawrence unslouring his waistcoat pocket. Lawrence, who plied Jeary with liquor and led him back to her house to rob him, was charged with theft and transported to New South Wales for a seven-year term.

UNTHIMBLE: To *unthimble* a man, is to rob, or otherwise deprive him of his watch.

UNTHIMBLED: Having been divested of one's watch.

When prostitute Mary 'Poll' Clarke was tried for unthimbling her clientele, the judge asked, 'What is the cant phrase, a *thimble*?' Constable Charles Humphreys replied, 'That is the ordinary name for a watch.' Clarke was charged with theft and transported to New South Wales for a seven-year term. Poll is slang for prostitute.

UP IN THE STIRRUPS: A man who is in *swell street*, that is, having plenty of money, is said to be *up in the stirrups*.

When, in 1830, Hugh Carberry was awarded his freedom, he was up in the stirrups. But when he was charged with stealing a horse, he was *the rider of a horse foaled by an acorn*—'a person sentenced to hang on the gallows'.

UPON THE CROSS. See: CROSS.
UPON THE SQUARE. See: SQUARE.
UPON THE SUIT, etc. See: SUIT.

UPPER-BEN, UPPER-BENJAMIN, UPPER-TOG: A great-coat.

292

In 1830, John Mahoney was arrested for '*milling*' a policeman. Because Mahoney tore the policeman's 'upper benjamin,' the newspaper report detailing his crime wryly referred to Mahoney as a 'sneider', a slang name for tailor derived from *schneider*, German for 'cutter'. Mahoney was punished with twenty-five lashes.

VARDO: A waggon.
VARDO-GILL: A waggoner.

Vardo is Romani for cart. Ex-convict George Burnett was employed as a vardo-gill to drive a vardo in Sydney. But in 1844, he drove over the head of a two-year-old girl, crushing her to death. The coroner ruled the tragedy an accident but admonished Burnett for his carelessness. When, in 1851, Burnett squashed another two-year-old, he was charged with manslaughter. But he was acquitted and, in summing up the case, the attorney-general rebuked the child's parents for their negligence, stating that 'Sydney, beyond any other part of the world, allowed young children to play in the most reckless manner in the most crowded thoroughfares.'

WACK: To share or divide any thing equally, as *wack the blunt*, divide the money, etc.

WACK: a share or equal proportion, as give me my *wack*, that is, my due part.

Waiter John Grayson was accused of stealing his co-worker's tips because he did not receive 'his whack'. Grayson was acquitted but he may have been guilty of another crime: receiving a wack of stolen goods. His lover, Catherine Johnson, was caught stealing cash and valuables from her co-workers. She was sentenced to two years' hard labour in Adelaide Gaol.

———

WALKER: An ironical expression, synonymous with bender, and used in the same manner. See: BENDER.

———

WALKING-DISTILLER. See: CARRY THE KEG.

———

WANTED: When any of the *traps* or runners have a private information against a *family person*, and are using means to apprehend the party, they say, such a one is *wanted*; and it becomes the latter, on receiving such intimation to *keep out if the way*, until the *stink* is over, or until he or she can find means to *stash the business* through the medium of *Mr. Palmer*, or by some other means.

The authorities published information in newspapers to alert the public to criminal activity. But information was also printed on posters displayed in public spaces. Some 'wanted posters', as they became known, advertised rewards to tempt the public to assist in catching criminals. One of the earliest rewards advertised in Australia appeared in the *Sydney Gazette* in March, 1803. Gaoler David White offered a cash reward for

the apprehension of thieves who broke into Sydney Gaol and stole his money and clothing. Convict James Hardwicke was charged with the theft and sentenced to death. But on the day of his execution, Governor Philip Gidley King granted him a reprieve.

WATER-SNEAK: Robbing ships or vessels on a navigable river, or canal, by getting on board unperceived, generally in the night. The water-sneak, is lately made a capital offence.

A capital offence is a crime punishable by death. In 1810, William Quelch was sentenced to death for perpetrating the water-sneak on the River Thames. But the judgment was respited and Quelch was released after serving just ten months' gaol. At this time, over two hundred crimes were punishable by death. Many people felt the judicial system, known as the Bloody Code, was harsh, immoral

and impossible to administer fairly. Over time the number of capital crimes were reduced—by the early 1860s, five crimes were punishable by death. Capital comes from *caput*, Latin for head, and alludes to execution by beheading.

WEAR IT: To *wear it upon* a person, (meaning to *wear a nose*, or *a conk*,) is synonymous with *nosing, conking, splitting*, or *coming it*, and is merely one of those fanciful variations so much admired by *flash people*. See: NOSE.

WEAR THE BANDS. See: BANDS.

WEDGE: Silver; as a *wedge-feeder*, a silver spoon, etc.; but silver coin, as well as silver plate, are both comprehended under the name of *wedge*. See: RIDGE, and: SPEAK TO.

Silverware may have been nicknamed wedge because silver ingots were called wedges. But wedge may also derive from wage, meaning 'silver money'. In 1802, Samuel Clarke approached Barnet Elias, a peddler, and offered to sell him 'wedge'. Clarke pulled a silver spoon from his pocket and explained that he had more silverware in a *'plant'*. Elias agreed to buy the items and arranged to meet Clarke later that day on Staines Bridge. To safeguard against Clarke getting caught with the stolen spoon, Elias instructed him to bury it. But after they  parted ways, Elias dug up the spoon, took it to the police and notified them of the robbery. When Clarke appeared on the bridge, he spotted the police and threw a bag containing the silverware into the River Thames. But it was recovered, the items were identified as stolen property and Clarke was charged with burglary. He was sentenced to death but the sentence was commuted to transportation for life.

WEED: Tobacco.

WEED: To pilfer or purloin a small portion from a large quantity of any thing; often done by young or timid predators, in the hope of escaping detection, as, an apprentice or  shopman will *weed* his master's *lob*, that is, take small sums out of the till when opportunity offers, which sort of peculation may be carried on with impunity for a length of time; but experienced thieves sometimes think it good *judgment* to *weed* a place, in order that it may be *good* again, perhaps for a considerable length of time, as in the instance of a warehouse or other depot for goods, to which they may possess the means of access by means of a false key; in this ease, by taking too great a *swag*, at first, the proprietors would discover the deficiency, and take measures to prevent future depredation. To *weed the swag* is to embezzle part of the booty, unknown to your *palls*, before a division takes place, a temptation against which very few of *the family* are proof, if they can find an opportunity. A *flash-cove*, on discovering a deficiency in his purse or property, which he cannot account for, will declare that he, (or it, naming the article,) has been *weeded to the ruffian*.

Tobacco may have been called weed because it is a noxious plant. Weeding, meaning 'pilfer', comes from weed, meaning 'to remove something without causing a disturbance'. Twelve-year-old William Johnson and thirteen-year-old Michael Desmond, for attempting to weed cigars while purchasing 'weed,' were sentenced to three months' hard labour in Sydney Gaol.

WEEDING DUES: Speaking of any person, place, or property, that has been *weeded*, it is said *weeding dues* have been concerned. See: DUES.

In 1854, brewer Henry Degraves tallied his accounts and discovered that he was short twenty tons of sugar. He suspected his convict servants of an 'extensive system of weeding', so he contacted the police. When police raided the brewery they caught Robert Worthington, John Smith and Bartlett Culvathy drawing a bucket out of a vat of ale. The trio was charged with stealing and sentenced to eighteen months' gaol with hard labour, with a recommendation that they be sent to Port Arthur Penal Station.

WEIGH FORTY: Term used by the police, who are as well versed in *flash* as the thieves themselves. It is often customary with the *traps*, to wink at depredations of a petty nature, and for which no reward would attach, and to let a thief *reign* unmolested till he commits a capital crime. They then *grab* him, and, on conviction, share (in many cases) a reward of 40£, or upwards; therefore these gentry will say, Let him alone at present, we don't *want* him till he *weighs his weight*, meaning, of course, forty pounds.

Ann Burton was arrested on suspicion of committing a violent robbery, but she swore to her innocence and complained that she 'did not weigh forty,' and that the arresting officer was a 'bloody thief'. She was cleared of all charges and released from gaol. In early nineteenth-century England, £40 was the standard reward paid for the apprehension of thieves, robbers, burglars and counterfeiters. Policemen caught instigating crimes to obtain the reward money faced stiff penalties. For enticing people to commit crime with a £40 value, Bow Street Policeman Benjamin Johnson was executed, and his colleague, George Vaughan, was sentenced to five years' gaol.

WELL: To *well* your accomplice, or *put him in the well*, is explained under the word GARDEN, which see.

WHIDDLE: To speak of, or mention any thing, as, Don't you *whiddle* about so and so, that is, don't mention it.
WHIDDLER: A talkative or tell-tale person, who is not fit to be trusted with a secret.
WHIDS: Words. See: CRACK A WHID.

Whid may derive from *cwide*, an Old English word meaning 'a statement'. William Astley, a nineteenth-century author who wrote under the pseudonym 'Price Warung,' specialised in convict fiction. To ensure his stories were authentic, he whiddled with 'old hands' and incorporated their slang and cant phrases into his writing. In *Tales of the Early Days*, a character states: 'Lord, ain't the *swell* a-crackin' a whid in *prime twig.*'

WHISTLERS. See: BROWNS AND WHISTLERS.

WIN, or WINCHESTER: A penny.

Because pennies were minted from silver, win may derive from *gwyn*, a Cymric word for white. But win may also come from *winnow*, meaning 'divide'. According to the *Swell's Night Guide*, a lodger paid between 'two win' and a '*tanner*' to rent a 'pad' (bed) for one night. But a night out could cost much more. James Holley, who paid prostitute Margaret Thompson six win to sleep with him, was robbed of three half-crowns, one shilling, one win and two halfpence. Thompson, however, paid the ultimate price. She was sentenced to fourteen years' transportation but died during the voyage to Van Diemen's Land.

WIND: A man transported for his natural life, is said to be *lag'd for his wind*, or to have *knap'd a winder*, or *a bellowser*, according to the humour of the speaker.

Wind, meaning 'breath,' is synonymous with life. And, because a sentence of life transportation was said to take away a person's breath, a convict serving a life sentence was called a 'winder'. Bellowser, derived from bellows, is slang for lungs. When Constable William Clifton arrested William Seymour for stealing, he remarked, 'I suppose this will be a bellowser for me this time, Clifton?' Seymour was lagged for his wind to New South Wales.

WOOLLY-BIRDS: Sheep.

When Thomas Addis spotted James Cadogan lugging a suspicious sheep-shaped sack, he accused him of stealing a 'woolly bird'. Cadogan insisted that the sack contained potatoes but when Addis looked inside and discovered a sheep, he alerted the police. Cadogan was sentenced to eighteen months' gaol with hard labour.

WORK. To *work upon* any particular *game*, is to practise generally, that species of fraud or depredation, as, He *works upon the crack*, he follows housebreaking, etc. An offender having been detected in the very fact, particularly in cases of coining, colouring base-metal, etc., is emphatically said to have been *grab'd at work*, meaning to imply, that the proof against him being so plain, he has no ground of defence to set up.

John Onely, for working upon the game, was murdered by three of his fellow convicts at Sarah Island Penal Station. When Onely swindled Samuel Higgins out of four pounds of bread, George Driver

pinned Onely to the ground and David McGee said 'Go to work,' which Samuel Higgins understood meant 'use the knife'—he stabbed Onely three times then cut his throat 'from ear to ear'.

WRINKLE: To lie, or utter a falsehood.
WRINKLE: An untruth.
WRINKLER: A person prone to lying; such a character is called also a *gully,* which is probably an abbreviation of Gulliver, and from hence, to *gully* signifies to lie, or deal in the marvellous.

A lie was called a wrinkle because a liar creases the truth. When convicts arrived in Australia, their names, physical features, next of kin, trades and criminal histories, were recorded in registers known as the Black Books. The authorities used this information to classify and identify convicts. But some convicts told wrinkles. Edward Johnson's real name was John Jackson. Not only was Johnson a wrinkler, he also was wrinkled—according to his description in the Black Books he had a 'face much wrinkled'. Gully, for 'liar', is a pun on Lemuel Gulliver, the central character in the popular fantasy-adventure book *Gulliver's Travels*.

X: Illiterate convicts signed their name with an 'x'.

John 'Rocky' Whelan, a Van Diemonian bushranger who murdered five men in a twenty-four-day period, signed his dictated statement with an 'x'. Because x is a sacred symbol, it reflected the signatory's sincerity. Whelan may have been nicknamed Rocky because he was 'calloused and hardened'. But his nickname is also attributed to his craggy facial features, and his skill in climbing the rocky cliffs of Norfolk Island. He was executed in 1855.

YACK: A watch (obsolete.)

When Alexander Thomas Gilderoy was arrested for burglary and '*frisked*' by police, they failed to discover a stolen 'yack' stashed in his pocket. Gilderoy then smuggled the yack out of gaol to his sweetheart, so she could '*fence*' it for cash. But she was caught and the yack was used as evidence to prosecute Gilderoy. He was sentenced to death and executed. Yack probably comes from *yakengeri*, a Welsh-Romani word for clock.

YARN: *Yarning* or *spinning a yarn* is a favourite amusement among *flash-people*; signifying to relate their various adventures, exploits, and escapes to each other. This is most common and gratifying, among persons in confinement or exile, to enliven a dull hour, and probably excite a secret hope of one day enjoying a repetition of their former pleasures. See: BONED. A person expert at telling these stories, is said *to spin a fine yarn*. A man using a great deal of

rhetoric, and exerting all his art to talk another person out of any thing he is intent upon, the latter will answer, Aye, Aye, you can *spin a good yarn*, but it won't do; meaning, all your eloquence will not have the desired effect.

Yarn, meaning story, comes from sailors' habit of telling stories to pass the time while they worked at yarn-twisting. In 1837, at the Parramatta

Female Factory, Mary Fogan was sentenced to one month in third class for her 'inveterate habit of yarning'. Prisons for women were called factories because the inmates manufactured goods and provided labour for colonists. Factory women were categorised into three classes according to their behaviour: those in first class could be assigned to colonists or work in positions of trust within the factory, including as overseers, cooks and hospital attendants; second-class women typically sewed and prepared linen; those in the third class did the most arduous work, such as laundry, wool work and unpicking old rope known as oakum.

YELLOW: Jealous; a jealous husband is called a *yellow gloak*.

Yellow is a pun on jealous. In 1865, at Boyle's Hotel in Howlong, New South Wales, Edward Ritherton claimed to be so 'tormented by the yellow demon jealousy' that he was driven to shoot Eliza Thomas. But because the gun was loaded with the wrong sized bullet, it misfired and Thomas was unharmed. Ritherton then attempted suicide by drinking a cup of strychnine. But the publican swiped the cup from Ritherton's hand, saving his life. He was punished with twelve months' hard labour at Albury Gaol.

YOKUFF: A chest, or large box.

Yokuff is derived from coffer, a 'strongbox' or 'lockable chest'. Convicts who misbehaved during the voyage from Britain to Australia could be punished with a stint in a wooden yokuff. The Black Box or Solitary Box, as it was known, measured approximately two feet, six inches wide, two feet, six inches deep and six feet, five inches high. Convicts could be

sentenced to stand in the box for between several hours and several days. Offenders were also doused with water while the box was suspended from ropes. During the voyage of the *East London* to Van Diemen's Land in 1843, Rose Carroll, a so-called 'very bad' convict, was confined to the Black Box for smoking in bed.

YORK: To stare or look at any person in an impertinent manner, is termed *yorking*; to *york* any thing, in a common sense, is to view, look at, or examine it.

YORK: a look, or observation; a *flash-cove* observing another person (a *flat*) who appears to notice or scrutinize him, his proceedings, or the company he is with, will say to his *palls*, That *cove* is *yorking as strong as a horse*, or, There is *York-street concerned*.

Because the people of Yorkshire were stereotyped as shrewd and perceptive, york, meaning stare, probably derives from Yorkshire. William Yeadon was a seventeen-year-old stable boy transported from Yorkshire, England, to New South Wales in 1832. Yeadon, who was just four foot, ten inches tall, was nicknamed 'Big Yorkey' because he was a fearless prizefighter.

Prizefighting was illegal, however, and in 1848, when Yeadon fought Richard Green, police stormed the ring. Green managed to escape but Yeadon was arrested. He may have been caught because he could not york—his face was 'greatly bruised' and his eyes were swollen and 'nearly closed'.

YOUKELL: A countryman, or clown.

Yokel may derive from *jacob*, meaning a stupid person. William Hawke, according to the South Australian press, was an 'unlucky yokel'. He was cheated in the three-card trick by a *'sharper'* named Thomas Long. But Long was caught and sentenced to six months' hard labour at Dry Creek Gaol. In the three-card gaff, also known as Monte and Find the Lady, the dealer places a queen and two number cards face down then switches them around and challenges the player to pick the queen from among the three cards. A skilled cardsharp was so accomplished in deception that not even his accomplices could pick the winning card.

ZOUNDS: An exclamation.

Zounds is a contraction of 'God's wounds'—a profane oath that refers to the crucifixion wounds of Jesus Christ. In 1784, Sir Godfrey Webster, Baronet, suspected an especially well-dressed theatregoer had brushed against him to pick his purse from his pocket. The suspect, who exclaimed 'zounds' when seized by Webster, was identified as George Barrington—a cunning pickpocket infamous throughout England. Police searched Barrington 'minutely,' even checking in his hair, but failed to discover the purse. Barrington was discharged from gaol for lack of evidence.

Index of historic penal sites in Australia

Index of further convict terms

Assigned *see* HANK, 114

Black Books *see* WRINKLE, 303

Bounding Pea *see* NOB-PITCHERS, 168

Cat-o'-nine-tails *see* TEAZE, 271

Chalks *see* PICK-UP, 183

Convict-Constable *see* ROLLERS, 209 and TRAPS, 283

Female Factory *see* YARN, 305

Flagellator *see* TEAZE, 271

Grog *see* THROUGH IT, 272

Hulk *see* DONE, 64

Jack Sheppard *see* NIX, 167

Leg Irons *see* BLEEDERS, 13 *and* SLANG'D, 233

Love Token *see* CROOK, 54

Magistrate *see* JUDGE, 125

Of the town *see* IN TOWN, 119

Pleaded her belly *see* QUEER SCREENS, 198

Postilion *see* JACK-BOY, 120

Pugilist *see* FIBBING-GLOAK, 85

Romani *see* ROMANY, 209

Scurvy *see* PRAD, 192

Shelta *see* BUZ-COVE, 32

Skeleton Key *see* SCREW, 222

Solitary Confinement *see* SINGLE-HANDED, 230

Stocks *see* BLUNT, 16

Thimblerig *see* NOB-PITCHERS, 168

Three-card trick *see* YOUKELL, 308

Ticket-of-leave *see* SCREEVE, 222

Treadmill *see* DANCERS, 57

Triangles *see* PUZZLING-STICKS, 197

Walnut shell *see* NOB-PITCHERS, 168

Watchhouse *see* SCOUT-KEN, 220

Weaned *see* TODDLER, 277

Acknowledgments

Thanks to James Hardy Vaux, Jonathon Green, Tuco, Amelie Mills, Lyn and Phil Barnard, Samantha Forge, Jess Horrocks, Imogen Stubbs, W. H. Chong, Philip Bryan and the Text Publishing team. Special thanks to Jo Bornemissza and Jane Pearson, to whom this book is dedicated.